Liberal Freedom

We seem to be losing the ability to talk to each other about – and despite – our political differences. The liberal tradition, with its emphasis on open-mindedness, toleration, and inclusion, is ideally suited to respond to this challenge. Yet liberalism is often seen today as a barrier to constructive dialogue: narrowly focused on individual rights, indifferent to the communal sources of human well-being, and deeply implicated in structures of economic and social domination. This book provides a novel defense of liberalism that weaves together a commitment to republican self-government, an emphasis on the value of unregulated choice, and an appreciation of how hard it is to strike a balance between them. By treating freedom rather than justice as the central liberal value this important book, critical to the times, provides an indispensable resource for constructive dialogue in a time of political polarization.

Eric MacGilvray is Professor of Political Science at Ohio State University.

Liberal Freedom

Pluralism, Polarization, and Politics

ERIC MACGILVRAY
Ohio State University

CAMBRIDGE
UNIVERSITY PRESS

University Printing House, Cambridge CB2 8BS, United Kingdom

One Liberty Plaza, 20th Floor, New York, NY 10006, USA

477 Williamstown Road, Port Melbourne, VIC 3207, Australia

314–321, 3rd Floor, Plot 3, Splendor Forum, Jasola District Centre, New Delhi – 110025, India

103 Penang Road, #05–06/07, Visioncrest Commercial, Singapore 238467

Cambridge University Press is part of the University of Cambridge.

It furthers the University's mission by disseminating knowledge in the pursuit of education, learning, and research at the highest international levels of excellence.

www.cambridge.org
Information on this title: www.cambridge.org/9781108836951
DOI: 10.1017/9781108873185

© Eric MacGilvray 2022

This publication is in copyright. Subject to statutory exception and to the provisions of relevant collective licensing agreements, no reproduction of any part may take place without the written permission of Cambridge University Press.

First published 2022

Printed in the United Kingdom by TJ Books Limited, Padstow Cornwall

A catalogue record for this publication is available from the British Library.

ISBN 978-1-108-83695-1 Hardback

Cambridge University Press has no responsibility for the persistence or accuracy of URLs for external or third-party internet websites referred to in this publication and does not guarantee that any content on such websites is, or will remain, accurate or appropriate.

for Ellie and Sydney
my freedom

The spirit of liberty is the spirit which is not too sure that it is right; the spirit of liberty is the spirit which seeks to understand the minds of other men and women.

>Learned Hand, "The Spirit of Liberty"

[T]he exercise of our freedom is a small piecemeal business which goes on all the time and not a grandiose leaping about unimpeded at important moments.

>Iris Murdoch, "The Idea of Perfection"

Contents

Preface	*page* ix
Acknowledgments	xv
Introduction: Why Liberalism? Why Freedom?	1
I.1 The Problem of Polarization	2
I.2 The Justice Paradigm	6
I.3 Overview	13
1 Free Actions and Free Persons	18
1.1 Choice and Responsibility	18
1.2 Freedom and Utility	24
1.3 Freedom and Justice	32
1.4 Freedom and Responsibility	40
1.5 Freedom and Nonresponsibility	46
2 Republican Freedom	52
2.1 Liberalism and Republicanism	52
2.2 Virtues and Interests	59
2.3 Reasons and Persons	65
2.4 Do Markets Dominate?	71
2.5 Do Markets Liberate?	78
3 Market Freedom	86
3.1 Liberalism and Markets	86
3.2 From Exchange to Competition	91
3.3 From Competition to Nonresponsibility	101
3.4 The Value of Market Freedom	107
3.5 The Limits of Market Freedom	118

4 The Liberal Tradition	122
4.1 The Liberal Problem	122
4.2 Democratization and Industrialization	128
4.3 Equality and Market Freedom: The "Classical" Liberals	134
4.4 Equality and Republican Freedom: The "New" Liberals	147
4.5 Liberals Before Liberalism?	158
5 Liberalism and the Problem of Polarization	165
5.1 Liberalism and Polarization	165
5.2 The Contractarian Turn	171
5.3 Corruption and Community	180
5.4 Capitalism and Empire	186
5.5 Liberal Boundaries	198
Conclusion	205
Index	210

Preface

You're speeding down the highway – ten miles over the limit, maybe fifteen. Night has just about fallen; no moon but a few stars poking through the amber haze off to the right. You'd be in that haze too if the traffic report hadn't warned you off. Drop a gear and drift left to get past the semi. The car laps up the center lines. You've been at this since lunchtime. The phone says there's a decent diner about half an hour up ahead, you could go for a burger. Maybe flirt with the waitstaff a little, what the hell, nobody knows you out here. Or just keep moving and make the coast by morning. A little coffee ought to do the trick. Back into top gear. *You could do anything.*

EMS finally found the car rolled over thirty feet off the shoulder. They would have found it a lot sooner up on the interstate. Then again if it wasn't for mobile GPS they'd still be looking. Three fatalities in a month on the same stretch, that ought to be enough to get the governor on TV. These country roads weren't built for long-haul driving but with the traffic in the city who can blame them? Could have been the bad light, loose gravel, oncoming traffic. Or maybe the driver nodded off – faulty steering actuator. Maybe all four. Air bags deployed but no seat belt – manufacturing defect or another bad call by the driver? There'll be a lot of money riding on that one. But first we have to notify the next of kin. They'll have the same question as the politicians, the insurance company, and the lawyers. *What could we have done?*

* * *

She has it coming, let's face it. Walking around with that smirk on her face like the last two years didn't happen, like it wasn't your best friend, like you don't matter. Well, there's a punishment to fit this crime – just the right photo, with just the right caption. That's why we save them, right? An open letter or a ransom note, depending how you play it. #slut. Your finger hovers over the screen for a few seconds, savoring the moment. A quick shudder, like vertigo. <Post> *Look what you did.*

No one saw it coming: a thousand hits by lunchtime. Ten thousand by dinner. How does anyone handle that kind of attention? Well, she didn't handle it, not for long. Sure, things live forever online – like Pandora we've all opened doors that we can't close again. But some things really thrive, jumping from screen to screen quicker than thought. That's what viral means: exponentially contagious, potentially deadly. A lesson we never seem to learn. *What have we done?*

* * *

The pickup makes a wide U-turn at the edge of town. Says he can get you over the border, no sweat. Done it dozens of times. After that it's up to you to find out where they need extra hands: strawberries, maybe almonds depending on the season. Hard work but it pays, and your folks could use the money. Thing is these days it's a one-way trip. It might take two, three, four tries to make it through, and once you're in you don't want to give the vigilantes another shot. So you'll make a new life there: new language, new friends, maybe a new family. At home you'll be a face on the wall and a check in the mail. You blink a few times and make like it's the dust in your eyes. *You can do this.*

The protests started back up on Labor Day: same rabble-rousers, same slogans, same spectacle. Things started to get ugly in October, several beatings and an arson, motive officially TBD but who are we kidding? It got worse after the election, and we all know what the election was about. So now the whole messy stew is back on the boil: basic decency smothered in the rule of law; nationalism with a side of profit. The sharp smell of fear, the bitter taste of violence. Home cooking. They might get a bill through this year, but the smart money is against it. *What are we going to do?*

* * *

The message pops up 2:32 am: <whats up cutie> Super sketch, check the profile. Not much but the photo catches your eye. Easy in his skin, hair pulled back, eyes coiled up like a watch spring or a pair of fists. A little sad, or angry maybe. New message: <saw your post about feeling lost i can relate> Sad, then. Reply: <wanna share?> It's been a while since you connected with someone. Thirty seconds, long ones. Finally: <lets meet> and an address. Red flag? It's been a while since someone looked at you like they really saw you. Steady breaths, don't overthink for once. One click and you can get away from all the bullshit. *Do what you want.*

They went missing for two months. No texts, no calls, social media dark, the usual story. A life that takes over the rest of life, like a cancer. Lucky we found them before it got really bad, what we saw was bad enough. Now for the hard questions. How does a person fall for someone like that? Who do they have to talk to, or not talk to? What butterfly's wings have to flap? Where were the family, the friends, the counsellors? What were they looking for? What kind of emptiness makes a person empty themselves out? How do we put them back together? *Where did we go wrong?*

* * *

6:30 am. Best time to be in the office. Your screen blinks on, the only light in the whole place. The second Adderall burning off the fumes from last night's bottle of wine. You don't feel good exactly, but you feel alive – like you're pushing back on something bigger than you and finally found the right grip. You get a feel for this kind of thing after a while, like a poker player or a dancer – always a fresh hand to play, new steps to try. Every second counts, and you're sitting on a cable with a direct line to the big board. Custom built. Pole fucking position. Time to borrow some money and make some trades. *Show them what you can do.*

When the market turns it turns hard, and the difference between losing big and losing everything is who jumps out of the burning building first. Someone won't be retiring this year after all. Someone won't be heading off to that fancy college. Someone will be driving that beater a little longer. A lot of someones. No bonuses for the bankers but they'll bounce back fine, they always do. And who do we point the finger at? The traders? The investors? The lenders? The regulators? The system, whatever that is? It's like trying to figure out which pebble caused a landslide. *Who did this?*

* * *

There are moments in our lives when ordinary constraints are thrown off and new paths are opened up, when opportunities that have always been in the background start to seem like real possibilities, when habit and routine give way to spontaneity and improvisation. These are the moments that we are likely to think of first when we think about what it means, or would mean, to be free, and the first half of each of these vignettes is meant to illustrate what it is like, for better or worse, for a person to "feel" free at such moments. These are also the kinds of moments that we are likely to think of first when we think about what freedom means as a political value: a free society – or, as I will call it, a *liberal polity* (liberal is one of the adjectival forms of liberty, as free is of freedom) – is, among other things, a society that makes these kinds of opportunities available to its members, whether they take advantage of them or not. But a liberal polity has to do more than that, and the second half of each vignette is meant to illustrate what it is like when this kind of freedom spins out of control; whether literally, as in the case of a car crash, or figuratively, as in the case of malicious gossip, a violent protest, an unhealthy relationship, or a market crash. Of course, the mundane behavior described in the first half of each vignette does not inevitably or even often lead to the dire consequences described in the second half. But the fact that it sometimes does, and the awareness that it always might, complicates our thinking about freedom in two important ways.

The first and most straightforward way is that it reminds us that freedom in a liberal polity is not just a matter of being left alone. Rather, our freedom is embedded in an intricate material, social, and legal infrastructure that simultaneously enables and limits its exercise. Consider, to take the first vignette as an example, the role that traffic rules, safety regulations, and liability laws (among other things) play in directly or indirectly shaping the behavior of the various actors in that narrative, and the role that a well-maintained system of roads, reliable communications technology, and an effective emergency response system (among other things) play in making that behavior possible in the first place. A similar kind of infrastructure enables and limits the freedoms of expression, movement, association, and exchange that are at play in the other vignettes: social media networks; labor, commodity, and equity markets; the physical and virtual spaces that make public protests and private solicitations possible; and so on. Consider also the political context in which narratives like these unfold: the political demands that cause the infrastructure of free action to be built up over time, and the political scrutiny that this infrastructure comes under when it is thought to have failed or fallen short in a given case. The point is not just that our freedom is always limited, which is obvious enough, but rather that the freedoms that we enjoy in a liberal polity are made possible by the cooperation and mutual restraint of the members of that society.

The second and more fundamental way that a recognition of the dangerous potential of free action complicates our thinking about freedom has to do with our understanding of what freedom is. When we make choices, we do not just want to be unconstrained, we also want to see ourselves as being responsible for what we do; we want to be active players and not just bystanders in the drama of our lives. (Often, but not always, we want others to see us this way as well.) When and to the extent that our choices are shaped by factors that we do not control – when, for example, we fall victim to unsafe road conditions, malicious gossip, politically motivated violence, manipulative people, or volatile markets – this sense of responsibility is diminished, and so too is our sense of being able to act, or of having acted, freely. In such cases, even though we may be the ones who decide what to do, we feel like we are being pushed around or swept along by the social environment in which our decisions are made. Of course, we never completely control our social environment, just as we are never completely unconstrained when we respond to it. Our freedom is in this sense always partial. Nevertheless, the desire to be responsible for what we do gives rise to a demand for a second, more obviously political, kind of freedom; a demand that is articulated, at least implicitly, in the second half of each of our vignettes. In each of these cases "we" – all of us – set out to remake the infrastructure of free action in such a way that "we" – each of us – are better able to control the conditions under which we act.

But here the argument comes full circle, because this demand for control cuts directly against the spirit of spontaneity and improvisation, of pushing boundaries, that we are likely to think of first when we think about what freedom means to us and why we find it valuable. After all, the greatest obstacle that we face in trying to control our social environment is the spontaneous behavior of other people. This is one reason why the boundary between the political and the nonpolitical – between "public" and "private" – is constantly being negotiated and redrawn. Here again our vignettes capture some of the messiness of the issues involved: for example, the fact that illegal behavior like speeding, the use of undocumented labor, and prescription drug abuse is nevertheless widely practiced and to some extent tolerated (within certain limits), and the fact that harmful behavior like petty revenge, hateful rhetoric, and excessive drinking is nevertheless legal (again, within certain limits). In each case the desire to contain the dangerous potential of free choice is at odds with the desire to preserve a space within which that kind of choice is permitted, consequences be damned. And in each case the question of whether the domain of free choice should grow or shrink is, for that reason, a live political question. A liberal politics is fundamentally concerned with managing the conflict between the two seemingly contradictory sets of intuitions about freedom that give rise to this dilemma. This is the kind of politics that this book sets out to defend.

I use the word "managing" advisedly. The most distinctive feature of the liberal politics that is defended here is its resolutely nonutopian character; the fact that the two sets of intuitions about freedom that it tries to accommodate can never be fully reconciled, but only provisionally balanced against each other. A liberal theory of politics can clarify the structure of the values that underlie those intuitions, show how those values come into conflict, and say something about how those conflicts are likely to play out in particular cases – and, of course, it can perform the traditional liberal task of warning against the dangers of utopianism – but it cannot (I will argue) offer a vision of a world in which this kind of conflict does not exist; at least, not without ceasing to be liberal. Put otherwise, liberals can and should strive to create a freer world or a more just world, but as liberals they cannot coherently set out to create a free or a just world, full stop. The fundamentally open-ended character of a liberal politics is captured, I hope, by the fact that each of our vignettes ends with a practical question addressed to a collectivity – a question that does not have an obvious answer. In the following chapters I explore the conceptual structure, the historical roots, and (more tentatively, of course) the practical implications of this distinctively liberal way of thinking about politics. First, though, I will formally introduce the argument that follows by saying something about how it speaks to the political challenges facing us today, and how it differs from – and seeks to improve upon – other recent efforts to respond to those challenges.

Acknowledgments

I am very fortunate to be part of a vibrant intellectual community at Ohio State University, and I would like to start by thanking my colleagues for the many ways in which they have shaped and supported this project. Justin D'Arms, Dana Howard, Don Hubin, Donghye Kim, Ben McKean, Michael Neblo, Grant Sharratt, Inés Valdez, Avery White, Dave Whitsett, and Brandon Zaffini each provided helpful comments and conversation on portions of the manuscript. Emma Saunders-Hastings and Piers Turner read larger swaths and were exceptionally generous – liberal, even – with their time and insight: in addition to helping me clarify my thinking on several important points they each tactfully corrected some notable bloopers. Chapters 1 and 3 had their first airings at our interdisciplinary Political Theory Workshop; thanks are due to Matthew Landauer and Jon Kingzette for serving as discussants on those occasions, and to the workshop participants for their challenging and constructive feedback. As Chairs of the Political Science Department Rick Herrmann and Greg Caldeira smoothed my path in many tangible and intangible ways.

The book started to come into focus during a sabbatical leave at the London School of Economics, and I am grateful to the Political Theory Group there – especially to Leigh Jenco – for welcoming me as a temporary member. I presented an early version of Chapter 2 to the LSE's Political Philosophy Research Seminar, and I thank the audience on that occasion, and Christian List and Laura Valentini in particular, for their comments.

Portions of the book were also presented at various annual meetings of the American Political Science Association, the Association for Political Theory, and the Philosophy, Politics, and Economics Society, and at conferences, lectures, or workshops at Cal Poly Pomona, Queens University Belfast, University College Dublin, the Inter-University Centre Dubrovnik, the University of North Carolina at Chapel Hill, the University of Vermont, the University of Wisconsin-Madison, and Yale University. Thanks are due to those audiences, and to David Grewal, Rafeeq Hasan, Alex Kirshner, Alexander Moon, Andrew Sabl, Emma Saunders-Hastings, Lucas Swaine, Andrew Valls, and Xinzhi Zhao for serving as respondents.

In addition to the above, Samuel Bagg, Leah Batstone, Brookes Brown, Devin Christenson, Michael Goodhart, Steven Klein, Daniel Layman, Jacob Levy, John McCormick, Philip Pettit, David Schmidtz, Melissa Schwartzberg, Peter Stone, Brandon Turner, Sarita Zaffini, and Alex Zakaras provided stimulating conversation and/or correspondence on many of the ideas that are developed here. Karen MacGilvray, Ellie MacGilvray, and Sydney MacGilvray offered encouraging words and candid advice on the Preface and Conclusion.

I am of course solely responsible for the errors that remain despite the efforts of these wonderful colleagues, friends, and family members, and I sincerely apologize if I have inadvertently left anyone off this list.

Finally, I would like to thank Robert Dreesen at Cambridge University Press, as well as the anonymous readers, for their enthusiasm and patience. I would also like to thank Raghavi Govindane for coordinating the production process, Matt Sparrow for copy-editing, and Jim Diggins for preparing the index.

In the following pages I argue that the pursuit of freedom requires that we strike a delicate and shifting balance between creating the conditions for responsible choice and carving out a space for nonresponsible or even irresponsible choice. Few experiences, if any, teach that lesson more profoundly than parenthood. As this book goes to press my older daughter is finishing college and my younger daughter is finishing high school. These milestones have brought home to me more clearly than ever the fact that letting go is a vital part of any loving relationship, and that my girls nevertheless are and always will be what I am proudest of in this world. This book, like my heart, belongs to them.

INTRODUCTION

Why Liberalism? Why Freedom?

> [A] criticism which has at heart the interests of liberalism might find its most useful work not in confirming liberalism in its sense of general rightness but in putting under some degree of pressure the liberal ideas and assumptions of the present time.
>
> Lionel Trilling, The Liberal Imagination

In this book I defend a liberal politics: one that treats liberty (or freedom – I will use the words interchangeably) as the first political value to be pursued. In doing so I hope to restore freedom to its proper place at the center of liberal political thought – a place that, despite the etymology of the word "liberal," has largely been ceded in recent years to the values of equality and justice. I also hope to show that the liberal conception of freedom is distinct from and superior to the two freedom-centered political ideals that have attracted the most scholarly attention in recent decades: the market-centered or "libertarian" (to its opponents, "neoliberal") view on the one hand, and the state-centered or "republican" (to its opponents, "socialist") view on the other. By showing that liberalism can absorb the insights and avoid the pitfalls of each of these positions, I hope to persuade the reader not only that freedom is the first political value to be pursued, but that the cause of freedom is best advanced under a liberal banner. Thus the title: *Liberal Freedom*.

Why do we need another (or any!) defense of liberalism, and why should the defense take this particular form? My answer is twofold: first, that a freedom-centered liberalism offers a promising set of resources for responding to what I take to be the most fundamental political challenge facing modern societies, and second, that the justice-centered understanding of liberalism that is currently dominant in the academy, and increasingly in public discourse, fails to take advantage of those resources. The purpose of this introduction is to briefly outline and defend each of these claims.

I.I THE PROBLEM OF POLARIZATION

First, the challenge. There is a growing sense – and mounting evidence – that we are losing the ability to talk to each other constructively across lines of political disagreement. The evidence takes many forms: the polarization of public opinion, even about seemingly nonpolitical matters, along partisan lines; the formation of ideological "bubbles" within which new information is tailored to fit preexisting narratives; the tendency to label one's political opponents as enemies, either of "people like us" or of the polity itself; low and declining trust in a variety of social institutions – government, the media, churches, universities, and so on – that used to be seen as sites or facilitators of civil discourse; and the inability of political leaders to respond to a wide range of pressing social problems, even when there is strong and consistent public support for doing so. Likewise, many explanations have been offered for these developments: the "sorting" of the population into increasingly homogeneous social spaces, meaning that we interact less often with people who look, think, or act differently than us; the emergence of communication technologies that make it easy to selectively distribute and consume information, and the corresponding decline of a "mainstream" media that once provided a common set of facts and narratives on which a shared public life could be built; the gradual but nevertheless dramatic decline in religious faith and practice, which once provided the ethical and institutional linchpin of a pluralistic civil society; the increasingly open expression of previously marginalized identities along lines of ethnicity, gender, and sexuality, and the resulting fragmentation of the public sphere; the rapid growth of the foreign-born population in many societies and the fear that "traditional" conceptions of national identity are being undermined; the emergence of a "winner take all" economy and the growing sense that life is a zero-sum game in which the stakes are high.

Needless to say, not all of these developments are entirely negative; indeed, some of them will appear to some people as unmixed goods. We can nevertheless agree, I think, that they have placed enormous strains on our civic culture, and that a society in which people are unwilling or unable to talk to each other about (and despite) their disagreements is not a healthy, and in the end not a sustainable, one. The problem of polarization, as I will call it for short, is therefore fundamental in a literal sense: whatever the most pressing problems facing us might be – and of course we disagree about that question too – we can only make headway on those problems if we first persuade our fellow citizens that they are real problems, and that despite our differences we can and should work together to try to solve them. I do not mean to suggest that politics is primarily about talk: it is not; it is primarily about the exercise of power. Nor do I mean to suggest that our problems could easily be overcome if we could just learn to get along: as a rule, social problems become political problems precisely because they are contentious and hard to solve. Still less do I mean to suggest that moderation and compromise are desirable for their own sakes: partisanship is not the same thing as principle; indeed, it typically corrupts it. I simply mean to assert the truism that the peaceful and constructive exercise of political power has to be mediated by communication. When power is exercised by people who cannot or will not communicate with each other, in pursuit of ends that are not mutually intelligible, then we can only submit to superior force – and, perhaps, look forward to a day when superior force is ours. Anyone who is comfortable with that kind of politics has to be confident that superior force is on their side, or that they can take steps to make sure that it is. That is a recipe, in the long run at least, for authoritarianism.

Communication consists in a kind of sharing, but it also presupposes a kind of sharing: we are only able to engage in conversation because there are certain things that we already have in common – a common language, obviously, but also common interests, common experiences, and common expectations. Those things cannot be completely shared, of course – otherwise there would not be anything to talk about – but taken together they form the matrix within which fruitful conversations become possible. The distinguishing feature of *political* communication is that it requires that we talk to people whose interests, experiences, and expectations are not only different from, but in conflict with, our own, and with whom we nevertheless have to act in common. At least two things have to be shared in order for this kind of communication to be possible: a set of moral norms that encourage peaceful and constructive engagement across lines of disagreement, and a shared moral vocabulary – a shared set of values – that makes such engagement possible. However, these two desiderata are in tension with each other: to the extent that we presuppose the existence of a shared set of values, we run the risk of excluding or failing to properly listen to those who do not share, or who are suspected of not sharing, those values. Conversely, to the extent that we commit ourselves to listening to people who embrace a wide and open-ended range of values, we run the risk of undermining the very conditions that make constructive disagreement possible.

The only viable strategy for responding to this dilemma, I will argue, is to identify a moral vocabulary that has more than one dimension – thus leaving room for constructive disagreement – but whose dimensions are broad and coherent enough to provide a common point of orientation. This is exactly what the liberal conception of freedom provides. As we will see, liberal freedom, like liberal society itself, has two distinct and complementary dimensions, which give rise to two distinct and complementary moral projects; on the one hand, to create the social conditions under which we are fit to be held responsible for what we do, and on the other hand, to carve out a domain of conduct within which we are not responsible to anyone else for what we do, except by choice.[1] For convenience, I associate each of these dimensions of liberal freedom with a particular institutional form: I use the term "republican freedom" to refer to the connection between freedom and responsibility, and the term "market freedom" to refer to the connection between freedom and nonresponsibility. In doing so I am of course imposing my own terminology on a complex and diverse tradition of thought. Some liberal thinkers organize the conceptual terrain in ways that superficially resemble but only partially overlap with this distinction; for example, by appealing to Isaiah Berlin's influential distinction between "negative" and "positive" liberty, or to Benjamin Constant's equally influential distinction between "ancient" and "modern" liberty.[2] Some reserve the word freedom (or liberty) for what I am calling market freedom, and use another term like "self-government" or "democracy" to refer to what I am calling republican freedom. As we will see, many domains of

---

[1] Despite first appearances, these two categories do not exhaust the domain of human conduct. The slave – the paradigmatically unfree person – cannot properly be held responsible for what he does because he is (at least in principle) a mere instrument of his master's will. Nor, of course, does the slave enjoy a domain of conduct in which he is *not* responsible for what he does, because there is no part of a slave's life that is not (in principle) subject to his master's will.

[2] Isaiah Berlin, "Two Concepts of Liberty" (1958/1969), in *Liberty*, ed. Henry Hardy (New York: Oxford University Press, 2002), pp. 166–217; Benjamin Constant, "The Liberty of the Ancients Compared with That of the Moderns" (1819), in *Political Writings*, ed. and trans. Biancamaria Fontana (New York: Cambridge University Press, 1988), pp. 309–28. I distinguish my typology of freedom from Berlin's and Constant's in Chapters 1 and 4, respectively.

nonresponsible conduct[3] are not "markets" in the colloquial sense, although it can be helpful to use commercial markets as a point of reference.

I nevertheless hope to show that, terminological differences aside, the republican-market freedom distinction provides the most perspicuous way of describing the values to which liberals are committed, and the most parsimonious way of accounting for the development of the liberal tradition over time. Liberalism as I understand it – and, I will argue, as it was understood by the most admirable and influential liberals of the past – is the political ideology that holds republican and market freedom together in a single political vision, defines their respective limits, and seeks to maintain a fruitful tension between them. As we will see, and as this initial formulation may already suggest, the two dimensions of liberal freedom complement and qualify one another: just as it is impossible to imagine a society in which everyone is always held responsible for everything that they do, so too is it impossible to imagine a society in which no one is ever held responsible for anything that they do. A liberal politics is therefore concerned not only with determining how the values of republican and market freedom can each be realized, but also with determining how far we should be willing to compromise one of them for the sake of realizing the other more fully. It will sometimes be appropriate on liberal grounds to sacrifice a certain amount of republican freedom for the sake of more market freedom, just as it will sometimes be appropriate to sacrifice a certain amount of market freedom for the sake of more republican freedom. Liberals do not give a single answer to the question of how these trade-offs should be made – that is what makes a liberal politics open-ended and capacious. However, they do agree in giving priority to republican freedom insofar as they insist that the trade-offs be made in publicly visible and contestable ways and for publicly avowable reasons – that is what gives a liberal politics its moral center of gravity (as we will see, acceptance or rejection of this latter proposition is what distinguishes *liberals* from *neoliberals*). Whatever balance we strike in practice, we should be willing to admit that the language of freedom does not belong exclusively on one side of the question or the other.

---

[3] I will occasionally refer to these as domains of "irresponsible" conduct, but it is important to keep in mind that while the term irresponsibility often connotes blameworthiness, I do not intend that connotation – although, as we will see, a key feature of market freedom is that it confers a freedom to act even when our actions seem blameworthy to (certain) others, and possibly even to ourselves.

Of course, not just any way of striking the balance will be accepted as liberal in a given time and place. There are domains of conduct in which we can agree, here and now, that it would be illiberal to hold people publicly accountable for their actions – for example, with regard to their religious beliefs and practices (within certain limits) – just as there are domains of conduct in which we can agree, here and now, that it would be illiberal *not* to do so – for example, with regard to their treatment of other people's property (again, within certain limits). These are, for the time being, matters of settled judgment in liberal thought. But the caveat is crucial: judgment is settled through experience, and the lessons of experience are subject to revision through further experience over time. Only through a gross reification of terms could we say that the property rights and religious freedoms that the citizens of liberal societies enjoy today are the same rights and freedoms, practically speaking, as the ones that were defended by the liberal thinkers of the seventeenth, eighteenth, or nineteenth centuries, and even the most nostalgic liberal today probably would not be willing, on reflection, to trade today's bundle of rights and freedoms for that of 1690, 1790, or 1890. One of the distinguishing features of a liberal politics is that the boundaries of liberal freedom can be expected to change over time: as John Stuart Mill reminds us, "it is as certain that many opinions, now general, will be rejected by future ages, as it is that many, once general, are rejected by the present."[4] Liberalism so understood does not stand for a particular set of political ends or a particular vision of the good or just society; it stands for a particular moral vocabulary and a particular value orientation, a particular way of talking to each other in public life. As is probably already clear, and as we will now see, this way of thinking about liberalism is sharply at odds with the mainstream of contemporary academic discourse.

I.2 THE JUSTICE PARADIGM

Contemporary academic liberals largely agree in thinking that political outcomes are only legitimate if they are governed by a set of principles – principles of justice – that are insulated from political contestation. These principles can be described in a number of ways: for example, as a system of natural law, a scheme of natural rights, a "basic structure" ordered by certain principles, or a constitutional framework within and through

---

[4] John Stuart Mill, *On Liberty*, in *Collected Works*, ed. J. M. Robson (Toronto: University of Toronto Press, 1963–91), vol. 18, p. 230.

The Justice Paradigm

which ordinary legislation is crafted – nor are these possibilities mutually exclusive. They can also be defended in a number of ways: for example, by appealing to the deliverances of right reason or properly cultivated sentiments, an ideal of human flourishing, or the necessary presuppositions of the use of language. Despite the important differences among these views, they share the common assumption that justice is, as John Rawls puts it, "the first virtue of social institutions, as truth is of systems of thought,"[5] and that principles of justice should therefore be placed beyond the reach of ordinary politics. Indeed, this understanding of liberalism is so widely shared, both by contemporary academic liberals and by their critics, that it is hard for many people to see how a political position could count as liberal (for better or worse) unless it took this form. As I have already suggested, the freedom-centered view defended here rejects this justice-centered view.[6] It will of course require an extended argument to defend this position, but let me start by raising two *prima facie* doubts about the justice paradigm, as I will call it; one historical and the other theoretical.

Liberalism, like all major political ideologies, has deep and contested historical roots, but even by these standards the justice paradigm rests on a highly selective reading of the tradition. It best fits the contractarian strand of liberal thought that is associated in the early modern period with John Locke and Immanuel Kant – and with nonliberals like Thomas Hobbes and Jean-Jacques Rousseau – and that was almost single-handedly revived by Rawls in the latter part of the twentieth century. It fits the liberal thinkers of the intervening period – figures like Montesquieu, Condorcet, David Hume, Adam Smith, Edmund Burke, Thomas Paine, Mary Wollstonecraft, Alexander Hamilton, James Madison, Jeremy Bentham, Wilhelm von Humboldt, Benjamin Constant, Germaine de Staël, Alexis de Tocqueville, François Guizot, John Stuart Mill, Frederick Douglass, T. H. Green, Henry Sidgwick,

---

[5] John Rawls, *A Theory of Justice* (2nd ed., Cambridge, MA: Harvard University Press, 1999 [1971]), p. 3 (§1).

[6] A number of scholars have recently challenged the central role that justice plays in contemporary political thought; for two contrasting efforts along these lines see Michael Goodhart, *Injustice: Political Theory for the Real World* (New York: Oxford University Press, 2018) and Katrina Forrester, *In the Shadow of Justice: Postwar Liberalism and the Remaking of Political Philosophy* (Princeton, NJ: Princeton University Press, 2019). Although I share their skepticism about a justice-centered politics, I do not agree with Goodhart or Forrester that this skepticism requires a rejection of liberalism – in fact, as I argue below, I believe that liberalism properly understood provides a powerful and flexible framework for thinking critically about politics without appealing to justice as an organizing value.

L. T. Hobhouse, J. A. Hobson, John Dewey, Max Weber, Isaiah Berlin, Friedrich Hayek, and Karl Popper – much more awkwardly, or not at all. Indeed it defines liberalism in a way that excludes utilitarians like Hume, Bentham, Mill, and Sidgwick out of hand, despite the fact that they each devoted their lives to liberal causes, and with considerable success.[7] (Mill's liberal credentials are weighty enough that a number of scholars have struggled to show how he might be admitted back into the fold, giving rise to the perception that he, one of the most systematic political thinkers of the nineteenth century, was fundamentally confused about the relationship between his moral and political commitments.) Less obviously but no less importantly, by placing the metaethical debate between contractarians and consequentialists at the center of attention this way of thinking effectively reads the other thinkers mentioned above – to whom such questions were of little if any interest – out of the tradition altogether.[8]

It is therefore hard to exaggerate the sea change in liberal political thought that the postwar turn back to social contract theory brought about. Since the middle of the eighteenth century, when Hume famously argued that the Lockean appeal to an original contract "leads to paradoxes, repugnant to the common sentiments of mankind, and to the practice and opinion of all nations and all ages,"[9] liberal thinkers had rarely mentioned the social contract except to disavow it. Smith, following his friend here as on other matters, held that government "arose, not as some writers imagine from any consent or agreement of a number of persons to submit themselves to such or such regulations, but from the natural progress which men make in society." Bentham observed tartly that "[c]ontracts came from government, not government from

---

[7] Jeremy Waldron, for example, finds that utilitarians like Bentham and Mill "stand ... in an ambiguous relation to the liberal tradition" because they "were always wary of the idea of social contract" – even though, as he admits, "[t]here *is* an obvious sense in which [utilitarianism] is a liberal theory": Jeremy Waldron, "Theoretical Foundations of Liberalism," *Philosophical Quarterly* 37 (1987), pp. 127–50, quoted at pp. 143–4 (original emphasis).

[8] Montesquieu, Condorcet, Smith, Humboldt, Constant, Tocqueville, Green, and Berlin each receive only passing mention in John Rawls, *Lectures on the History of Political Philosophy* (Cambridge, MA: Harvard University Press, 2007); Burke, Paine, Wollstonecraft, Hamilton, Madison, de Staël, Guizot, Douglass, Hobhouse, Hobson, Dewey, Weber, Hayek, and Popper are not mentioned at all. Needless to say, Rawls and his students have played a central role in educating the current generation of liberal political philosophers.

[9] David Hume, "Of the Original Contract" (1748), in *Essays Moral, Political, and Literary*, ed. Eugene F. Miller (Indianapolis: Liberty Fund, 1985), p. 486.

The Justice Paradigm

contracts," and that the contrary view "does mischief, by involving the subject in error and confusion, and is neither necessary nor useful to any good purpose." Mill agreed that "no good purpose is answered by inventing a contract in order to deduce social obligations from it," and Green found that social contract theory is "generally admitted untenable" and "conveys a false notion of rights." In the twentieth century Dewey held that "the contract theory of the origin of the state is a theory whose falsity may easily be demonstrated both philosophically and historically," while at the opposite end of the ideological spectrum Hayek praised Hume, Smith, and Adam Ferguson for rejecting "the Cartesian conception of an independent and antecedently existing human reason that invented [social] institutions," and thus by extension "the conception that civil society was formed by some wise original legislator or an original 'social contract.'"[10] Examples could easily be multiplied.

The jump from Kant to Rawls therefore cuts us off from the rich set of resources that liberalism provides in areas like economic and social theory, moral and political psychology, and institutional design. More fundamentally, it cuts us off from the sense of historical perspective and intellectual humility that we can get by working within a continuous tradition of thought; continuous not only in terms of time but also in terms of connecting high theory with practical politics.[11] The period in which social contract theory was moribund is also the period, running roughly from the French Revolution to the Second World War, in which liberals won their greatest political victories: the elimination of hereditary privilege and the opening of careers to talents, the separation of political from ecclesiastical authority and the advent of religious toleration, the abolition of slavery and the

---

[10] Adam Smith, *Lectures on Jurisprudence* (Oxford: Clarendon Press, 1978 [1763]) (A) iv.19; Jeremy Bentham, "Nonsense Upon Stilts" (1795), in *Collected Works: Rights, Representation, and Reform: Nonsense Upon Stilts and Other Writings on the French Revolution*, ed. Philip Schofield, Catherine Pease-Watkin, and Cyprian Blamers (New York: Oxford University Press, 2002) pp. 331–2; Mill, *On Liberty*, p. 276; T. H. Green, *Lectures on the Principles of Political Obligation* (1885), in *Lectures on the Principles of Political Obligation and Other Writings*, ed. Paul Harris and John Morrow (New York: Cambridge University Press, 1986), §§9, 49; John Dewey, *Reconstruction in Philosophy* (1920), in Jo Ann Boydston, ed., *The Middle Works of John Dewey* (Carbondale: Southern Illinois University Press, 1976–83), vol. 12, p. 104; Friedrich Hayek, *The Constitution of Liberty* (Chicago: University of Chicago Press, 1960), p. 57.

[11] This is a prominent theme in the work of the political theorist Michael Freeden; see, for example, the essays collected in his *Liberal Languages: Ideological Imaginations and Twentieth-Century Progressive Thought* (Princeton, NJ: Princeton University Press, 2005).

establishment of universal suffrage, the breaking down of trade barriers and the building of a welfare state. Each of the thinkers mentioned above played a key role, both intellectually and practically speaking, in winning one or more of those victories, and the freedom-centered liberalism that is defended here allows us to make better sense and use of the rich tradition of thought that they represent. The fact that the contractarian canon centers around (and is nearly exhausted by) Kant and Rawls – two of the least politically engaged and politically influential thinkers in the tradition – should give us pause. Whatever we make of the fate of liberalism as a political project over the last fifty years – most would describe it, I think, as a period of retrenchment – it would be hard to argue that it has been guided, still less advanced, by the principles of social contract theory, Rawlsian or otherwise. Indeed, it is hard to think of a time when the gulf between those who are doing the practical work of advancing liberal aims and those who are doing the intellectual work of providing a systematic rationale for pursuing those aims has been as wide as it is now.

This brings us to the second *prima facie* doubt about the justice paradigm, this one theoretical rather than historical in nature.[12] Social contract theorists have held since the time of Locke that a political order is only legitimate if its authority rests on the consent of those who are subject to it. Contemporary contractarians take this to mean that a legitimate political order is one whose terms of cooperation could be accepted (or not reasonably rejected[13]) by all who are bound by them. Rawls calls this "the liberal principle of legitimacy"; that "our exercise of political power is fully proper only when it is exercised in accordance with a constitution the essentials of which all citizens as free and equal may reasonably be expected to endorse in the light of principles and ideals acceptable to their common human reason."[14] The freedom alluded to here is a version of the

---

[12] Portions of the following paragraphs are drawn from Eric MacGilvray, "Liberalism Before Justice," *Social Philosophy and Policy* 32 (2016), pp. 354–71, which develops this line of argument in more detail.

[13] The latter formulation is due to T. M. Scanlon, who defends it as a general principle of moral reasoning: see his "Contractualism and Utilitarianism," in Amartya Sen and Bernard Williams, eds., *Utilitarianism and Beyond* (New York: Cambridge University Press, 1982), pp. 103–28, and more generally his *What We Owe to Each Other* (Cambridge, MA: Harvard University Press, 1998). It is made the basis for a liberal politics in Thomas Nagel, "Moral Conflict and Political Legitimacy," *Philosophy and Public Affairs* 16 (1987), pp. 215–40. Its roots lie, as both Scanlon and Nagel acknowledge, in Rawls's theory of justice as fairness.

[14] John Rawls, *Political Liberalism* (2nd ed., New York: Columbia University Press, 1996 [1993]), p. 137.

so-called positive conception of liberty: it consists not just in the capacity to form and pursue one's own ends, but also in the capacity to adjust those ends and the way in which they are pursued to the demands of fair cooperation with others. A free person is, in Rawls's terms, reasonable as well as rational, and to be treated as a free person – to enjoy freedom in society – is to be bound only by social rules and obligations to which all reasonable people would consent (or not withhold consent).[15]

Needless to say, few if any political principles would pass this test in a modern society, even if we suppose (optimistically) that all of its members are reasonable in the sense of being sincerely motivated to identify and abide by such principles.[16] The goal of unanimity can therefore only plausibly be pursued if we idealize the consenting parties and the conditions under which they offer their consent. Rawls's famous "original position" and the various other thought experiments that contractarian liberals have devised are designed to accomplish this task. As both defenders and critics of these devices have pointed out, the idealizations that they propose place a strain on the liberal credentials of the resulting theories of justice. That is, to the extent that we define consent counterfactually – as something that *would* or *should* have been given under the right conditions – it becomes doubtful that we have shown our actual, nonideal fellow citizens the kind of respect that contractarian liberals insist they are owed. (This is simply a version of the standard liberal critique of positive liberty views.[17]) Contractarian liberals therefore spend a lot of time and energy on the metapolitical project of trying to show that their way of constructing consent – of defining reasonableness – is in fact reasonable. A justice-centered liberalism is in this sense a *justification*-centered liberalism.

Justification – the exchange of reasons with the aim of persuading others – is, as I have already emphasized, a central part of any politics, liberal or otherwise. However, the justice paradigm raises the stakes of

---

[15] Ibid., pp. 29–35; in an alternate statement of the liberal principle of legitimacy Rawls substitutes the phrase "reasonable and rational" for the phrase "free and equal": ibid., p. 217. See also Waldron's "Theoretical Foundations of Liberalism," cited above, which gives more attention than Rawls does to the role that the appeal to freedom plays in defining the contractarian position.

[16] This is Scanlon's definition of reasonableness; see, for example, "Contractualism and Utilitarianism," pp. 110–11. Rawls holds that reasonable people must also assume the "burdens of judgment"; that is, they have to accept that uncertainty about how to weigh conflicting evidence, define key terms, and balance competing value claims limits our ability to reach agreement on fundamental moral questions: see especially Rawls, *Political Liberalism*, pp. 54–8.

[17] Most famously laid out in Berlin's "Two Concepts of Liberty."

justification to (we might say) an unreasonable level; one that exacerbates instead of alleviating the problem of polarization. Those who refuse to accept one's own favored principles of justice – who do not recognize themselves in the idealized conditions under which their consent is said to have been given – must after all be deemed "unreasonable" if their refusal is not to call the legitimacy of those principles into question. This is not a very constructive stance to take with someone who disagrees with you, nor is it a very liberal one. After all, there are few if any interesting political questions – not even regarding "constitutional essentials" – on which all people of good will can be expected to agree. Contractarian political thought is therefore marked by a strange mixture of diffidence and insularity; intensely preoccupied with the kind of immanent critique that we would expect from people who take universal agreement as their ideal, but largely uninterested in engaging with political views that do not begin from liberal premises as it defines them. This may help to explain why the justice paradigm has made so little headway with the broader public, to whom the premises are not as self-evident as contractarians often like to suppose, and to whom the appeal to counterfactual consent is likely to seem mysterious at best.

I therefore think that it is time for a fresh start, and I propose to make such a start by returning to the etymological roots of the word "liberalism" in the word "liberty," treating freedom rather than justice as the "first virtue" of social institutions. Instead of trying to identify a set of principles that all reasonable people would or should have consented to, and against which the legitimacy of actual polities and policies can be measured, liberalism so understood is committed to the messy and contentious project of balancing the claims of responsibility and non-responsibility – of republican and market freedom – against one another. In the language of moral philosophy, liberal freedom is more like an Aristotelian virtue than a contractarian side-constraint or a utilitarian maximand, and, like an Aristotelian virtue, its meaning can often be clarified, and its aims advanced, as much through persuasive rhetoric or exemplary action as through reasoned argument. I hope to show that this way of thinking about politics is more faithful than the justice paradigm is to the central concerns of the liberal tradition, and that it allows us to make better sense of the development of that tradition over time: liberal thinkers do not speak with one voice, but historically speaking they have agreed in placing freedom rather than justice at the center of political life, and in defining freedom (at least implicitly) in the double-barreled sense that I have described. More importantly, this approach offers a more promising response to the problem of polarization, because it detaches the question of what should be done from the question of what all reasonable people could accept, or not reasonably reject. By reviving a tradition of liberal thought that is freedom- rather than justice- (and justification-) centered, I want to encourage liberal thinkers to make better use of their past, and to put their energies to more constructive use in the present. Liberalism is too important to be left to the Rawlsians.

1.3 OVERVIEW

Any effort to put freedom at the center of a liberal politics has to start by coming to terms with the bewildering variety of meanings that liberals – and political philosophers more generally – have assigned to the word "freedom," and the equally bewildering variety of criticisms that those definitions have attracted. This is the task of Chapter 1, which introduces and defends the key conceptual claim on which the rest of the argument is built: that instead of treating freedom as a property of *actions*, as in the familiar negative – positive liberty framework, we should treat it as a property of *persons*, or more precisely of the social position that persons occupy. This is what freedom meant in premodern and early modern political thought: a free person was someone who held a privileged social status, and who displayed the qualities of character – the virtues – that were expected of someone holding that status. The liberal conception of free personhood is distinctive, as we have already seen, in that a liberal citizen is free by virtue of occupying two distinct social positions that complement and qualify one another: that of being constituted and recognized as a responsible agent, and that of being granted a domain of nonresponsible conduct. This way of thinking about freedom improves on the positive liberty position by shifting our focus away from the metaphysical question of whether human beings "really" exercise agency and toward the practical question of when we should hold them responsible for the things that they do. It likewise improves on the negative liberty position by providing a clear explanation of why unconstrained choice is socially and politically valuable – a question that liberals have sometimes found surprisingly difficult to answer. The result is a great gain in conceptual clarity, as we are no longer obliged to shore up our theory of freedom by placing *ad hoc* conditions on what counts as a free action or as a freedom-reducing constraint.

Chapters 2 and 3 look more closely at the relationship between these two conceptions of freedom – republican and market freedom, as I call them. Chapter 2 examines the relationship between republican freedom and the market, with particular focus on the work of Philip Pettit, the leading contemporary philosopher of republicanism. Republicans have traditionally tried to keep the political and economic domains distinct by limiting citizenship to the economically independent. It is easy to see why: the pursuit of republican freedom requires that we create the social conditions under which people are fit to be held responsible for what they do, and markets generate outcomes for which no one in particular can be held responsible, and that nevertheless profoundly shape the choices that we make. It would seem to follow that republican freedom is not available to those who participate in or depend upon them. Pettit, departing from this tradition of thought, argues that while the inequalities that markets generate can undermine republican freedom, markets themselves do not pose a direct threat to our freedom because they do not involve the imposition of an alien will. The distinction between intentionally and nonintentionally imposed constraints on which this line of argument rests dissolves once we treat freedom as a property of persons rather than actions: the salient question is not how a constraint was imposed, but rather whether its presence diminishes people's fitness to be held responsible for what they do – and whether it is within the power of human beings to remove. Thus, while republicans have good prudential reasons to delegate decision-making authority to markets – in order to prevent the state itself from posing a threat to republican freedom – they do not give us any positive reason to value market freedom. A republican theory of freedom is therefore qualitatively different from a liberal one.

Chapter 3 examines the meaning and value of market freedom more closely. I have already described market freedom as a person-centered conception of freedom which consists in holding the privileged status of being a nonresponsible social actor. Here I define that privilege more precisely as the ability to impose costs on other people without being accountable to them for doing so. A market is a domain of conduct in which people who enjoy this privilege interact with each other. Every choice that a market actor makes has at least a marginal effect on the overall pattern that the market generates, but we enjoy market freedom not because we are accountable to each other for what that pattern is, but rather precisely because we are not: we do as we please and let the chips fall where they may. Normative evaluations of "the market" that take commercial markets as the paradigm case overlook the fact that nonresponsibility is a key feature of behavior in many other domains, making it harder to appreciate the full range of reasons that we have for allowing markets (understood in this broader sense) to decide certain social outcomes. Broadening the definition of markets also allows us to rebut the charge that they are simply "neoliberal" instruments of social control by helping us to see how rights of possession and exchange, systems of incentives, and other elements of "control," far from being constitutive features of markets, are in fact exogenous constraints on them. In a liberal polity these constraints are imposed in the name of republican freedom: they set clear but contestable boundaries on nonresponsible choice. Markets themselves, by contrast, are sites of independence, innovation, and idiosyncrasy, and are therefore a necessary (though not of course a sufficient) means for the pursuit of traditional liberal ends such as limited government, social progress, and personal development.

Chapter 4 explores how the liberal tradition arose, historically speaking, out of the effort to strike an appropriate balance between republican and market freedom. The key development here was the gradual but ultimately decisive collapse of traditional economic, political, and social hierarchies over the course of the nineteenth and twentieth centuries – a collapse that forced political thinkers and actors to move beyond the contractarian claim that people are equal in theory and start wrestling with the implications of the fact that they were becoming equal in practice. The liberal response to this development came in two overlapping stages. First, the democratization of public and private life made it increasingly clear that the power that we exercise over each other in modern societies is reciprocal, insidious, and pervasive, and thus gave new urgency to the problem of carving out a domain of nonresponsible conduct. Second, the rise of industrial capitalism exposed the fundamental tension between the dependence that we experience in our "private" lives and the independence that we are expected to display in public life, and thus gave new urgency to the problem of creating the material and social conditions under which people are fit to be held responsible for what they do. The liberal tradition was born out of the effort to respond to these interrelated problems, and the key liberal insight, which was worked out over the course of this period, is that efforts to promote republican freedom often require that we limit market freedom, and vice versa. To say that the liberal tradition was "born" in this period is not to deny or downplay the obvious fact that earlier thinkers and ideas have been incorporated into it. Rather, it allows us to see that this incorporation was retroactive, as nineteenth and twentieth century liberals drew selectively on influential precedents that could be used to support their cause. In doing so they reconfigured the lines of alliance and opposition that those thinkers had used to orient themselves, giving rise to apparent paradoxes that intellectual historians are still working to unravel.

Chapter 5 returns to the problem of polarization and argues that a freedom-centered liberalism provides us with a better set of resources for responding to it than the going alternatives, liberal or otherwise. I begin by arguing that liberalism so understood allows us to sort anti-liberals into two basic groups: those who deny that republican and market freedom are important political values – *authoritarians* of various stripes; and those who hold that one or the other of them is a sufficient political value taken in itself – *utopians* of various stripes. We can further distinguish *socialist* utopians, who embrace republican freedom to the exclusion of market freedom, from *market* utopians, who embrace market freedom to the exclusion of republican freedom. I then consider two influential contemporary critiques of liberalism, each of which calls attention to an important source of political polarization: the claim, most closely associated with the political right, that it corrodes the ethical foundations of social life and promotes an empty, anomic individualism; and the claim, most closely associated with the political left, that it is complicit in the power structures of capitalism and imperialism. In each case we find that a freedom-centered liberalism puts its critics on the horns of a dilemma: they either have to admit that they occupy a position within the liberal fold – that is, that they are also committed to striking an appropriate balance between republican and market freedom, albeit one that is substantially different from the status quo – or embrace one of the authoritarian or utopian positions that I have just described. I conclude by considering whether and on what terms a freedom-centered liberalism can accommodate its contractarian counterpart.

The defense of liberalism that is offered here will be viewed with suspicion by those who hold that liberal ideals are only secure if their validity can somehow be shown to transcend the beliefs and desires of those who are subject to them. The appeal of the justice paradigm lies, after all, in its claim to place certain values on firmer ground than the shifting sands of public opinion and public discourse. A freedom-centered liberalism asks us to treat this as a quixotic and counterproductive aim, and to see politics instead as an arena in which the proper bounds of public authority and the proper ends of public life are open to revision at any time and to substantial change over time. As I have pointed out, the ideals that liberal polities stand for today are not the same ideals, practically speaking, that they stood for in the past, and there is every reason to expect that some of the ideals that they stand for today will not be attractive or even fully intelligible in the future. The liberalism that is defended here is therefore itself an object of political contestation, and not just the background against which such contestation takes place. If we can look to the past achievements of liberal polities – the widespread (but still imperfect) acceptance of religious toleration and free inquiry, the relative (but still woefully incomplete) deconstruction of class, gender, and racial hierarchies, the (possibly temporary) defeat of totalitarianisms, left and right – to remind ourselves of the promise of a liberal politics, we can look to our many remaining failings, and to the fact that even our achievements are preserved only through our own vigilance, to remind ourselves how fallible our ideals, and the institutions that we have built upon them, actually are. Liberal freedom is, in short, both a richer and a more fragile ideal than many of its supporters – and critics – realize.

I

Free Actions and Free Persons

> The subject of this Essay is not the so-called Liberty of the Will, so unfortunately opposed to the misnamed doctrine of Philosophical Necessity; but Civil, or Social Liberty: the nature and limits of the power which can be legitimately exercised by society over the individual.
>
> John Stuart Mill, *On Liberty*

1.1 CHOICE AND RESPONSIBILITY

Mill begins his treatise *On Liberty* – probably the best-known and most influential defense of individual liberty ever written – by detaching the question of what the limits of individual liberty should be from the question of whether individual liberty is possible, and, if so, what it consists in metaphysically speaking. His instincts in doing so were sound, but he was at best only partly successful: even now political debates about freedom typically converge on – and quickly diverge over – the question of what it means for a person to make a choice. As a result, practical questions about the proper scope of individual liberty – the kinds of questions that Mill wanted to focus on – are entangled with theoretical questions about the nature of human agency – exactly the kinds of questions that he hoped to avoid. In this chapter I pursue Mill's intuition that these two lines of inquiry should be kept distinct; not because I believe (as he did) that questions about "the so-called Liberty of the Will" are otiose, but because I think they lead us astray when we take up what he called "the practical controversies of the age."[1]

---

[1] John Stuart Mill, *On Liberty*, in *Collected Works*, ed. J. M. Robson (Toronto: University of Toronto Press, 1963–91), vol. 18, p. 217. Mill discusses the "doctrine of Philosophical

In pursuing this line of argument I rely on one of the oldest distinctions in Western political thought: the distinction between being free to act and being a free person.[2] Freedom of *action* has traditionally been associated with the absence of preventing conditions, where these may be either physical or moral in nature: the Justinian *Digest* of Roman law defines freedom as "the natural ability to do as one pleases unless prohibited by force or right."[3] As the word "natural" suggests, freedom in this sense can be predicated of any creature that possesses the faculty of choice, and so to talk about free action we have to say something about what agency consists in and how it is distributed. The familiar modern language of "negative" and "positive" liberty grew out of this juristic conception of freedom. Being a free *person*, by contrast, has traditionally been associated with holding a privileged social status and with the quality of the choices that one is thereby in a position to make. A free man (freedom in this sense was originally only fully available to men) was a member of a dominant class – paradigmatically, a master as opposed to a slave – whose dominance was justified, ideologically speaking, by the superior qualities – the virtues – that its members were said to possess. The language of free personhood therefore has an ethical as well as a status-based dimension, although it is not bound up, as the language of free action is, with the question of willing: virtue in the classical tradition is a matter of disposition, not volition. Traces of this mingling of ethical and status-based ways of thinking can be found in modern English words like "liberal" (in the sense of generous or magnanimous), "frank" (a quality with which the Germanic conquerors of Gaul credited themselves), and "ingenuous" (derived from the Latin word for free-born) – and in contrasting words like "base," "common," "low," "mean," "servile," "villainous," and "vulgar."[4]

Not surprisingly, the language of free personhood has traditionally been the politically salient one: it provides an ideological basis not only

---

Necessity" most notably in book 6, chapter 2 of *A System of Logic Ratiocinative and Inductive*, in *Collected Works*, vol. 8, pp. 836–43.

[2] Here and in the following paragraph I draw on the more detailed discussion in Eric MacGilvray, *The Invention of Market Freedom* (New York: Cambridge University Press, 2011), chapters 1–2.

[3] *Digest* 1.5.4. The *Digest* was compiled in the sixth century CE; its definition of freedom is drawn from the *Institutes* of Gaius, which date from the second century, but the view that it expresses is much older than that.

[4] For a useful survey of the Greek, Latin, and English roots of the language of freedom see C. S. Lewis, *Studies in Words* (2nd ed., New York: Cambridge University Press, 1960), chapter 5.

for frankly hierarchical political orders, but also, as we will see, for the more complicated republican ideal of virtuous self-government. Indeed, many linguists believe that the language of free personhood is not only politically but etymologically prior to the language of free action; that the association of freedom with the absence of constraint was a metaphorical extension of its original status-based meaning, inspired by the privileges and immunities that were available to free men.[5] It is clear in any case that the mere freedom to act did not have any special political significance prior to the modern period: an action has to be freely chosen in order to count as moral, but the properly political question from a premodern point of view (and from many modern points of view as well) is not the number of choices that are available, but whether the right choices are made.[6] Free action and free personhood are thus qualitatively different things: free persons may have fewer constraints on their actions than slaves, but this is not what qualifies them as free, and we cannot determine whether someone is a free person simply by counting up the number of things that he or she is able to do, even comparatively speaking. Indeed, in the classical tradition a "servile" person is sometimes said to be *less* constrained than a free man, in the sense that he or she is said to lack the capacity and training, and thus to be unbound by the ethical and social norms, that are necessary for the cultivation of individual virtue and the preservation of social order. This is why giving people of unfree status access to choices that were normally reserved for free men is so often associated with disorder and anarchy in premodern political thought.[7]

Any effort to incorporate the language of free personhood into a liberal theory of freedom faces two basic challenges. The first and most obvious challenge arises from the fact that the hierarchical structure of the classical

---

[5] The etymological debates are explored in Hanna Fenichel Pitkin, "Are Freedom and Liberty Twins?" *Political Theory* 16 (1988), pp. 528–44.

[6] Thomas Aquinas, for example, describes liberty as "one of the foremost blessings" of human life, not because he thinks that people should be allowed to do as they please, but rather because right actions are only moral actions if they are done freely: "a deed is rendered virtuous and praiseworthy and meritorious," he argues, "chiefly by the way in which it proceeds from the will," and actions can be done freely in this sense "even where there is a duty of obedience"; for example, even when the action in question is required by law: Thomas Aquinas, *Summa Theologiae* 2a2ae q 104 art 1 ad 3, in *Political Writings*, trans. R. W. Dyson (New York: Cambridge University Press, 2002), p. 58.

[7] The most famous example is the satirical description of democracy as a regime of extreme freedom tending toward anarchy in book 8 of Plato's *Republic* (557a–564a), but this view is pervasive in Greek and Roman political thought: see, for example, Aristotle, *Politics*, 1310a30–35 and 1317b10–18; Polybius, *Histories*, book 6 §57; Livy, *Ab urbe condita*, book 24, chapter 25 §8; and Cicero, *De re publica*, book 1 §§52–3.

language of free personhood is at odds with the egalitarian norms that underlie a liberal politics: from a liberal point of view people are properly treated as being not only free, but also equal. This is why contemporary liberals typically associate freedom with qualities that are, unlike classical virtue, said to be within the reach of all people, at least in principle: with the mere fact of being unconstrained, as in the case of negative liberty views, or with action in accordance with a rational will, as in the case of positive liberty views. The second challenge is to take into account the distinctively liberal claim that unconstrained choice is a core political value; that, as Mill put it, "the only freedom which deserves the name, is that of pursuing our own good in our own way."[8] In short, any effort to put the language of free personhood to liberal use must be able to show that this language can be both egalitarian and libertarian – and that it does a better job of honoring those commitments than the familiar negative and positive liberty approaches.

The key to meeting these challenges is to recognize that there are two distinct social positions that qualify a person as free in a liberal polity: the position of republican citizen and of market actor. This is because from a liberal point of view the question of why I should want the *freedom* to do or choose x, as opposed to simply wanting x, has two different and seemingly contradictory answers: "Because I want to be held responsible for doing or choosing x," and "Because I *don't* want to be held responsible for doing or choosing x." That is, on the one hand we might hold that we act freely only insofar as our actions are not shaped or determined by factors – such as ignorance, poverty, or subjection to arbitrary power – that tend to diminish our fitness to be held responsible for what we do. On the other hand, we might hold that we act freely only insofar as our actions are not subject to the interference – or even, in the limit, to the scrutiny – of other people; that is, if we are not responsible to anyone else for what we do, unless we choose to be.[9] The liberal idea of free personhood embraces both of these conceptions of freedom and seeks to strike an appropriate balance between them. As my use of the phrase "insofar as" suggests, each kind of freedom can in principle be measured, at least ordinally: it is

---

[8] Mill, *On Liberty*, p. 226.
[9] As I pointed out in the Introduction, the social positions of responsibility and nonresponsibility do not exhaust the domain of human conduct: a slave, for example, cannot properly be held responsible for what he does because he is (in principle) a mere instrument of his master's will, and he does not enjoy a domain of conduct in which he is *not* held responsible for what he does, because there is no part of his life that is not (in principle) subject to his master's will.

possible to be more or less fit to be held responsible for what one does, and it is possible for the domain of conduct within which one is *not* held responsible for what one does to be more or less extensive. But neither kind of freedom can be reduced to the quantity or quality of the choices that a person has, or to the number or significance of the constraints that he or she faces. On this view a person is not free because he or she is able to perform a certain range of actions; rather an action is free (in different senses) because it is performed by a responsible or a nonresponsible person.

Why adopt a person-centered instead of an action-centered theory of freedom? In the first half of this chapter, I examine the conceptual and normative blind spots of the action-centered negative and positive liberty views when considered as political values. On the one hand, any effort to treat negative liberty – unconstrained choice – as a political value has to take into account the fact that constraint is a ubiquitous feature of human experience (thus Mill's doubts about "the so-called Liberty of the Will") and that choices not only have different values, they often have negative value – especially (but not only) if they are available to everyone. Indeed, the idea that freedom should be thought of in negative terms was originally promoted by thinkers, such as Thomas Hobbes and Jeremy Bentham, who denied or were skeptical about the existence of free will, and who argued that freedom does not have any independent political value (Section 1.2). On the other hand, thinkers who, like John Locke and Immanuel Kant, follow the mainstream of the juristic tradition in equating free action with rightful rather than with unconstrained choice – who define freedom in "positive" rather than "negative" terms – subordinate the value (and often the meaning) of freedom to whatever conception of "rightness" they use to define its proper boundaries. Such views fail to take account of the fact that any effort to define what rightful choice consists in will be deeply contested, and (pardon the expression) rightly so. Indeed, despite its formally egalitarian character, the language of rightful choice has been used to support the same kinds of hierarchies that defined the classical conception of free personhood (Section 1.3).

In the second half of the chapter, I argue that a person-centered theory of freedom can capture the intuitions that make the negative and positive liberty approaches attractive while avoiding their pitfalls. I argue, first, that the association of freedom with responsibility – republican freedom, as I call it – allows us to take into account the quality of the choices that people are in a position to make while being less vulnerable than positive liberty views to concerns about hierarchy and paternalism (Section 1.4).

We have already seen that in order to create the conditions under which people are fit to be held responsible for what they do we have to make sure that they are not subject to factors, such as ignorance, poverty, or subjection to arbitrary power, that tend to diminish that possibility. To this extent proponents of republican freedom and of positive liberty agree, practically speaking. However, republican freedom has a built-in bias toward inclusivity that does not depend on a particular theory of what human agency consists in or how it is distributed. This is because in politics we often detach the metaphysical question of whether people are "really" responsible for what they do from the practical question of whether we should treat them as if they are. In a republican polity the latter question cannot be settled by philosophical fiat, it has to be negotiated by all of the members of the political community. To exclude anyone from the process of defining the conditions and determining the boundaries of public responsibility is *ipso facto* to diminish their fitness to be held responsible for the various ways in which the resulting decisions shape their behavior, and thus to take away their republican freedom.

I argue, finally, that the association of freedom with nonresponsibility – market freedom, as I call it – allows us to treat the absence of constraint as a core political value without overlooking the fact that constraint is a ubiquitous feature of human action, or that different choices have different values (Section 1.5). The key insight here is that market freedom can be used for purposes – that people can and do make choices – whose consequences cannot be foreseen, or in some cases even conceived of, in advance. A liberal polity is one in which people are, in certain areas of their lives and with regard to certain kinds of issues, free to make these kinds of choices, and in which the resulting uncertainty about outcomes is tolerated and even celebrated. An appreciation of the open-ended quality of free action, and thus of the open texture of a free society, must therefore be a central feature of any liberal theory of freedom. To this extent proponents of market freedom and of negative liberty agree, practically speaking. However, because the defining feature of market freedom is not the absence of constraint but rather the absence of responsibility, it is not subject, as the idea of negative liberty is, to the charge of conceptual incoherence, nor does it require that we make question-begging stipulations about what "counts" as a constraint. Moreover, the fact that the political value of market freedom consists largely in the unforeseeable consequences to which it can lead means that its value cannot simply be reduced to the current or expected value of the particular choices that are permitted. The idea of market freedom therefore allows us to distinguish between more and less valuable choices while still treating freedom itself as something that is independently valuable. As we will now see, this distinctively liberal case for noninterference stands in sharp contrast to the early modern view that negative liberty is not a political value at all.

1.2 FREEDOM AND UTILITY

The traditional distinction between being free to act and being a free person was notoriously collapsed by Thomas Hobbes, who argues in fairly traditional terms that "LIBERTY, or FREEDOME, signifieth (properly) the absence of Opposition," that is, of "externall Impediments of motion," and then adds, more daringly, that "a FREE-MAN, is he, that in those things, which by his strength and wit he is able to do, is not hindred to doe what he has a will to." For Hobbes the relativist, a free man is not a man of superior status or character, but simply a man who is free to act. And for Hobbes the materialist and determinist, the prerequisite of free action is not a rational will, but rather the absence of "externall" (i.e., physical) impediments. Indeed, he emphasizes that this definition of freedom "may be applyed no lesse to Irrationall, and Inanimate creatures, than to Rationall"; that freedom so understood can just as well be predicated of stones or insects as of people. He goes on to argue that actions that are done out of fear of punishment are nevertheless done freely, since fear is not an "externall Impediment," and draws the startling conclusion that the desire for freedom provides no grounds for resisting political authority. On the one hand, since laws are "made to hold, by the danger, though not by the difficulty of breaking them," and since actions undertaken out of fear are nevertheless free actions, it follows that laws do not limit our liberty, and that "it were very absurd for men to clamour as they doe, for the Liberty they so manifestly enjoy." On the other hand, even if we treat laws as "Artificiall Chains" and "take Liberty, for an exemption from Lawes," it is nevertheless the case that law – backed by an overawing fear of the sovereign – is a necessary condition for social order. It would therefore be "no lesse absurd, for men to demand as they doe, that Liberty, by which all other men may be masters of their lives."[10]

---

[10] Thomas Hobbes, *Leviathan*, ed. Richard Tuck (New York: Cambridge University Press, 1996 [1651]), pp. 145–7 (chapter 21, emphasis removed). This definition of a "free man" is not found in Hobbes's earlier writings; for a useful analysis of the development of his theory of freedom over time see Quentin Skinner, *Hobbes and Republican Liberty*

Hobbes's views on liberty, like many of his views, attracted a lot of attention but did not win many supporters. A more influential defense of an action-centered theory of political freedom was set out by the utilitarian thinkers of the late eighteenth century. It is not clear whether they owed a debt to Hobbes in doing so: Jeremy Bentham, who was in a position to know better, credited himself with having made "a kind of discovery"; namely that "the idea of liberty [is] merely a negative one," properly defined as "the absence of restraint."[11] Bentham's "discovery" was first published in 1776 in an anonymous pamphlet written by his friend John Lind, who credited it (at Bentham's request) to "a very worthy and ingenious friend, whose name I am not now permitted to mention."[12] Like Hobbes – and like the earlier natural jurists – Lind draws a distinction between "physical" and "moral" constraints: "A man is deprived of his physical liberty," he argues, "when he is constrained, by physical force, to do, or to forbear, certain acts; he is deprived of his moral liberty, when by moral motives, that is, the threat of painful events, to happen in consequence of his doing or forbearing, he is constrained to do or to forbear."[13] This idea is stated more formally in William Paley's influential *Principles of Moral and Political Philosophy* – published in 1785 but based on lectures delivered some years earlier[14] – and remained the official utilitarian position for more than a century. The young John Stuart Mill writes, for example, that "[l]iberty, in its original sense, means freedom from restraint," and that "[i]n this sense, every law, and every rule of morals, is contrary to liberty." Henry Sidgwick, writing near the end of the

---

(New York: Cambridge University Press, 2008). Skinner calls Hobbes's elision of the distinction between free actions and free persons "perhaps the most outrageous moment of effrontery in the whole of *Leviathan*": ibid., p. 151.

[11] Bentham lays claim to this "discovery" in a letter to John Lind dated March 27–April 1, 1776: *The Correspondence of Jeremy Bentham*, ed. Timothy L. S. Sprigge (London: Athlone Press, 1968), vol. 1, pp. 309–11, quoted at p. 310 (emphasis removed). For a useful analysis of Bentham's treatment of liberty see Douglas G. Long, *Bentham on Liberty: Jeremy Bentham's Idea of Liberty in Relation to His Utilitarianism* (Toronto: University of Toronto Press, 1977).

[12] Bentham was preparing to anonymously publish his *Fragment on Government* – he hoped to promote sales by encouraging speculation about its authorship – and presumably did not want to blow his cover.

[13] John Lind, *Three Letters to Dr. Price* (London: T. Payne, J. Sewell, and P. Elmsly, 1776), pp. 17n, 20.

[14] William Paley, "Of Civil Liberty," in *Principles of Moral and Political Philosophy* (Indianapolis: Liberty Fund, 2002 [1785]), pp. 311–16. On the relationship between the *Principles* and Paley's earlier lectures at Cambridge see the editorial introduction: ibid., pp. xii–xiii, and see also Long, *Bentham on Liberty*, p. 253n.

nineteenth century, likewise holds that freedom "signifies primarily the absence of physical coercion or confinement," but can also refer to "the moral restraint placed on inclination by the fear of painful consequences resulting from the action of other human beings."[15]

In advancing this line of argument Hobbes and the utilitarians attacked the traditional person-centered conception of political freedom on two fronts. On the one hand, they vigorously rejected the republican identification of freedom with self-government. Hobbes is especially scathing on this point, arguing that the classical republicans created

> a habit (under a falseshew of Liberty,) of favouring tumults, and of licentious controlling the actions of their Soveraigns; and again of controlling those controllers, with the effusion of so much blood; as I think I may truly say, there was never any thing so deerly bought, as these Western parts have bought the learning of the Greek and Latine tongues.[16]

Lind used Bentham's "negative" conception of liberty as the opening salvo of a long polemic against Richard Price's influential republican case for American independence[17] – arguing that Price "gives us, as principles of *government*, such unguarded assertions, as are *destructive* of all government."[18] Bentham himself attacked what he called the "Terrorist language" of the French revolutionaries in the same terms, arguing that their appeal to *liberté* served only "to excite and keep up a spirit of resistance to all laws, a spirit of insurrection against all governments."[19]

---

[15] Mill, "Periodical Literature: Edinburgh Review" (1824), in *Collected Works*, vol. 1, p. 296; Henry Sidgwick, *The Elements of Politics* (2nd ed., London: Macmillan, 1897 [1891]), p. 45 (chapter 4 §1).

[16] Hobbes, *Leviathan*, pp. 149–50 (chapter 21).

[17] Richard Price, *Observations on the Nature of Civil Liberty, the Principles of Government, and the Justice and Policy of the War with America* (London: T. Cadell, 1776). John Lind published two other anonymous pamphlets arguing against American independence, both written in collaboration with Bentham: *Remarks on the Principal Acts of the 13th Parliament of Great Britain* (London: T. Payne, 1775) and *Answer to the Declaration of the American Congress* (London: T. Cadell, J. Walter, and T. Sewell, 1776). Neither contains an analysis of the meaning of liberty.

[18] Lind, *Three Letters to Dr. Price*, p. 45 (original emphasis).

[19] Jeremy Bentham, "Nonsense Upon Stilts," in *Rights, Representation, and Reform: Nonsense Upon Stilts and Other Writings on the French Revolution*, ed. Philip Schofield, Catherine Pease-Watkin, and Cyprian Blamers (New York: Oxford University Press, 2002), pp. 330–1. This withering commentary on the French *Déclaration des droits de l'homme et du citoyen* was written in 1795 but published – in French translation under the title "Sophismes Anarchiques" – only in 1816. It first appeared in English as "Anarchical Fallacies" in vol. 2 of the posthumous *Works of Jeremy Bentham*, ed. John Bowring (London: Simpkin, Marshall, 1843), and was reprinted in the Bentham Project's critical edition under Bentham's preferred title

Paley argued more soberly, but no less bitingly, that "those definitions of liberty ought to be rejected, which, by making that essential to civil freedom which is *unattainable* in experience, inflame expectations that can never be gratified, and disturb the public content with complaints, which no wisdom or benevolence of government can remove."[20]

On the other hand, Hobbes and the utilitarians also rejected the view, first articulated by the natural jurists and now associated with the idea of positive liberty, that freedom does not consist in unconstrained choice but rather in rightful choice. Here they collapse the traditional distinction between liberty and license – or, to put the point the other way around, they introduce a distinction between free action and rightful action. Hobbes's reasoning on this point is straightforward: if I act freely whenever I am not physically prevented from carrying out my will, and if my will is necessarily determined by my (perhaps momentarily) strongest appetite, then it follows that whatever I do, I do freely, and that actions that are harmful to myself or to others are nevertheless free actions.[21] The utilitarians reach a similar conclusion without endorsing the deterministic premise: "Is not the liberty of doing mischief liberty?" Bentham asks. "[I]f not, what is it? and what word is there for it in the language, or in any language, by which it can be spoken of?"[22] (The word he is looking for, again, is "license.") Sidgwick puts the point more diplomatically: "I am sensible," he writes, "of the gain in effectiveness of moral persuasion which is obtained by ... enlisting the powerful sentiment of Liberty on the side of Reason and Morality." Nevertheless, he insists, "it is obvious that the Freedom [often] connected with Responsibility is not the Freedom that is only manifested or realised in rational action, but the Freedom to choose between right and wrong which is manifested or realised equally in either choice."[23]

Like their juristic predecessors, Hobbes and the utilitarians insist that the absence of constraint does not have any value taken in itself and point

---

"Nonsense Upon Stilts" in 2002. On the composition and publication history of the essay see the editorial introduction to the Bentham Project edition, pp. xlv–liii.

[20] Paley, "Of Civil Liberty," p. 315 (original emphasis).

[21] "In Deliberation, the last Appetite, or Aversion, immediately adhaering to the action, or to the omission thereof, is that wee call the WILL," and "[b]y this it is manifest, that not onely actions that have their beginning from Covetousnesse, Ambition, Lust, or other Appetites to the thing propounded, but also those that have their beginning from Aversion, or Feare of those consequences that follow the omission, are *voluntary actions*": Hobbes, *Leviathan*, pp. 44–5 (chapter 6, original emphasis).

[22] Bentham, "Nonsense Upon Stilts," p. 339.

[23] Henry Sidgwick, *The Methods of Ethics* (7th ed., London: Macmillan, 1907 [1874]), p. 58 (book 1, chapter 5 §1).

out that constraint is often a good thing, even (and sometimes especially) for the person being constrained. Unlike the earlier jurists – who did not overlook or dismiss the political meaning of the word[24] – they conclude that those who treat freedom as a political value confuse it with something else that *is* of value, and that therefore defines the proper bounds of individual liberty.[25] For Hobbes this "something else" is of course security and its necessary condition, sovereign power: on his view we ought to have just as much freedom as it is safe for us to have, and "such Liberty is in some places more, and in some lesse; and in some times more, in other times lesse, according as they that have the Soveraignty shall think most convenient."[26] The utilitarians, as we might expect, define the proper bounds of individual liberty by appealing to social utility: "The liberty which the law *ought* to allow of," Bentham argues, "is the liberty which concerns those acts only by which, if exercised, no damage would be done to the community upon the whole ... or none but what promises to be compensated by at least equal benefit."[27] These two lines of argument are not as far apart as they might seem: Hobbes agrees that it is the sovereign's duty to pursue the common good; he just insists that it is a necessary condition of peace – which is a necessary condition for the enjoyment of all other goods – that a single person (natural or artificial) be empowered to decide what the common good is and how it should be pursued.[28] Bentham, for his part, after arguing that the bounds of individual liberty are properly defined by social utility, adds the Hobbesian caveat that "[t]he marking out of these bounds ought not to be left to any body but him or them who are acknowledged to be in possession of the sovereign power."[29]

---

[24] Aquinas, for example, who stands at the head of the natural law tradition, defines a "free community" as one "which may make its own laws": *Summa Theologiae* 1a2ae q 97 art 3 ad 3 (*Political Writings*, p. 155).

[25] Bentham found this kind of confusion to be so pervasive that he resolved to abandon the language of liberty altogether: "I would no more use the word liberty in my conversation when I could get another that would answer the purpose, than I would brandy in my diet, if my physician did not order me: both cloud the understanding and inflame the passions": unpublished MS c. 1776, quoted in Long, *Bentham on Liberty*, p. 173.

[26] Hobbes, *Leviathan*, p. 152 (chapter 21). Hobbes's position is complicated by the fact that he holds that there are "things, which though commanded by the Soveraign, [a subject] may neverthelesse, without Injustice, refuse to do," most notably "to kill, wound, or mayme himselfe" and (more problematically) "to execute any dangerous, or dishonourable Office": ibid., pp. 150–1. These complications, though interesting and important in their own right, do not affect the line of argument that I am pursuing here.

[27] Bentham, "Nonsense Upon Stilts," p. 340 (original emphasis).

[28] See especially Hobbes, *Leviathan*, chapter 30.

[29] Bentham, "Nonsense Upon Stilts," p. 340.

Hobbes and the utilitarians pose two fundamental challenges to any brand of liberalism that treats unconstrained choice as a core political value. The first challenge arises from the fact that different choices have qualitatively different values, and that we have to take these differences into account in order to say how much freedom a person has or should have.[30] As we have seen, distinguishing between more and less valuable choices in this way subordinates the value of freedom to whatever criteria we use to draw the distinctions. From this point of view freedom is just an all-purpose means that we use to pursue our ends, and the interesting political question is not how many choices we have, but rather what our ends should be. The second challenge is more fundamental. All human action takes place under conditions of constraint: the physical constraints that are imposed by the natural world, the legal penalties that are imposed by the government, and the social costs that are attached to various courses of action. If we define freedom as the absence of constraint, then we also have to stipulate which constraints "count" as freedom-reducing: otherwise my inability to leap six feet in the air or walk through walls, my submission to laws against assault and theft of whose existence I heartily approve, and my fear of being criticized for expressing unpopular opinions or acting in unconventional ways (for example) would all count equally as reductions of my freedom.

An especially sophisticated effort to respond to these challenges has been mounted by the philosopher Ian Carter, who sets out to articulate a "pure" conception of negative liberty, and thus of constraint, that is politically salient, morally neutral, and objectively measurable. Building on a line of argument that was first proposed by Hillel Steiner,[31] Carter shows that the seemingly crude Hobbesian definition of freedom as the absence of physical constraint can yield a subtle means of measuring the

---

[30] Even Isaiah Berlin, who is largely responsible for the contemporary association of liberalism with negative liberty, and who famously insists that negative liberty should not be confused with other values – that "everything is what it is" – admits that in order to say how much negative liberty a person has we cannot simply ask "how many possibilities are open." Rather, we also have to ask, *inter alia*, "how important in [his] plan of life, given [his] character and circumstances, [the] possibilities are when compared with each other" and "what value not merely the agent, but the general sentiment of the society in which he lives, puts on the various possibilities": Isaiah Berlin, "Two Concepts of Liberty" (1958/1969), in *Liberty*, ed. Henry Hardy (New York: Oxford University Press, 2002), pp. 172, 177n.

[31] Hillel Steiner, *An Essay on Rights* (Oxford: Basil Blackwell, 1994), for example, pp. 2–3, 33, 86–101; Steiner himself credits the idea of compossibility to Gottfried Leibniz: ibid., p. 2n.

overall freedom of agents if we take into account the "compossibility" – the joint realizability – of various courses of action. This line of argument makes it possible to say (*pace* Hobbes) that a person may be free – that is, physically able – to perform an illegal action, but nevertheless made less free by the existence of the legal prohibition because and insofar as the resulting punishment would reduce the number of actions that he or she is physically able to perform in the future. It also helps to untangle a number of other conceptual problems with the idea of negative liberty, such as the problem of accounting for constraints that make an action difficult but not impossible to perform, the problem of accounting for constraints that are (like legal punishment) only probabilistically imposed, and the problem of distinguishing between offers and threats. Carter argues that even though this way of measuring freedom requires that we perform the unwieldy task of translating ordinary-language descriptions of free action into the abstract terms of physical movement through space, it will nevertheless yield results that are "isomorphic" with our common-sense intuitions about the relative amounts of freedom that people have.[32]

Although the appeal to compossibility provides an ingenious means of handling some of the thorniest problems that are raised by the idea of negative liberty, many equally thorny problems remain, and here it must be said that Carter's proposed solutions, while no less ingenious, are considerably less satisfying. For example, he holds that the question of where a constraint comes from – whether its source is human or nonhuman, or whether it is imposed intentionally or unintentionally – is irrelevant to the question of how much freedom a person has; that one is made no less unfree by an earthquake or a traffic jam than by a mugger. He also admits that by treating the extent of one's freedom as a function of the size of the "spatio-temporal regions" through which one is able to move one's body we threaten to "under-represent" important liberties, such as those of thought and speech, that involve very small movements.[33] In each of these cases – and in several others – Carter defends his rather strained theoretical conclusions by appealing, implicitly or explicitly, to the imperative of developing a tractable method of measuring freedom objectively – that is, in physical terms. This raises the obvious question of why we should want such a method in the first place: after all, in cases where the resulting measurements clash with our common-sense intuitions about

---

[32] Ian Carter, *A Measure of Freedom* (New York: Oxford University Press, 1999), esp. chapters 4 and 8.
[33] Ibid., pp. 220–3, 204–8.

how much freedom people have, surely it is the measurements, and not the intuitions, that would give way.[34]

Carter's response to this objection contains his most valuable insight. Only a "pure" conception of negative liberty, he argues, can take into account the fact that freedom has what he calls "non-specific value"; that is, value that cannot simply be reduced to the value of the ends that it is used to pursue. Carter does not deny that different values can and should be assigned to the freedom to pursue different ends; that particular freedoms of association, expression, and movement (for example) can have more or less of what he calls "specific value." He simply insists that the mere existence of options has value over and above these considerations, because it is often the case that "*some* specific option or set of options (we just do not know which) will serve ... an end the exact nature of which has yet to become clear, or an end which we are aware might change in the future." Consider, for example, the possibilities that are opened up when we learn a new skill or overcome a physical handicap, or when we are able to associate with a new group of people or gain access to a previously restricted area. "Our ignorance about the future," Carter argues, "gives value to specific freedoms in the present that otherwise would not have value"; indeed, "[t]hose freedoms have value *in virtue* of our ignorance." He concludes that the value of freedom cannot be directly captured by a utilitarian calculus, and that we should treat it instead as something to be independently and generically measured.[35]

The appeal to freedom's "non-specific value" gives political salience to the apparently sterile conception of negative liberty that we find in Hobbes and the utilitarians, and despite the special role that it plays in Carter's argument the appeal is not idiosyncratic to him. Indeed, by

---

[34] Carter himself admits that empirical measurements of freedom would need to be brought into "reflective equilibrium" with our "common-sense comparisons" of the overall amount of freedom that various individuals and societies enjoy: ibid., pp. 98–100, 208–11. The idea of "reflective equilibrium" is of course borrowed from John Rawls; see in particular his *A Theory of Justice* (2nd ed., Cambridge, MA: Harvard University Press, 1999 [1971]), §9.

[35] Carter, *Measure of Freedom*, esp. chapters 2–3, quoted at p. 45 (original emphasis). Carter refers to the nonspecific value of freedom as "the basic idea running through [his] book": ibid., p. 4. I set aside for the purposes of this discussion the "pure" conception of negative liberty that is developed by Matthew Kramer, which also draws on the idea of compossibility, because Kramer weights the amount of overall freedom that a person has according to the value of the particular freedoms that he or she enjoys, and thus does not treat freedom as something that is nonspecifically valuable: Matthew H. Kramer, *The Quality of Freedom* (New York: Oxford University Press, 2003), for example, p. 9 and chapter 5 *passim*.

calling attention to the open-ended appeal to values like growth, progress, and perfectibility that we find in liberal thinkers as diverse as Condorcet, Kant, Humboldt, Mill, Hobhouse, and Hayek, Carter is able to show that this insight has always played a central role in the liberal tradition – though not, he points out, in its recent justice-centered incarnation.[36] It plays an equally central role in the freedom-centered liberalism that I am defending here. According to this way of thinking, individual liberty in the sense of unconstrained choice is a necessary (though not of course a sufficient) condition for the pursuit of a variety of ends – such as knowledge and understanding, progress and development, civilization and culture, and self-discovery and self-realization – that we can name as aspirations for the future but whose content we cannot describe in the present. However, although Carter's views about freedom's *value* are not idiosyncratic, his analysis of its *meaning* is: few if any liberal thinkers have embraced the "pure" negative conception of freedom as the absence of physical constraint. Carter struggles in particular to account for the fact that many combinations of physical movements seem highly unlikely, even on the most generous estimate of the extent of human myopia, to contribute to the pursuit of any valuable end – and that many seem pretty clearly to have negative value.[37] As we will see, a person-centered conception of freedom provides a more elegant means of capturing this distinctively liberal appreciation of the value of negative liberty.

1.3 FREEDOM AND JUSTICE

According to a familiar line of argument, when the limits of individual liberty are defined through an appeal to social utility, we have reason to worry that individuals will be treated as means to the realization of a larger social end. As John Rawls has influentially argued, such a view "does not take seriously the distinction between persons," because "there is no reason in principle ... why the violation of the liberty of a few might not be made right by the greater good shared by many."[38] We might therefore be tempted to think, as Rawls did, that the claims of individual liberty will be better respected in a justice-centered than in a utility-centered politics.

---

[36] Carter, *Measure of Freedom*, pp. 45–54; cf. pp. 68–74 for his critique of justice-centered conceptions of freedom.
[37] See, for example, ibid., pp. 61–5, 130–40, and 198–204, where he confronts this problem in different forms.
[38] Rawls, *Theory of Justice*, pp. 23–4 (§5).

Such a politics defines the proper limits of freedom by appealing to a moral standard whose terms are fixed in advance: it endows people with rights, and thus with liberties, that cannot be infringed except in extraordinary cases. This way of thinking, unlike the tradition of thought that descends from Hobbes and the utilitarians, gives special weight to individual liberty and is thus often taken to be the distinctively liberal view. However, as we will now see, it does not treat individual liberty as an independent political value. Rather, it defines freedom for political purposes as action in accordance with the demands of justice, and thus subordinates the value of freedom to the value of creating or sustaining a just society. Because the question of what justice requires is hotly contested, this "positive" conception of freedom is vulnerable to the charge that it protects individual liberty at the cost of imposing a particular conception of justice – and of right reasoning about justice – on those who are subject to it.

The association of freedom with justice is at least as old as the juristic formula which defines freedom as "the natural ability to do as one pleases unless prohibited by force *or right [iure]*." However the origins of the justice-centered theory of freedom, like the origins of liberalism itself, are now typically traced to John Locke, who defines "the natural liberty of men" as "a State of perfect Freedom to order their Actions, and dispose of their Possessions, and Persons as they think fit, *within the bounds of the Law of Nature*," and "the Liberty of Man, in Society" as "a Liberty to dispose, and order, as he lists, his Person, Actions, Possessions, and his whole Property, *within the Allowance of those Laws under which he is*" – laws which, he emphasizes, "are only so far right, as they are founded on the Law of Nature, by which they are to be regulated and interpreted." Although these passages seem at first blush to follow Hobbes in treating law and liberty as antithetical, Locke actually holds the opposite view: "Law, in its true Notion," he argues, "is not so much the Limitation as the direction of a free and intelligent Agent to his proper Interest ... So that, however it may be mistaken, the end of Law is not to abolish or restrain, but to preserve and enlarge Freedom."[39] As the reference to "proper Interest" suggests, a free agent for Locke is not a person whose actions are unconstrained, but rather a person who acts in accordance with reason, and thus with the law of nature; indeed, he argues in the *Essay Concerning Human Understanding* that "[i]f to break loose from the conduct of Reason, and to want that restraint of Examination and

---

[39] John Locke, *Second Treatise of Government*, §§4 (emphasis added), 57, 12, 57 (emphasis removed).

Judgment, which keeps us from chusing or doing the worse, be Liberty, true Liberty, [then] mad Men and Fools are the only Freemen."[40] (We may be reminded here of Auden's Rake, "Whom neither Passion may compel/ Nor Reason can restrain."[41]) Anyone who rejects the "rule of right" therefore forfeits the equal freedom to which Lockean citizens are otherwise entitled and is to be treated instead like a "wild beast, or noxious brute with whom Mankind can have neither Society nor Security."[42] In short, Locke holds exactly the view that Hobbes and Bentham mocked so roundly: that the liberty to do wrong is no liberty at all.

This association of freedom with action in accordance with moral law is deepened and intensified in the practical philosophy of Immanuel Kant. Kant was of course centrally preoccupied with what Mill called the "doctrine of Philosophical Necessity," and in particular with the problem of how rational beings can be regarded as free despite the deterministic workings of the natural world. The crux of his position is what he takes to be the undeniable fact that human beings hold themselves to be morally responsible for what they do; that we have a sense of right and wrong, and a moral conscience that troubles us when we fail to abide by it. This practical stance is incoherent, he argues, if we suppose that human actions are simply natural events, since all natural events are determined by some prior natural cause, and since we can only be morally responsible for our actions if they are performed freely; that is, if we could have chosen to do otherwise (Kant's position is in this sense diametrically opposed to Hobbes's). In order to make sense of our practices of moral judgment, he concludes, "a rational being must regard himself... as belonging not to the world of sense but to the world of understanding... under laws which, being independent of nature, are not empirical but grounded merely in reason." These laws must be unconditional – categorical – and universal, because only then will their dictates be untainted by empirical desires, and thus unbound by the deterministic workings of nature. "A free will and a will under moral laws," Kant concludes, "are one and the same."[43] At this level of abstraction

---

[40] Locke, *Essay Concerning Human Understanding*, book 2, chapter 21 §50 (emphasis removed).
[41] W. H. Auden, *The Rake's Progress* (1951), act 2, scene 1; the Mephistophelian Nick Shadow prefaces this description by declaring that "he alone is free/Who chooses what to will, and wills/His choice as destiny."
[42] Locke, *Second Treatise*, §172.
[43] Immanuel Kant, *Groundwork of the Metaphysics of Morals* (1785), in *Practical Philosophy*, trans. and ed. Mary J. Gregor (New York: Cambridge University Press, 1996), section 3, quoted at pp. 99, 95 (4:452, 4:447).

Kant's theory of freedom has the same structure as Locke's, and like Locke he draws on the idea of free will to argue that legitimate political authority (public right, as he calls it) must be derived from an idealized "original contract": "legislative authority," he insists, "can belong only to the united will of the people," and the legislator must therefore "give his laws in such a way that they could have arisen from the united will of a whole people."[44]

As we saw in the Introduction, the social contract tradition on which Locke and Kant built their respective theories of political freedom was moribund throughout the nineteenth and much of the twentieth century, only to be revived by Rawls, who begins his seminal book *A Theory of Justice* by proposing to "generalize and carry to a higher order of abstraction the traditional theory of the social contract as represented by Locke, Rousseau, and Kant."[45] It is therefore not surprising to find that while he eschews their metaphysics, Rawls follows Locke and Kant in subordinating the claims of freedom to those of justice or right. However, this is not how things appeared at first: in the original formulation of his doctrine of "justice as fairness" Rawls defended what he called the "equal liberty principle," which says that "[e]ach person is to have an equal right to the most extensive total system of equal basic liberties compatible with a similar system of liberty for all," and that these basic liberties can only be restricted when doing so would increase the overall amount of liberty that is equally enjoyed. Moreover, the equal liberty principle, as the first of Rawls's two principles of justice, is "lexically prior" to the second principle, which governs the distribution of wealth, income, and positions of authority and responsibility. This means that "infringements of the basic equal liberties protected by the first principle cannot be justified, or compensated for, by greater social and economic advantages"; rather, they "can be limited and compromised only when they conflict with other basic liberties."[46] The idea that the scope of the basic liberties should be as extensive as possible, taken together with the claim that they can be limited only for the sake of a greater amount of overall liberty, seems to suggest that Rawls, unlike Kant, Locke, and the earlier natural jurists, does in fact treat freedom in the sense of unconstrained choice as a core political value.

---

[44] Kant, *The Metaphysics of Morals* (1797), ibid., pp. 456–7, 459 (6:313, 6:315); Kant, "On the Common Saying: That May Be Correct in Theory, But It Is of No Use in Practice" (1793), ibid., p. 296 (8:297).

[45] Rawls, *Theory of Justice*, p. xviii (preface).

[46] Ibid., pp. 220 (§39), 266 (§46), 53–4 (§11); the last quoted passage does not appear in the original (1971) edition. On the "lexical priority" of the first principle of justice see ibid., §8.

However, Rawls was soon led to fundamentally revise this line of argument in the face of strong criticism of the "equal liberty principle." Most notably, the legal philosopher H. L. A. Hart pointed out, as Hobbes and the utilitarians had, that "whether or not it is in any man's interest to choose that any specific liberty should be generally distributed depends on whether the advantages for him of the exercise of that liberty outweigh the various disadvantages for him of its general practice by others." It follows, Hart argued, that "some criterion of the value of different liberties must be involved in the resolution of conflicts between them," and that any resolution "must involve consideration of the relative value of different modes of conduct, and not merely the extent or amount of freedom." He concluded that the idea of restricting liberty only for the sake of greater overall liberty – and indeed the idea of maximizing liberty at all – is incoherent, and that we can only judge the value of a "total system" of liberty by appealing to extra-libertarian criteria.[47] Rawls saw the force of Hart's criticism and revised his first principle of justice accordingly; most notably by substituting the phrase "fully adequate" for "most extensive," and by specifying that a "fully adequate" system of liberties is one that "guarantee[s] equally for all citizens the social conditions essential for the adequate development and the full and informed exercise" of what he calls the two "moral powers": the capacity for a sense of justice and the capacity to form a conception of the good – with the former, of course, enjoying priority over the latter.[48] According to this revised line of argument freedom is not something whose equal enjoyment is to be maximized; rather it is to be permitted only insofar as its enjoyment contributes to – or at least does not conflict with – the more fundamental aim of living in a just society.

Other academic liberals have generally followed Rawls's lead in subordinating the claims of freedom to those of justice, though of course they disagree about what justice requires. Robert Nozick's libertarian theory of justice rests, as G. A. Cohen has pointed out, on a "moralized" definition

---

[47] H. L. A. Hart, "Rawls on Liberty and Its Priority," *University of Chicago Law Review* 40 (1973), pp. 534–55, quoted at pp. 543–4, 550. For a generalization of this line of argument see Onora O'Neill, "The Most Extensive Liberty," *Proceedings of the Aristotelian Society* 80 (1979–80), pp. 45–59.

[48] John Rawls, "The Basic Liberties and Their Priority" (1982), revised and reprinted as lecture 8 of *Political Liberalism* (2nd ed., New York: Columbia University Press, 1996 [1993]), quoted at pp. 332–3. Rawls also made a number of revisions to *A Theory of Justice* itself in response to Hart's criticisms; see the discussion in the preface to the revised edition, pp. xii–xiii. The subordination of freedom to justice is already hinted at in the original text; see, for example, p. 12 (§3).

of freedom, since it counts the violation, but not the enforcement, of property rights as freedom-reducing.[49] Ronald Dworkin's resource-egalitarian theory of justice holds that "we cannot, in good conscience, press for any right to liberty that conflicts with the demands of equality,"[50] while Joseph Raz's autonomy-centered view holds that "[i]n judging the value of negative freedom one should never forget that it derives from its contribution to autonomy."[51] Susan Okin builds her feminist theory of justice on the claim that "[p]ublic policies must respect people's views and choices ... only insofar as it can be ensured that these choices do not result, as they now do, in the vulnerability of women and children."[52] The pattern is clear: in each case freedom is treated, as it is in utilitarian political thought, as an all-purpose means, and the salient political question is not how much freedom we have but rather what our ends should be. Indeed Will Kymlicka, after a lengthy survey of libertarian views, concludes that "the very idea of a liberty-based [political] theory is confused," and that "[t]he question we should ask is which specific liberties are most valuable to people, given their essential interests, and which distribution of those liberties is legitimate, given the demands of equality or mutual advantage": "The idea of freedom as such, and lesser or greater amounts of it," he argues, "does no work in political argument."[53]

This is a surprising conclusion for a liberal to reach, given the close historical and etymological connection between liberalism and liberty, and we do not have to deny the attractiveness of the values that these thinkers promote, or the ingenuity with which they defend them, in order

---

[49] Robert Nozick, *Anarchy, State, and Utopia* (New York: Basic Books, 1974), for example, p. 262, where he points out that "[o]ther people's actions place limits on one's available opportunities," and adds that "[w]hether this makes one's resulting action non-voluntary depends upon whether these others had the right to act as they did." For G. A. Cohen's observation that Nozick's conception of freedom is "moralized" see, for example, his "Freedom, Justice, and Capitalism" (1980), reprinted in *History, Labour, and Freedom: Themes from Marx* (Oxford: Clarendon Press, 1988), pp. 295–6. Cohen later preferred to say that Nozick held a "rights definition of freedom": see, for example, G. A. Cohen, *Self-Ownership, Freedom, and Equality* (New York: Oxford University Press, 1995), p. 62n, and see also Serena Olsaretti, "Freedom, Force and Choice: Against the Rights-Based Definition of Voluntariness," *Journal of Political Philosophy* 6 (1998) pp. 53–78.
[50] Ronald Dworkin, "The Place of Liberty" (1987), reprinted in *Sovereign Virtue* (Cambridge, MA: Harvard University Press, 2000), quoted at p. 131.
[51] Joseph Raz, *The Morality of Freedom* (New York: Oxford University Press, 1986), p. 410.
[52] Susan Moller Okin, *Justice, Gender, and the Family* (New York: Basic Books, 1989), p. 172.
[53] Will Kymlicka, *Contemporary Political Philosophy: An Introduction* (New York: Oxford University Press, 2002), chapter 4, quoted at p. 153.

to have doubts about it. The most significant doubts arise, I think, from the fact that contemporary liberal theories of justice make extraordinary epistemic demands on those who are charged with realizing them. Rawls famously requires that we reason about justice from behind a "veil of ignorance"; that is, we detach ourselves from any personal qualities, circumstances, experiences, or commitments that are "irrelevant from the standpoint of justice."[54] Nozick requires that we be able to show that current holdings have descended to their owners through an unbroken series of just (i.e., voluntary and nonfraudulent) transfers, and that when they have not the existing distribution be adjusted to approximate the counterfactual scenario in which no unjust transfers had taken place.[55] Dworkin holds that a distribution of resources is just insofar as it approximates the results of an iterated auction from a starting point of equal resources, and that in order to control for externalities we should imagine this auction as having been preceded by a "superimaginary pre-auction" in which "all motives are transparent, all transactions are predictable, and organizational costs are absent."[56] Raz defends a "perfectionist" state that is "duty-bound to promote the good life" – not the life, he emphasizes, that it *considers* good, but the one that is actually so.[57] Okin makes "the disappearance of gender ... a prerequisite for the complete development of a nonsexist, fully human theory of justice," even though, as she admits, "there are no currently shared meanings in this country about the extent to which differences between the sexes are innate or environmental, about the appropriate roles of men and women, and about which family forms and divisions of labor are most beneficial for partners, parents, and children" – that is, even though we do not have a clear idea of what a world without gender would look like or how it might best be achieved.[58]

---

[54] Rawls, *Theory of Justice*, p. 17 (§4) and §24 *passim*. Rawls holds in particular that behind the veil of ignorance "no one knows his place in society, his class position or social status ... his fortune in the distribution of natural assets and abilities, his intelligence and strength, and the like ... his conception of the good, the particulars of his rational plan of life, or even the special features of his psychology such as his aversion to risk or liability to optimism or pessimism"; moreover "the parties [behind the veil] do not know the particular circumstances of their own society ... its economic or political situation, or the level of civilization or culture it has been able to achieve," and "have no information as to which generation they belong": ibid., p. 118 (§24).

[55] Nozick, *Anarchy, State, and Utopia*, pp. 150–3.

[56] Dworkin, "The Place of Liberty," p. 157.

[57] Raz, *Morality of Freedom*, pp. 426, 412.

[58] Okin, *Justice, Gender, and the Family*, pp. 105, 172 (emphasis removed).

These epistemic demands do not just pose a theoretical challenge; they have profound political implications. Indeed, despite its formally egalitarian character the "positive" association of freedom with rightful choice has been used to support the same kinds of hierarchies that were a defining feature of the classical conception of free personhood. As we have seen, Locke argues that those who depart from the "rule of right" should be treated like "wild beast[s], or noxious brute[s]," a stipulation that sounds rather sinister when we recall that there is likely to be disagreement about what the rule of right requires – and when we consider his entanglements with the slave trade and his notoriously draconian poor law proposal.[59] Kant goes even further, arguing that apprentices, domestic servants, wage laborers, and "all women" lack the independent judgment that is necessary to reason about matters of right, and should therefore be treated as "passive citizens."[60] The political exclusion of women, the poor, non-European peoples, and the ideologically deceived (for example) has routinely been justified on the grounds that they allegedly lack or are deficient in the necessary rational faculties, and are therefore in need of paternalistic supervision of and interference with their choices.[61]

Although few contemporary academic liberals would countenance, let alone try to enforce, such exclusions, the structure of their position makes them all too easy to justify. After all, if justice is an "uncompromising" virtue, as Rawls suggests, then those who reason wrongly about it – for example, those who deny (*pace* Rawls) that talent and the willingness to make an effort are irrelevant from the standpoint of justice, or (*pace* Nozick) that property rights are sacrosanct; or those who hold (*pace* Raz) that there is no truth of the matter about what constitutes a good life, or (*pace* Okin) that gender differences are in some sense innate – must be deemed "unreasonable," and their beliefs about justice disregarded or overridden. Adam Swift states the inner logic of this way of thinking with unusual candor: "I live in a democracy," he complains,

---

[59] Locke, *Second Treatise*, §172; John Locke, "An Essay on the Poor Law" (1697), in *Political Essays*, ed. Mark Goldie (New York: Cambridge University Press, 1997), pp. 182–98. On Locke's involvement with the slave trade see, for example, James Farr, "'So Vile and Miserable an Estate': The Problem of Slavery in Locke's Political Thought," *Political Theory* 14 (1986), pp. 263–89, and "Locke, Natural Law, and New World Slavery," *Political Theory* 36 (2008), pp. 495–522.
[60] Kant, *Metaphysics of Morals*, pp. 458–9 (6:314–5).
[61] See, for example, Carole Pateman, *The Sexual Contract* (Stanford, CA: Stanford University Press, 1988); C. B. Macpherson, *The Political Theory of Possessive Individualism: Hobbes to Locke* (New York: Oxford University Press, 1962), chapter 5; Uday Singh Mehta, *Liberalism and Empire: A Study in Nineteenth-Century British Liberal Thought* (Chicago: University of Chicago Press, 1999), chapters 1–2; and Berlin, "Two Concepts of Liberty," respectively.

containing too many people who are: (i) too unreflective or ignorant to understand the conceptual distinctions that would allow them properly to understand the place of fairness in any overall evaluation of policy or individual action; and/or (ii) too selfish to value fairness as much as they should, and hence to vote for policies that would promote it, or to be motivated by it when deciding on their actions as individuals.

One is not entirely reassured by the tongue-in-cheek disclaimer that "since, as well as valuing fairness, I am a democrat, and a liberal [sic!], I wouldn't really *want* to be an omnipotent dictator."[62]

Again, this a surprising conclusion for a liberal to reach, given that liberalism has always stood, colloquially speaking, for the qualities of open-mindedness and toleration. We are very far here from the kind of epistemic modesty that underlies Carter's appeal to the "non-specific value" of freedom – although it is presumably a kind of epistemic modesty that prevents contemporary academic liberals from embracing the kinds of exclusion that their theories of justice would otherwise seem to commit them to. I will now argue that the concerns that I have raised about action-centered conceptions of political freedom – whether "negative" or "positive" – give us strong reasons to adopt a more traditional person-centered view. In light of the argument so far, a person-centered *liberal* theory of freedom should have two key features: first, it should capture the intuitive connection between freedom and autonomy without appealing to a full-blown, and therefore controversial and potentially exclusive, theory of human agency; and second, it should treat the mere fact of being unconstrained as a distinct (though not absolute) political value without relying on stipulative, and therefore conceptually or ideologically dubious, claims about what "counts" as a constraint. I will use the remainder of this chapter to sketch a person-centered theory of freedom that succeeds, I think, in meeting both of these conditions. I turn in the following chapters to a more detailed examination of the two distinct kinds of freedom that this theory gives us reason to value, and of the relationship between them.

1.4 FREEDOM AND RESPONSIBILITY

I began this chapter (and this book) by suggesting that when we ask whether a person is free to do something – or whether, having done it, they did it freely – we may be asking two different and seemingly contradictory things. The first, whose contours we will start to examine now, is

---

[62] Adam Swift, "The Value of Philosophy in Nonideal Circumstances," *Social Theory and Practice* 34 (2008), quoted at pp. 383–4, 382 (original emphasis).

whether it would be appropriate to hold them responsible for what they have done, or whether they can properly take responsibility (for example, in the form of credit or blame) for having done it.[63] In other words, we may want to know whether the person in question is properly subject to what the philosopher P. F. Strawson calls the "reactive attitudes" on which our practices of holding people responsible depend.[64] In unpacking the implications of this conception of freedom we should start by distinguishing two kinds of "reactive attitudes" from each other: those that arise from *holding* someone responsible, and those that arise from holding someone *to be* responsible – what the philosopher Gary Watson has influentially referred to as "accountability" and "attributability," respectively.[65] An action is *attributable* to a person if it is connected in some intelligible way to the actor's ends or purposes – if he or she is not simply moved, for example, by neurosis or compulsion; by ignorance, deception, manipulation, or coercion; or by severe emotional or physical distress. A person is *accountable* for a given action, by contrast, if other people have a reasonable expectation that they act in one way rather than another and are prepared to respond in tangible ways – say, through praise or blame, reward or punishment – to what they do. Moral philosophers disagree about whether the distinction between attributability and accountability accurately captures the *phenomenology* of holding others responsible; some have argued, for example, that we always expect responsible persons to be able to account for what they do, at least implicitly.[66] However, it provides a good description of the *social practice* of holding others responsible: we do in fact distinguish the question of whether someone is properly regarded as having acted in a given case from the question of whether they are accountable to others for acting as they did.

---

[63] This position should not be confused with the claim that a person can only be made *unfree* by constraints for which *other* people can be held morally responsible: see especially David Miller, "Constraints on Freedom," *Ethics* 94 (1983), pp. 66–86, and S. I. Benn and W. L. Weinstein, "Being Free to Act, and Being a Free Man," *Mind* 80 (1971), pp. 194–211.

[64] P. F. Strawson, "Freedom and Resentment," *Proceedings of the British Academy* 48 (1962), pp. 1–25.

[65] Gary Watson, "Two Faces of Responsibility," *Philosophical Topics* 24 (1996), pp. 227–48.

[66] See, for example, Marina A. L. Oshana, "Ascriptions of Responsibility," *American Philosophical Quarterly* 34 (1997), pp. 71–83; T. M. Scanlon, *What We Owe to Each Other* (Cambridge, MA: Harvard University Press, 1998), chapter 6; Angela M. Smith, "Attributability, Answerability, and Accountability: In Defense of a Unified Account," *Ethics* 122 (2012), pp. 575–89.

The distinction between attributability and accountability raises two sets of questions about the association of freedom with responsible choice. One set of questions has to do with the actor him- or herself: whether they are capable of making responsible choices in general (Are they a child, an addict, or mentally deficient in some way?), whether they were in full possession of their faculties when they made a particular choice (Were they intoxicated, sleepwalking, or hypnotized?), whether they were aware of the consequences of the choices that they made (Were they ignorant, manipulated, or deceived?), and so on. In other words, one thing that we could be saying when we say that we want to make someone free (or more free) is that we want to put them in a position to make choices that are properly attributable to them: to make sure that they are mentally sound, adequately informed, not subject to manipulation, and so on. A second and more straightforwardly political set of questions has to do with the social context in which we act. Most if not all of our choices are shaped, implicitly or explicitly, by the expected costs and benefits of acting in one way rather than another. Do we act freely – can our actions properly be attributed to us – insofar as we are influenced by these kinds of considerations? Do I act freely when I pay my taxes, take a detour to avoid a traffic jam, use "proper" table manners, or call my sister on her birthday? What about when I pay off an extortionist, take a detour to avoid an unsafe neighborhood, observe "proper" gender norms, or refrain from expressing an unpopular opinion? According to one traditional view, I can only answer these questions in the affirmative – I only act freely – if and to the extent that the people who create or influence the conditions under which I act are accountable to me, in the sense that I have authorized and am able to control or influence their actions in turn. In other words, I am free in this sense if and to the extent that I am *self-governing* in one of the many possible senses of that term.

For the sake of convenience, and following much precedent, I call this first kind of freedom *republican freedom,* because it is concerned with the question of how we govern ourselves and thereby create the social conditions under which we are fit to be held responsible for what we do. Philip Pettit, the leading contemporary philosopher of republicanism, goes so far as to argue that "there is an *a priori* connection" between freedom and responsibility; that "[s]omeone who did not see why that connection had to obtain would fail to understand what freedom was or what holding someone responsible was."[67] I take a broader view of what we can

---

[67] Philip Pettit, A *Theory of Freedom: From the Psychology to the Politics of Agency* (New York: Oxford University Press, 2001), p. 18. Pettit's republicanism is described

understand freedom to mean here, but Pettit undeniably puts his finger on an important insight. He goes on to emphasize, as I have, that freedom so defined "has a social as well as a psychological aspect" which "takes us beyond the realm of free will, traditionally conceived, and into politically relevant matters": "in any [republican] collectivity," he argues, "the things that the social integrate judges and intends are things that *we* judge and intend; they are not matters of merely impersonal record."[68] The philosopher Thomas Nagel argues along similar lines that autonomy requires "the extension of ethics into politics," and in particular that we "find ourselves faced with the choices we want to be faced with, in a world that we can want to live in."[69] The converse is true in cases where we did not choose and do not control the social conditions under which we act: all things being equal, we are less likely to think that it is appropriate to hold people responsible for the consequences of their actions if they are obeying the (possibly implicit) wishes of the secret police under a repressive regime than if they are acting within a properly enforced system of law which they played (or could have played) a role in making, and whose content they can contest.[70]

Of course, responsible agency and republican government are not coextensive and do not necessarily entail one another. As the examples mentioned above suggest, some of the conditions that tend to diminish responsibility, such as the presence of mental illness, are agent specific. Others are the product of factors such as upbringing, environment, and personal experience that it may not be feasible or desirable for a republican polity to regulate. Many people fail to take advantage of the conditions for responsible agency even when they are present, and again it may not be feasible or desirable for a republican polity to compel them to do so. It would therefore be more accurate to say that republican

---

and defended at greater length in his *Republicanism: A Theory of Freedom and Government* (2nd ed., New York: Oxford University Press, 1999 [1997]), and more recently in *On the People's Terms: A Republican Theory and Model of Democracy* (New York: Cambridge University Press, 2012). For my own understanding of republican freedom, which is largely consonant with Pettit's, see my *Invention of Market Freedom*, esp. chapter 1, and Chapter 2 of this volume.

[68] Pettit, *Theory of Freedom*, pp. 4, 118 (emphasis added).
[69] Thomas Nagel, *The View from Nowhere* (New York: Oxford University Press, 1986), pp. 135–6. Nagel takes a Kantian position on the meaning of autonomy, but as I point out below republicans need not be committed to such a view – as indeed Pettit is not.
[70] There is an interesting asymmetry here, since we probably *would* credit someone with responsible agency if they were to *resist* a repressive regime, although (or because?) we would probably view such resistance as supererogatory.

government is a necessary but not a sufficient condition for personal responsibility in certain domains of conduct. The converse is also true, which is why questions about the abilities, education, and conduct of free citizens – often discussed collectively under the heading of "civic virtue" – play such an important role in republican political thought. The devil is in the details: what it means to be free in this sense will depend on what kind of story we tell about what self-government requires, and not all such stories are equally plausible. Indeed, as my use of the word "story" may suggest, any claim that a people is collectively or jointly responsible for (some of) the social conditions under which its members act – for example, because they played a role, or could have played a role, in creating those conditions, because they approve of their form, or would do so on reflection, or because they are able to challenge them when they disagree – will be contestable in principle and almost certainly contested in fact.

The history of republican political thought and practice is in effect a series of efforts to get this story straight. On the one hand, the enjoyment of republican freedom requires that citizens be in a position to make attributable choices; that when we have reason to doubt that someone is *actually* fit to be held responsible for what they do, we nevertheless treat them as a *potentially* responsible person and try to remove whatever impediments stand in the way of their becoming responsible in fact. Practically speaking, this means that a republican polity must see to it that its citizens are adequately educated and informed, not physically or economically vulnerable, not subject to power relationships that limit or distort their ability to pursue their own ends and purposes, and so on. On the other hand, the enjoyment of republican freedom requires that we and our fellow citizens be accountable to each other for (some of) the social conditions under which we act. Practically speaking, this means that republican freedom depends on the existence of inclusive political processes and responsive political institutions, and on the use of those processes and institutions to regulate the unchosen costs – the externalities, as economists call them – that we impose on each other through our actions. The distinctively republican insight is that these two kinds of responsibility are reciprocally related: certain actions can only properly be attributed to people who stand in a relationship of accountability to one another, and this kind of accountability is only possible if those people bring their attributable beliefs and preferences to bear in creating and preserving that relationship. In more traditional language, republican freedom is only possible if virtuous citizens check the arbitrary exercise of power, and virtuous citizenship is only possible if the arbitrary exercise of power is checked.[71]

Although a republican polity is committed to creating the conditions under which its citizens are responsible in both of these senses, it is important to emphasize that attributability and accountability often come apart in practice, especially in the politically salient domains of law and public policy. In particular, a republican polity will often hold its citizens accountable for actions that are not, or that may not be, attributable to them. For example, we may hold lessees accountable for damage to rented property regardless of fault because this makes certain kinds of contracts possible, or less costly. We may hold addicts accountable for the things that they do while intoxicated because we expect that an addiction "loophole" would be abused or inequitably applied. We may hold inexperienced or uneducated people accountable for the consequences of their bad choices because we hope that this will encourage them to choose more prudently over time. We may ignore variation in the extent to which people are "really" responsible for what they do for reasons of administrative simplicity and predictability. More generally, we may not think that we can reliably distinguish between autonomous and heteronomous choices – or we may not be willing to give the state the power to draw such distinctions – and adopt a "naive" position about attributability on epistemic or prudential grounds.

It is here that the distinction between free actions and free persons becomes crucial. From a republican point of view a free *person* is a person who holds the privileged status of citizen in a republican polity, and who is therefore entitled to take part in the processes through which the polity decides when and how to hold its members accountable for what they do. Because those decisions are often made, and known to be made, for practical reasons like the ones that I have just mentioned, debates about what *actions* republican citizens should be free to perform will often set aside the question of whether those actions are "really" attributable to the people who perform them and focus instead on the advantages and disadvantages of treating them as if they were. It follows that these debates, unlike debates about the nature and extent of "positive" liberty, do not need to appeal to full-blown conceptions of reasonableness or rationality – conceptions which are, as we have seen, deeply controversial and (therefore) potentially exclusive. Instead, a commitment to republican

---

[71] On the reciprocal relationship between civic virtue and republican freedom see my *Invention of Market Freedom*, chapter 1 and *passim*.

freedom – an appreciation of the interdependence of responsible agency and responsive political institutions – creates a strong presumption in favor of political *in*clusion because the mere fact of being excluded diminishes to that extent a person's fitness to be treated as a responsible agent. This is not to deny, of course, that debates about when and how a given polity should hold its citizens accountable will themselves be controversial; it is simply to say that in a republican polity these controversies are *political* controversies; to be worked out, directly or indirectly, by and among the citizens themselves. We will explore some of the ways in which republicans have responded to (often by dodging) the inclusive implications of their conception of freedom in Chapter 2.

1.5 FREEDOM AND NONRESPONSIBILITY

As I have pointed out, we rarely if ever act in the absence of constraint, even if we only take into account constraints that are directly or indirectly imposed by other people, as most theories of freedom do. For example, I may be free to choose how to spend my money, but what I can afford to buy is constrained by the choices of all of the other buyers (including the buyers or potential buyers of my own labor and other resources), which add up to an overall pattern of prices that I do not control. I may be free to choose what route to take when I drive to work, but how long it takes me to get there is constrained by the choices of all of the other drivers, which add up to an overall pattern of traffic that I do not control. I may be free to choose whom to associate with and how to act in a wide range of contexts, but I do not control how other people will react, for better or worse, to the company that I keep or the things that I do. In such cases I am free in the sense that I am the one who decides what to do given what everyone else is doing or given what I expect them to do; I decide how to respond to the pattern of potential costs and benefits that is created by other people's choices. But I am not free in the sense that I control the pattern itself; indeed, when (or to the extent that) people enjoy this kind of freedom in roughly equal measure, a pattern of outcomes – and a corresponding pattern of potential costs and benefits – is realized that *no one* can predict or control, and often that no one intended. The exercise of this kind of freedom gives rise, for better or worse, to the open-endedness and unpredictability that is a distinguishing feature of life in a liberal polity.

Of course, just as other people's choices affect me in ways that I do not control, so too do my choices affect other people in ways that they do not control. When I decide what to spend money on, which way to drive to work, whom to associate with, or how to act, my choices have a marginal effect on the overall pattern of prices, traffic, association, and behavior – and, again, often an effect that I did not intend. The distinguishing feature of this kind of freedom is thus not the absence of constraint *on* choice: my choices are constrained by everyone else's choices. Nor is it the exercise of control *over* choice, in the sense of "attributability" that we just examined: I can act recklessly, compulsively, ignorantly, or out of sheer habit and still act "freely" in this sense. Freedom consists here in the absence of responsibility *for* choice: I am free if and to the extent that I am not accountable to anyone else for what I do, unless I choose to be (say, by making a promise or signing a contract). To put the point in slightly more technical terms, one is free in this sense if one is able to impose certain costs on other people without being accountable to them for doing so. I decide what price I am willing to sell my house for, and if I lower my neighbors' property values or raise their property taxes in doing so then that is my business. I decide which way to drive to work, and if I waste gas or contribute to a traffic jam in doing so then that is my business. I decide how to respond to the various social pressures that I face – whom to associate with, whose approval to seek, and whose disapproval to ignore – and if I offend some people or encourage what some people see as bad behavior in doing so then that is my business.

For the sake of convenience, and again following much precedent, I call this kind of freedom *market freedom*, because it is concerned with allowing people to decide for themselves how to respond to the pattern of potential costs and benefits that they face, even when there is no meaningful sense in which they are responsible for that pattern. As we have seen, the word "market" is used here to refer to a wide range of social spaces, many of which have little if anything to do with the exchange of commodities. From the standpoint of the individual actor[72] a market is, again, any domain of conduct in which we can decide for ourselves how to respond to the various risks and opportunities that social life presents, thereby imposing certain costs on other people without being accountable to them for doing so. From the point of view of society as a whole a market is any domain of conduct in which the unregulated and uncoordinated behavior of individual actors gives rise to an overall pattern of outcomes that no one

---

[72] The "individual actor" may of course be a corporate entity rather than a "natural" individual, for example, a firm or a voluntary association. I leave aside the difficult question of what morally relevant differences there might be between these two kinds of actors.

is responsible for; one that is, as Adam Ferguson famously put it, "the result of human action, but not the execution of any human design."[73] Every decision that we make in a market has a marginal effect on the overall pattern, but we enjoy market freedom not because we are accountable to others for what that pattern is, but rather precisely because we are not. From the standpoint of market freedom, a free person is someone who holds the privileged status of being permitted to affect other people in this way. Market freedom is in this sense the antithesis of republican freedom.

Of course, our nonresponsible choices are not immune to evaluation: as Watson emphasizes, choices are a form of "self-disclosure" and are therefore subject to "aretaic appraisal"; they allow us to draw conclusions about the virtues (or lack thereof) of the people who make them.[74] We may silently judge other people's choices; for example, when we stand in the checkout line at the grocery store (let's be honest). We may openly question the choices of friends and family members; for example, if they act in ways that we consider to be dangerous, unhealthy, wasteful, or offensive. We may shun those who make choices that we find objectionable or join with others to protest their choices – and, perhaps, to protest the fact that they are not held publicly accountable for making them. And such protests sometimes succeed: there are choices that were once permissible for which we are now held publicly accountable; for example, we regulate the sale of alcohol, tobacco, and firearms, and prohibit the sale of leaded gasoline, narcotics, and people. In short, our nonresponsible choices can trigger a wide range of responses, ranging from indifference to astonishment, from acceptance to irritation, from praise to protest. These responses represent some of the most significant costs and benefits that we impose on other people through our own nonresponsible choices and are therefore among the most important factors that we have to take into account when we choose to pursue one course of action rather than another. We will explore some of the complexities to which these "private" practices of holding people responsible give rise in Chapter 3.

---

[73] Adam Ferguson, *An Essay on the History of Civil Society* (1767), ed. Fania Oz-Salzberger (New York: Cambridge University Press, 1995), p. 119 (part 3, section 2); cf. Friedrich Hayek, *Law, Legislation and Liberty*, vol. 1: *Rules and Order* (Chicago: University of Chicago Press, 1976), p. 20, and Edna Ullmann-Margalit, "Invisible Hand Explanations," *Synthese* 39 (1978), pp. 263–91.

[74] Watson, "Two Faces of Responsibility," pp. 227–31; *aretē* is the Greek word that is often translated as "virtue."

The idea of market freedom nicely captures the intuition that an action can be attributable to a person without that person being accountable to anyone else for what they have done. However, just as the enjoyment of republican freedom leaves room for the possibility that a person might be accountable for making a choice without that choice necessarily being attributable to them, so too can the enjoyment of market freedom make it harder to attribute choices to the people who make them. By permitting the sale of alcohol and tobacco we probably increase the overall amount of addiction that exists. By permitting the use of advertising and other marketing techniques we probably increase the overall amount of deception and manipulation that exists. By permitting the existence of labor markets we probably increase the overall amount of material insecurity that exists. By permitting the criticism of opinions and lifestyles we probably increase the overall amount of social conformity that exists. In each case, one possible side effect of allowing nonresponsible choice in a given domain is to reduce the extent to which the resulting choices are attributable to the people who make them. There may be good prudential reasons for doing this: for example, to promote administrative efficiency and predictability, or because we think that the power to interfere paternalistically with market choices would be abused if it were granted. There may be good instrumental reasons as well: for example, we may think that on the whole productive resources will be more efficiently allocated, and individual preferences more efficiently satisfied, if we let people respond to their social environment as they see fit, despite the predictable errors and oversights that occur in particular cases. More fundamentally, we may appeal to the distinctively liberal appreciation of freedom's "non-specific" value and seek to promote a social order in which the idiosyncrasy and creativity of nonresponsible choice generates unforeseen and unforeseeable opportunities for progress and growth. Again, we will explore some of these issues in Chapter 3.

For now, I simply hope to have brought to light the seemingly contradictory answers that a liberal can give to the question of when a person is free, or under what conditions it becomes possible for a person to do something freely. The first, which I have associated with the term republican freedom, says that a free person is someone who is fit to be held responsible for what he or she does, and the second, which I have associated with the term market freedom, says that a free person is someone who is not responsible to anyone for what he or she does, except by choice. In the following chapters I will argue that, far from being contradictory, republican and market freedom are in fact complementary ways of thinking about freedom, and that a liberal polity is one that makes both kinds of freedom available to its members. The pursuit of liberal freedom therefore gives rise to two complementary political projects: first, that of creating the social conditions under which we are able to make choices for which we are fit to be held responsible, and second, that of carving out a domain of conduct in which we are not responsible to anyone else for what we do unless we choose to be. In other words, just as there is more than one kind of freedom that liberals have reason to value, so too is there more than one social position – more than one conception of free personhood – that a liberal polity aims to secure for its members. The challenge is not to choose, but rather to strike an appropriate balance, between them: this is not only the task of liberal political thought, but the substance of liberal politics itself.

I also hope to have shown that this person-centered theory of freedom provides a more perspicuous way of thinking about political freedom than the more familiar action-centered negative and positive liberty views, while still capturing the intuitions that motivate those views. On the one hand, by shifting our conceptual focus from autonomy, understood as a faculty that a person may or may not possess, to responsibility, understood as a social position that a person may or may not occupy, this approach makes it possible to treat freedom as a property of human agents without appealing, as positive liberty theories do, to a particular theory of what human agency consists in. On the other hand, the shift from an action-centered to a person-centered theory of freedom allows us to sidestep a number of conceptual problems that bedevil the appeal to negative liberty: for example, how we should enumerate choices and the corresponding liberties to make them – and what counts as a choice; whether a constraint has to be man-made in order to count as freedom-reducing – and what counts as a man-made constraint; and whether a constraint has to be recognized as such – and what counts as recognition. As we have seen, it is perfectly consistent on this view to hold that someone is not "really" responsible for what they do – or for the formation of the beliefs, habits, and preferences that lead them to act as they do – and still hold that we have good reason to treat them as if they were. Conversely, it is perfectly consistent to hold that someone is in fact responsible for what they do and for the consequences that follow, but nevertheless allow them to behave "irresponsibly" in a given domain.

I do not mean to say that the ideal of autonomous agency is illusory – though neither do I mean to deny that it might be. Still less do I mean to deny that our practices of holding others responsible often track our intuitions about the autonomy, or lack thereof, of the people concerned. I simply want to distinguish, as Mill did, between a political and a metaphysical theory of freedom, and to insist that questions about rational agency and autonomy do not enjoy privileged status *a priori* in political inquiry. Rather than start with the question of which constraints count as freedom-reducing and then turn to the question of which constraints should or should not be allowed to exist, we should start with the question of which social conditions qualify a person as free and then turn to the question of how far the boundaries of freedom so understood should be extended. As we will see, the shift from an action-centered to a person-centered theory of freedom requires that we rethink existing views about both republican and market freedom. On the one hand, it calls into question the efforts of contemporary republicans to show that a republican theory of freedom, taken on its own, can be both egalitarian and friendly toward markets. On the other hand, it calls into question the association of markets and market freedom with a regime of competition via economic exchange. It requires, more fundamentally, that we change our accounting practices as we place various social practices on one side of the freedom ledger or the other. We turn now to a closer examination of these two kinds of freedom, and of the relationship between them.

2

Republican Freedom

> If, in accord with traditional political thought, we identify tyranny as government that is not held to give account of itself, rule by Nobody is clearly the most tyrannical of all, since there is no one left who could even be asked to answer for what is being done.
>
> Hannah Arendt, *On Violence*

2.1 LIBERALISM AND REPUBLICANISM

The explosion of scholarship on republican political thought over the past several decades has gradually converged on two conclusions. On the one hand, there is now widespread agreement about what republicans stand for: where republicanism was once described as a "vague and supple" ideology – an open-ended political "language" or "paradigm" – it is now widely regarded as a "research program" that centers on an analytically distinctive and normatively fertile conception of freedom.[1] On the other hand, there is also widespread agreement that republicanism and liberalism are complementary rather than competing political ideologies; that the differences between them are matters of emphasis and approach, not

---

[1] Robert E. Shalhope, "Toward a Republican Synthesis: The Emergence of an Understanding of Republicanism in American Historiography," *William and Mary Quarterly* 29 (1972), p. 72; on languages and paradigms see especially J. G. A. Pocock, *The Machiavellian Moment: Florentine Political Thought and the Atlantic Republican Tradition* (Princeton, NJ: Princeton University Press, 1975) and the essays collected in his *Politics, Language and Time* (New York: Atheneum Press, 1971). On republicanism as a "research program" see, for example, Frank Lovett and Philip Pettit, "Neorepublicanism: A Normative and Institutional Research Program," *Annual Review of Political Science* 12 (2009), pp. 11–29.

of principle or fundamental aims. In this chapter I argue that these two conclusions are at odds with one another; that a clear understanding of what republican freedom means makes it equally clear that republicanism and liberalism cannot easily be reconciled. In particular, I will argue that republican-liberal syncretism is only possible if we paper over the complicated and contentious relationship between republicanism and the market – as indeed many contemporary republicans have done. Because markets have a central role to play in any liberal polity – and because we have good reasons to value the kind of freedom that they provide – I conclude that liberals should treat republican freedom as an attractive but partial political value, one that needs to be complemented and qualified by the contrasting value of market freedom.

The revival of scholarly interest in the republican tradition dates back to the 1960s, when intellectual historians began to challenge the widely held view that early modern political thought was predominantly "Lockean" or "liberal." These historians highlighted the central role that the language of self-government, virtue, and the common good – and of tyranny, corruption, and faction – played in the early modern period, and showed that this way of thinking drew on an older "republican" or "civic humanist" tradition.[2] This renewed interest in the historical influence of republican ideas soon led some scholars to consider what lessons the republican tradition might hold for the present day. Not surprisingly, given the motivations and findings of the historical scholarship, these contemporary applications of republican ideas focused at first on what many saw as the key shortcomings of liberalism: its excessive individualism, its tendency to "privatize" social conflicts, its reluctance to admit religious and other "comprehensive" worldviews into the public sphere, and its tendency to privilege rights and interests over duties and responsibilities. In short, republican political thought provided a colorful backstory for the so-called communitarian critique of

---

[2] See, in addition to Pocock's *Machiavellian Moment*, Bernard Bailyn, *The Ideological Origins of the American Revolution* (Cambridge, MA: Harvard University Press, 1967); Gordon S. Wood, *The Creation of the American Republic, 1776–1787* (New York: W. W. Norton, 1969); Quentin Skinner, *The Foundations of Modern Political Thought* (New York: Cambridge University Press, 1978), vol. 1. The "liberal" reading of American political thought was influentially set out in Louis Hartz, *The Liberal Tradition in America: An Interpretation of American Political Thought Since the Revolution* (New York: Harcourt, Brace, 1955). The term "civic humanism" (*Bürgerhumanismus*) was coined by the historian Hans Baron ; see in particular his *The Crisis of the Early Italian Renaissance: Civic Humanism and Republican Liberty in an Age of Classicism and Tyranny* (2nd ed., Princeton, NJ: Princeton University Press, 1966 [1955]).

liberalism.[3] This republican revival therefore attracted criticism from liberals who found the lofty but rather vague appeals to civic virtue and the common good – not to mention the clear historical connections between republicanism, patriarchy, and slavery – to be more insidious than inspiring.[4]

Despite this unpromising beginning, a number of liberal thinkers over the course of the 1990s called attention to the central role that republican ideas like limited government, the rule of law, a commitment to public deliberation, a concern to minimize asymmetries of power among citizens, and an orientation toward the common good play in liberal polities. John Rawls, the most influential liberal political philosopher of this period, insisted that there is "no fundamental opposition" between political liberalism and "classical republicanism," which he defined as the view that "[t]he safety of democratic liberties requires the active participation of citizens who possess the political virtues needed to maintain a constitutional regime."[5] The legal scholar Cass Sunstein, describing himself as a "liberal republican," argued along similar lines that "the opposition between liberal and republican thought" is built on "a caricature of the [liberal] tradition," and that "the most powerful versions of republicanism are not antiliberal at all." The political theorist Richard Dagger, describing himself as a "republican liberal," agreed that "to oppose republicanism to liberalism" is to overlook "the common ground that republicanism and liberalism share."[6] Even Michael Sandel, the most prominent republican critic of liberalism, conceded that "[a]t a certain level of generality, there is no necessary conflict" between the two schools

---

[3] See, for example, Michael J. Sandel, *Democracy's Discontent: America in Search of a Public Philosophy* (Cambridge, MA: Harvard University Press, 1996); Benjamin R. Barber, *Strong Democracy: Participatory Politics for a New Age* (Berkeley: University of California Press, 1984); Robert N. Bellah et al., *Habits of the Heart: Individualism and Commitment in American Life* (Berkeley: University of California Press, 1985).

[4] For an especially pointed example of this line of criticism see Don Herzog, "Some Questions for Republicans," *Political Theory* 14 (1986), pp. 473–93; for a more measured version see Ian Shapiro, *Political Criticism* (Berkeley: University of California Press, 1990), chapter 6.

[5] John Rawls, *Political Liberalism* (New York: Columbia University Press, 1993), p. 205.

[6] Cass R. Sunstein, "Beyond the Republican Revival," *Yale Law Journal* 97 (1988), pp. 1539–90, quoted at pp. 1567, 1569, 1589; Richard Dagger, "The Sandelian Republic and the Encumbered Self," *Review of Politics* 61 (1999), pp. 181–208, quoted at pp. 184, 207. As its title suggests, the latter essay is a critical response to Sandel's *Democracy's Discontent*; see more generally Richard Dagger, *Civic Virtues: Rights, Citizenship, and Republican Liberalism* (New York: Oxford University Press, 1997).

of thought, and emphasized that his quarrel was not with liberalism *tout court*, but rather with its "procedural" or "Kantian" variant.[7]

This shift from a competitive to a complementary understanding of the relationship between republicanism and liberalism was accompanied by an emerging consensus about the core commitments of republicanism itself. The central figure here was the philosopher Philip Pettit, who argued that the defining feature of republican political thought is its commitment to freedom understood as the absence of domination, where domination means "having to live at the mercy of another, having to live in a manner that leaves you vulnerable to some ill that the other is in a position arbitrarily to impose." Dominated people are unfree on the republican view even when they are not interfered with, because they can never be sure if and when interference will come: the power that dominates them is arbitrary in the sense that it can be exercised at will (*ad arbitrium*) by those who hold it. Pettit emphasizes that this kind of vulnerability often causes the dominated party to distort his or her behavior – in traditional republican language, to adopt a "slavish" or "servile" disposition – in order to anticipate and, if possible, forestall the interference of the dominating party. Republican freedom – "non-domination," as Pettit calls it – is therefore to be valued because it

> goes with being able to look the other in the eye, confident in the shared knowledge that it is not by their leave that you pursue your innocent, non-interfering choices; you ... do not have to live either in fear of that other, then, or in deference to them. The non-interference you enjoy ... is not enjoyed by their grace and you do not live at their mercy. You are a somebody in relation to them, not a nobody. You are a person in your own legal and social right.[8]

---

[7] Michael J. Sandel, "Liberalism and Republicanism: Friends or Foes? A Reply to Richard Dagger," *Review of Politics* 61 (1999), pp. 209–14, quoted at p. 209.

[8] Philip Pettit, *Republicanism: A Theory of Freedom and Government* (2nd ed., New York: Oxford University Press, 1999 [1997]), pp. 4–5, 71. Unlike Rawls, Sunstein, and Dagger, Pettit often portrays republicanism and liberalism as opposing political traditions, primarily because on his account liberals define freedom as "non-interference," not as "non-domination": see, for example, Pettit, *Republicanism*, pp. 8–11; Philip Pettit, *On the People's Terms: A Republican Theory and Model of Democracy* (New York: Cambridge University Press, 2012), p. 11, and *Just Freedom: A Moral Compass for a Complex World* (New York: W. W. Norton, 2014), pp. 16–26. As is already clear I reject this characterization of liberal freedom, but in any case Pettit also emphasizes that there is a great deal of overlap between the two traditions; indeed he once remarked, in response to a suggestion by Dagger, that "there is no good reason" why his own position should not be described as "liberal republicanism" or "republican liberalism": Philip Pettit, "On Republicanism: Reply to Carter, Christman and Dagger," *The Good Society* 9 (2000), p. 57.

As this passage makes clear, and as we saw in Chapter 1, republican freedom so understood is a person-centered rather than an action-centered conception of freedom: it consists in the possession of a privileged social status. The paradigmatic case of unfreedom that it identifies is the relationship between a master and a slave. No matter how indulgent a given master may happen to be, no matter how little he or she may interfere with the slave's choices, there is still a profound kind of unfreedom in any master-slave relationship; an unfreedom that consists in, rather than simply resulting from, the dependence of the slave on the master's arbitrary will. It is a short step, conceptually speaking, from personal to political domination, where the tyrant rather than the master is the paradigmatic wielder of arbitrary power. However, because a republican politics (like any politics) entails the exercise of authority by some people over others, the political enjoyment of republican freedom requires that citizens work together to make collective decisions about how that authority should be constituted and used. Pettit holds that two conditions have to be met in order for political rule to be consistent with the enjoyment of republican freedom. First, its exercise has to be grounded in reasons that are made known to and endorsed by all citizens; and second, citizens have to be willing and able to challenge political authorities when they fail to meet that standard: "it must always be possible," he argues, "for people in the society, no matter what corner they occupy, to contest the assumption that the guiding interests and ideas really are shared and, if the challenge proves sustainable, to alter the pattern of state activity."[9] In more traditional language, republican citizens have to display civic virtue in order to ensure that their polity pursues the common good.

Pettit's work has expanded the scope of republican political thought by calling attention to the potential presence of arbitrary power not only in the relationship between rulers and ruled, but also in relationships that classical and early modern republicans saw as extra-political, such as those between men and women, between employers and employees, between different cultures, and even between human beings and the environment.[10] However, he retreats from the republican tradition in one important way: by denying that participation in or dependence on markets poses a threat to republican freedom. Pettit is of course aware

---

[9] Pettit, *Republicanism*, p. 63. For a more detailed discussion of the political arrangements that support republican freedom see Pettit, *On the People's Terms*, chapters 3–5.
[10] For a useful overview see Pettit, *Republicanism*, chapter 5.

that concentrations of wealth and other kinds of economic power increase the threat of domination, and that unregulated markets tend to concentrate wealth in this freedom-threatening way. Indeed, he suggests that republicans have reason to endorse the "socialist" aim (as he calls it) of ensuring that workers are not subject to the arbitrary power of their employers, not only by promoting their economic independence through social welfare programs, but also by limiting the power of employers to hire and fire at will.[11] Nevertheless, he insists that "[t]here is no particular threat to people's freedom as non-domination associated with participation in the market": "Like the natural environment," he argues, the market "will certainly affect the range or the ease with which people enjoy their status as undominated agents, and it may warrant complaint on that account, but it will not itself be a source of domination"; indeed, properly regulated markets may actually "strengthen ... people's undominated standing in relation to one another."[12]

Pettit's position on this question is puzzling at first blush, not only because republicans have historically been suspicious of markets, but also because even the staunchest defenders of markets admit, and indeed emphasize, that we cannot enjoy the material benefits of a market economy unless people are made systematically vulnerable to adverse changes of fortune. Friedrich Hayek, for example, argues that it is futile to try to "protect individuals or groups against diminutions of their income, which although in no way deserved yet in a competitive society occur daily, against losses imposing severe hardships having no moral justification yet inseparable from the competitive system."[13] The philosopher Gerald Gaus concludes that a consistent republican should reject the "competitive system": "the right to private property," he argues, "makes each person a mini-sovereign, able to unilaterally alter the rights and duties of others," and so from a republican point of view the market "is much closer to a realm of domination than it is to one of freedom."[14] Where Gaus intends to criticize republicanism from the right, the political theorist Alex Gourevitch praises it from the left, calling attention to the

---

[11] Ibid., pp. 158–63 and 140–3, respectively; cf. Pettit, *On the People's Terms*, pp. 114–17.

[12] Philip Pettit, "Freedom in the Market," *Politics, Philosophy and Economics* 5 (2006), pp. 131–49, quoted at pp. 142, 139, 147; cf. Pettit, *Republicanism*, pp. 204–5.

[13] Friedrich Hayek, *The Road to Serfdom* (Chicago: University of Chicago Press, 1944), p. 135.

[14] Gerald Gaus, "Property, Rights, and Freedom," *Social Philosophy and Policy* 11 (1994), p. 226, and "Backwards into the Future: Neorepublicanism as a Postsocialist Critique of Market Society," *Social Philosophy and Policy* 20 (2003), p. 68.

apparent incompatibility between the enjoyment of republican freedom and the dependence of wage laborers on their employers. The nineteenth century "labor republicans" whose ideas he examines held that the liberal ideal of a labor market constituted by "free" contracts should be replaced by "shared ownership and control of productive resources"; they "did not accept the range of opportunities that commercial society made available to them," and sought "to replace [the] existing economic and social logic with a new one."[15]

Contemporary republicans are therefore caught on the horns of a dilemma: they must either claim, implausibly and in the face of the tradition, that markets do not pose a threat to republican freedom, or else admit that they *do* pose a threat, and that the pursuit of republican freedom is at odds with some of the central norms and practices of a liberal polity. In the first half of this chapter, I explore this dilemma by considering three strategies that republicans have used to try to square the political demands of republican freedom with the economic demands of social life. I start by examining two prominent approaches drawn from the history of political thought – what I call the "virtue" and "interest" models – and show that neither succeeds in reconciling the existence of a market economy with the contemporary republican commitment to the equal enjoyment of nondomination (Section 2.2). I then look more closely at Pettit's position, which I call the "discourse" model. On this view the pursuit of republican freedom requires that we create the social conditions under which people are fit to be held responsible for their actions – a condition that Pettit calls "discursive control" – and that we identify "common avowable interests" – in traditional republican language, a common good – against which those actions are measured (Section 2.3). Although the discourse model is a distinct improvement over the virtue and interest models, it raises two questions about the relationship between republicanism and the market: first, whether markets themselves satisfy the conditions of discursive control, and second, whether the association of freedom with discursive control overlooks or undervalues the distinct

---

[15] Alex Gourevitch, *From Slavery to the Cooperative Commonwealth: Labor and Republican Liberty in the Nineteenth Century* (New York: Cambridge University Press, 2015), quoted at pp. 119, 148. Republican concerns about wage labor are not new; Cicero held, for example, that "all those workers who are paid for their labour and not for their skill have servile and demeaning employment," and that "the very wage is a contract to servitude": Cicero, *On Duties*, book 1 §150, quoting Margaret Atkins's translation (New York: Cambridge University Press, 1991), p. 58.

kind of freedom that markets provide; a freedom that consists, as we have seen, not in responsibility but rather in nonresponsibility.

In the second half of the chapter, I take up each of these questions in turn. First, I contrast Pettit's position with Hayek's, which also defines freedom as the absence of arbitrary power, and which also holds that markets do not pose a threat to freedom so defined. As we will see, despite their superficial similarities Hayek and Pettit hold diametrically opposed views about the nature of a free society: for Hayek any effort to exercise collective control over social outcomes is inherently freedom-threatening, and the anonymity and impersonality of market outcomes is therefore desirable for its own sake. In other words, Hayek rejects the appeal to "common avowable interests" that lies at the heart of Pettit's republicanism (Section 2.4). Finally, I argue that while republicans have good grounds for wanting to decentralize economic decision-making, those grounds do not exhaust the full range of reasons that we have to value market freedom. In particular, the ideal of discursive control overlooks the various ways in which we can properly be described as free when we disregard, fall short of, or even exceed (at least in our own eyes) the social expectations that are placed upon us – when, in short, we act irresponsibly in the eyes of our fellow citizens. The discourse model, instead of insulating markets from republican criticism, therefore exposes a fundamental tension between republican and market freedom (Section 2.5). The liberal solution, as I have already indicated, is to treat these two kinds of freedom as complementary political values, and to focus on the practical question of how they should be balanced against each other. I conclude that republicanism and liberalism are, despite recent claims to the contrary, qualitatively different political ideals – although the issues that divide them are not the ones that "communitarian" republicans have identified.

2.2 VIRTUES AND INTERESTS

The challenge of reconciling the enjoyment of republican freedom with the imperatives of economic life is not new: the arts of production and trade, while less sophisticated, were of course no less central to life in the premodern and early modern periods than they are today. Historically republicans have responded to this challenge in two basic ways.[16] The

---

[16] Here and in the following paragraphs I draw on the more detailed discussion provided in Eric MacGilvray, *The Invention of Market Freedom* (New York: Cambridge University Press, 2011), especially chapters 1 and 3.

first, which I will call the *virtue model,* and which is of much longer standing, holds that active participation in economic affairs is incompatible with the enjoyment of republican freedom. According to this way of thinking, the economy is not a realm of freedom but of necessity, in the Aristotelian sense that it is concerned with the goods, such as food, shelter, and clothing that make life possible, and not the goods – above all the virtues – that make it worth living. While the secure ownership of property has always been a key marker of free status, the virtue model holds that direct involvement in economic activity is incompatible with the cultivation of civic virtue and thus beneath a free man's station. On this view the enjoyment of republican freedom requires a strict division of labor between politics, which is the proper domain of free and presumptively virtuous men, and economics, which is the proper domain of women, slaves, menial laborers, and the various other classes of unfree and presumptively unvirtuous people. The traditional division of labor between these two domains of conduct is reflected in the very word "economics," which is derived from the Greek work *oikos,* or household – in contrast to "politics," derived from *polis,* or city.

Two basic lines of argument have been offered in support of the virtue model. The first and more far-reaching says that active participation in economic affairs not only prevents us from cultivating our virtue in "higher" pursuits like politics, warfare, and the "liberal" ("free") arts, but also involves us in activities that tend to corrupt whatever virtue we might originally have had. For Aristotle the connection between paid labor and the loss of virtue was definitional: "One should consider a vulgar [*banausos*] task, art, or sort of learning," he argues, "to be any that renders the body, the soul, or the mind of free persons useless with a view to the practices and actions of virtue" – a category that includes "wage-earning sorts of work, for they make the mind a thing abject and lacking in leisure."[17] The second and more distinctively republican argument in support of the virtue model emphasizes that the market is a place where people compete against each other for personal gain, and concludes that this will inevitably lead to the corruption of public life. Plato's Athenian Stranger remarks, for example, that "proximity to the sea ... infects a place with commerce and the money-making that comes with retail trade, and engenders shifty and untrustworthy dispositions in souls ... thereby tak[ing] away the trust and friendship a city feels for

---

[17] Aristotle, *Politics* 1337b9–14 (book 8, chapter 2), quoting Carnes Lord's translation (2nd ed., Chicago: University of Chicago Press, 2013), p. 224.

itself and for the rest of humanity." Cicero agrees in thinking that "[m]aritime cities are ... subject to corruption and alteration of character," because "the desire for trade and travel" leads citizens to "abandon ... the cultivation of fields and of military skill": "Nothing did more to weaken gradually, and ultimately to destroy, Carthage and Corinth," he insists, "than this wandering and dissipation of their citizens."[18]

The association of commerce with corruption persisted until well into the eighteenth century, by which time commercial relations had developed to such an extent that they promised (or threatened, in the eyes of some) to replace war as the primary mode of interaction between states. Jean-Jacques Rousseau finds, for example, that the citizen of a commercial society "must ... constantly try to interest [others] in his fate and ... make them really or apparently find their own profit in working for his," and argues that this "makes him knavish and artful with some, imperious and harsh with the rest."[19] Adam Ferguson agrees in thinking that "nations under a high state of the commercial arts, are exposed to corruption, by their admitting wealth, unsupported by personal elevation and virtue, as the great foundation of distinction, and by having their attention turned on the side of interest, as the road to consideration and honour."[20] Even in the famously commerce-friendly United States, Thomas Jefferson argued that "corruption of morals ... is the mark set on those, who not looking up to heaven, to their own soil and industry ... for their subsistence, depend for it on the casualties and caprice of customers," and John Adams – Jefferson's political nemesis – warned that "the Spirit of Commerce," because it leads to "Servility and Flattery," is "incompatible with that purity of Heart and Greatness of soul which is necessary for a happy Republic."[21]

Despite the long history and imposing pedigree of republican skepticism toward commerce, the second half of the eighteenth century saw the emergence of a distinctively modern brand of republicanism which treated

---

[18] Plato, *Laws* 705a (book 4), quoting Thomas L. Pangle's translation (Chicago: University of Chicago Press, 1988), p. 90; Cicero, *De re Republica*, book 2 §7, in *On the Commonwealth and On the Laws*, trans. and ed. James E. G. Zetzel (New York: Cambridge University Press, 1999), p. 35.

[19] Jean-Jacques Rousseau, *Discourse on the Origins and Foundations of Inequality Among Men* (1755), in *The Discourses and Other Early Political Writings*, trans. and ed. Victor Gourevitch (New York: Cambridge University Press, 1997), pp. 170–1.

[20] Adam Ferguson, *An Essay on the History of Civil Society* (1767), ed. Fania Oz-Salzberger (New York: Cambridge University Press, 1995), p. 241 (part 6, section 3).

[21] Thomas Jefferson, *Notes on the State of Virginia* (1785), query 19; John Adams, letters to Mercy Otis Warren, April 16 and January 8, 1776.

the market as a means rather than an obstacle to the enjoyment of republican freedom – a way of thinking that I will call the *interest model*. Like the virtue model, the interest model rests on two related claims about the relationship between politics and economics. The first is that commerce provides a new tool for checking the arbitrary power of the state. Charles de Montesquieu influentially argued, for example, that in the modern age "experience itself has made known that only goodness of government brings prosperity"; a thought that was expressed more clearly by the Scottish mercantilist James Steuart, who suggested that "a modern œconomy... is the most effectual bridle ever was invented against the folly of despotism" because "the sovereign... finds himself so bound up by the laws of his political œconomy, that every transgression of them runs him into new difficulties."[22] As Benjamin Constant later observed, the reliance of modern states on credit "places authority itself in a position of dependence," since "to obtain the favours of wealth one must serve it."[23] Moreover, the mobility of capital makes it easy for investors to punish states that do not respect and support the commercial activities of their citizens, and easy to see which states are failing in this regard. Modern governments therefore have an interest in treating their subjects nonarbitrarily, at least as far as economic matters are concerned. In short, in a world where wealth rather than virtue is the key to national greatness, competitive and acquisitive behavior, far from distracting citizens from the common good, provides the most efficient means of securing it.

The second argument in favor of the interest model is most famously laid out in Adam Smith's seminal treatise on *The Wealth of Nations*. Smith found that the rise of commerce had "gradually introduced order and good government, and with them, the liberty and security of individuals among the inhabitants of the country, who had before lived in a continual state of war with their neighbours, and of servile dependency upon their superiors." He goes on to emphasize that it is the impersonal nature of market transactions that gives them this freedom-promoting

---

[22] Charles de Montesquieu, *The Spirit of the Laws* (1748), trans. Anne Cohler, Basia Miller, and Harold Stone (New York: Cambridge University Press, 1989), p. 389 (book 21, chapter 20); James Steuart, *An Inquiry in the Principles of Political Economy* (1767), book 2, chapters 22, 13. See also Albert O. Hirschman, *The Passions and the Interests: Political Arguments for Capitalism Before Its Triumph* (Princeton: Princeton University Press, 1977), where these passages are quoted at pp. 72 and 83–5, respectively.

[23] Benjamin Constant, "The Liberty of the Ancients Compared With That of the Moderns" (1819), in *Political Writings*, ed. Biancamaria Fontana (New York: Cambridge University Press, 1988), p. 325.

quality. A feudal tenant "is as dependent upon the proprietor as any servant or retainer whatever and must obey him with as little reserve," because "[t]he subsistence of both is derived from his bounty, and its continuance depends upon his good pleasure." In a commercial economy, by contrast, "[e]ach tradesman or artificer derives his subsistence from the employment, not of one, but of a hundred or a thousand different customers," so that while he is "in some measure obliged to them all ... he is not absolutely dependent upon any one of them." The same can be said of the "customers": although "the produce of [a wealthy man's] estate may be sufficient to maintain, and may perhaps actually maintain, more than a thousand people, yet as those people pay for everything they get ... there is scarce any body who considers himself as entirely dependent upon him."[24] According to this line of argument, the multiplication and diversification of economic relationships, and the space that is thereby created for the pursuit of economic gain, is favorable to republican as well as to market freedom.

Despite their obvious attractions, Pettit rejects each of these models – and for good reason. The virtue model was developed by and for a leisured elite: even the most "democratic" republics in the ancient world excluded most men and all women from citizenship, which is of course how they were able to keep politics and economics separate from each other. Moreover, this brand of republicanism places a premium on unity of purpose, and therefore looks with suspicion on any form of allegiance – religious, ethnic, socioeconomic, or whatever – that might divide the polity and thereby distract citizens from the pursuit of the common good. It is not clear how a virtue-centered republicanism could be pursued in a large and diverse polity where almost everyone has to work for a living, unless we are willing to follow the ancients in practicing massive political exclusion and indoctrination. It is therefore not surprising that "communitarian" republicans, who come closest among contemporary republicans to endorsing the virtue model, tend to be rather vague about what civic virtue consists in and how it should be promoted. As Pettit points out, Sandel – the most prominent advocate of this approach, at least among academics – "remains studiously uncommitted on what the content of [republican] virtue is supposed to be"; a "worrying indeterminacy" that "carries over into a similar, breezy vagueness about the institutions and programs that such freedom and virtue are going to support" – giving rise to the reasonable worry that, whatever his

---

[24] Adam Smith, *An Inquiry into the Nature and Causes of the Wealth of Nations* (Oxford: Clarendon Press, 1979 [1776]), III.iv.4, 6, 12; V.i.b.7.

intentions, such a politics would in practice simply "let loose the dogs of moralistic enthusiasm."[25]

Where the virtue model appeals to an idealized past, the interest model plays a central role in the self-understanding of contemporary democracies – though it is now typically referred to as "interest-group pluralism" rather than as a species of republicanism.[26] According to this way of thinking it is self-interest and not civic virtue that draws people into politics, and the public sphere is an arena in which groups of various kinds compete for power in order to defend and advance their interests. From this point of view politics itself is a kind of market, and the proper aim of institutional design is, as the political scientist Robert Dahl puts it, to "increase the size, number, and variety of minorities whose preferences must be taken into account," thus preventing any particular group or coalition of groups from acquiring monopolistic or oligopolistic market power.[27] As we have already seen, republicanism as Pettit conceives of it requires that citizens state their political views publicly and defend them in other-regarding terms, that political power be exercised in the name of shared public reasons, and that citizens be able to challenge its exercise when it fails to live up to this standard. Pettit therefore rejects the interest-centered conception of politics in the strongest terms, because it treats any (legal) motivation that one might have for voting or otherwise exercising political power as legitimate, and thus makes all citizens potentially subject to the arbitrary power of the majority coalition, whatever it happens to be: "[t]he backgrounding of reason which interest-group pluralism would recommend," he argues, "is inherently inimical to the goal of promoting freedom as non-domination," and so "nothing could be further from the republican ideal."[28]

---

[25] Philip Pettit, "Reworking Sandel's Republicanism," *Journal of Philosophy* 95 (1998), pp. 73–96, quoted at pp. 81, 90. The Herzog and Shapiro essays cited in note 4 above pursue a similar line of argument.

[26] The literature on interest group pluralism is too vast to summarize here; early landmarks include David Truman, *The Governmental Process: Political Interests and Public Opinion* (New York: Knopf, 1951); Robert A. Dahl, *A Preface to Democratic Theory* (Chicago: University of Chicago Press, 1956); Anthony Downs, *An Economic Theory of Democracy* (New York: Harper & Row, 1957); and Theodore J. Lowi, *The End of Liberalism: The Second Republic of the United States* (New York: Norton, 1969).

[27] Dahl, *Preface to Democratic Theory*, p. 132.

[28] Pettit, *Republicanism*, pp. 202–5, quoted at p. 205; cf. Pettit, *On the People's Terms*, pp. 248–51 and chapter 5 *passim*. Here Pettit follows a broader strand of contemporary republican thought; Sunstein argues, for example, that "[t]he purpose of politics is not to aggregate private preferences, or to achieve an equilibrium among contending social forces," but rather "to achieve a measure of critical distance from prevailing desires and

We might wonder how Pettit can object on republican grounds to the "backgrounding of reason" that interest-group pluralism entails without also objecting to the "backgrounding of reason" that takes place in the market. We will consider his response to this apparent inconsistency below, after we look more carefully at the model of republican politics that he defends. Given his rejection of the virtue and interest models, we can already see that this model should have three basic features: (1) it should be *substantively nonarbitrary*, allowing only commonly shared interests to shape political outcomes; (2) it should be *procedurally nonarbitrary*, operating in a reason-guided and contestable way; and (3) it should be *egalitarian*, giving all normally functioning adults equal access to and influence over the political process. The virtue model violates condition (3), and the interest model violates condition (2). It is a matter of dispute whether either model satisfies condition (1) since they each rest on a particular and contestable conception of which interests are commonly shared: in the case of the virtue model, the pursuit of human flourishing through the practice of civic virtue, and in the case of the interest model, the pursuit of wealth or power through the exercise of strategic rationality. As we will now see, Pettit turns to discourse – the practice of intersubjective reason-giving – as a means of guiding political outcomes that is both reason-guided and inclusive, and that leaves the question of which interests are commonly shared to be answered through public deliberation, not ideological fiat.[29]

2.3 REASONS AND PERSONS

One of the central claims of Pettit's book *Republicanism* (1997) is that interference is nonarbitrary, and thus nondominating, if it "tracks the relevant interests" of the agent who is being interfered with.[30] Pettit is not entirely clear in that book how we should determine whether an interest is "relevant" or not; in particular whether he is appealing to a conception of

---

practices, subjecting these desires and practices to scrutiny and review": Sunstein, "Beyond the Republican Revival," pp. 1548–9. Dagger puts the point more succinctly, pointing out that "the so-called consumer-citizen is, in traditional republican terms, a corruption of what a citizen should be": Richard Dagger, "Neo-Republicanism and the Civic Economy," *Politics, Philosophy and Economics* 5 (2006), p. 159.

[29] Pettit is not the only republican to emphasize the importance of public deliberation – Sunstein in particular has made this a central theme – but his is the most thoroughly worked-out view.

[30] See, for example, Pettit, *Republicanism*, pp. 55, 58, 63, 68, 120, 185, 186, 188.

genuine or "real" interests, or whether he sees the question of which interests are "relevant" as a matter to be worked out politically. He decisively embraced the latter position with his turn to the idea of *discursive control*, which lies at the center of his book *A Theory of Freedom* (2001) and much of his subsequent work on agency and freedom. There he argues that an agent can only be said to have done something freely if he or she can properly be held responsible for having done it, and vice versa. Indeed, as we saw in Chapter 1, he argues that "there is an *a priori* connection" between freedom and responsibility; that "[s]omeone who did not see why that connection had to obtain would fail to understand what freedom was or what holding someone responsible was."[31] Because, as Pettit emphasizes, holding people responsible is a social practice, it follows that the question of which kinds of interference count as nonarbitrary has to be worked out through a process of public deliberation. In other words, our "relevant" interests are, as he now prefers to say, our "avowable" interests – the interests that we can legitimately assert and successfully defend in discourse.[32]

In developing this line of argument Pettit considers and rejects two conceptions of free agency before settling on a third, within which the first two are absorbed or taken up. The first conception, which he calls freedom as *rational control*, counts as free any agent whose actions are properly directed by the intentional states – the beliefs and desires – that he or she has, where those intentional states have been properly formed and updated in light of the information gained from past actions. The second conception, which he calls freedom as *volitional control*, counts as free the subset of rational actions that are performed willingly, in the sense that the agent identifies with or "owns" the beliefs and desires on behalf of which they are undertaken. Where the attribution of rational control depends on a quality of the action itself – whether it contributes to achieving its *intended* end – the attribution of volitional control depends on a quality of the actor – whether he or she pursues his or her *considered* ends. In Pettit's language, a rationally controlled actor counts as a mere

---

[31] Philip Pettit, *A Theory of Freedom: From the Psychology to the Politics of Agency* (New York: Oxford University Press, 2001), pp. 70, 18.
[32] Pettit adopted the language of "avowability" in the course of developing the "contestatory" model of democracy that he first introduced in *Republicanism*, chapter 6; see in particular Philip Pettit, "Republican Freedom and Contestatory Democratization," in Ian Shapiro and Casiano Hacker-Cordon, eds., *Democracy's Value* (New York: Cambridge University Press, 1999), pp. 163–90, and Philip Pettit, "Democracy, Electoral and Contestatory," *NOMOS* 42 (2000), pp. 105–44.

agent, whereas a volitionally controlled actor counts as a *self*. I act neither rationally nor willingly when there is no discernible connection between my behavior and my intentional states; for example, when I am moved by a nervous tic or compulsion. I act rationally, but not willingly, when I successfully pursue ends that I would not endorse on reflection; for example, when I procure and consume a pack of cigarettes despite my considered desire to quit smoking. And I act both rationally and willingly when I successfully pursue ends that I reflectively endorse and thereby "own."[33]

Pettit rejects each of these conceptions of free agency on the grounds that it is possible to do something rationally and even willingly without being fit to be held responsible for having done it. This is clearest in the case of rational control, since agents can be said to act rationally not only when they act contrary to their considered ends, but even when they do not reflect on their ends at all – and even if they are not aware that they have adopted a rational means of pursuing them, as in the case of nonhuman animals or robots. As Pettit puts it, rational agents often appear to others and even to themselves as bystanders to, rather than as authors of, their actions.[34] The appeal to volitional control tries to avoid this possibility by counting as free only those actions that are guided by what the philosopher Harry Frankfurt calls a "second-order volition" to be moved by certain beliefs and desires; for example, when my first-order desire to have a cigarette is overridden by my second-order desire to quit smoking. However, Pettit points out that we may be bystanders even to our own second- (or higher-) order volitions – as, to borrow his example, when my first-order desire to keep my desk clean is endorsed by my second-order allegiance to the Victorian maxim that cleanliness is next to godliness, a maxim that I disapprove of on reflection. In short, volitional control not only requires that we identify with our first-order beliefs and desires, but that we also identify with the second-order process (say, of socialization or habit-formation) that gave rise to them, the third-order process that gave rise to that second-order process, and so on. Taken

---

[33] I use the word "successfully" here as a shorthand for "in a way that is guided by the best available information"; needless to say, action that is so guided does not always succeed in achieving its intended ends. The rational and volitional control models are discussed in Pettit, *Theory of Freedom*, chapters 2 and 3, respectively.

[34] Ibid., pp. 40–2. On the possibility that a robot might count as an agent in this sense see Philip Pettit, "Joining the Dots," in Geoffrey Brennan, Robert Goodin, Frank Jackson, and Michael Smith, eds., *Common Minds: Themes from the Philosophy of Philip Pettit* (New York: Oxford University Press, 2007), p. 229.

in itself the appeal to volitional control does not tell us where this regress should stop, and thus which of our higher-order volitions we are fit to be held responsible for.[35]

A more immediate practical worry about the appeal to volitional control is that it makes it possible to say that we act freely even in the face of coercion. After all, I might willingly hand over my wallet to a mugger – that is, in doing so I might live up to my considered belief that I should value my personal safety over my desire to keep my money or to appear heroic – but it would be odd to say that I could properly be held responsible for doing so. This seemingly absurd implication reveals a broader problem with the idea of volitional control when considered as a conception of political freedom: the threat of coercive force lies at one end of a continuum that includes a wide range of lesser material and psychic sanctions, from financial ruin to mild embarrassment. As we saw in Chapter 1, almost everything that we do is influenced by our expectations about how other people will react, and it is not obvious how the standard of "willingness" can be used to determine when this kind of influence should count as freedom-reducing. On the other hand, it would be counterintuitive in the extreme to say that being influenced by other people is *always* freedom-reducing, and that the freest person is one who is not bound by social ties or expectations of any kind. An adequate theory of political freedom therefore not only has to identify which of our higher-order volitions we are fit to be held responsible for, it also has to specify the conditions under which we can be recognized as free and responsible agents despite the fact that both our will and our actions are constantly shaped by the actual or anticipated reactions of other people.

Pettit argues that discourse can perform both of these tasks. A discursively controlled agent is one who is willing and able to own up to (some of) his or her past commitments in discourse with others. Such an agent – a *person*, in Pettit's terminology – is, in short, someone who can be moved by reason, defined roughly as self-consistency in discourse over time, and whose ability to do so is recognized by other people who are similarly able. On this view my actions count as free not simply because I did them, but rather because other people treat me as someone who is fit to be held responsible for doing them – and because I live up to their expectations over time. By shifting the focus from the beliefs and desires of

---

[35] Pettit, *Theory of Freedom*, pp. 53–7; cf. pp. 97–100. On second-order volitions see Harry Frankfurt, "Freedom of the Will and the Concept of a Person," *Journal of Philosophy* 68 (1971), pp. 5–20.

the acting agent to the relationships in which that agent stands with other people, the discourse model allows us to avoid the regress that the volitional model creates. As Pettit puts it, "the regress bottoms out with the type of agent that we take the person to be: the reason-responsive type to which we assign the person in discursively authorizing them." The shift to an intersubjective point of view also makes it possible to distinguish, at least in principle, between forms of social influence that we discursively authorize, and for which we can therefore be held responsible, and forms that we do not; to distinguish, for example, between getting taxed and getting mugged. Under conditions of discursive control "[i]f we are moved by others ... we will only be moved in a way that we would want to be moved; we will ourselves retain discursive determination of where those movements take us." The discourse model is therefore consistent with the association of freedom with responsibility, since in order to represent oneself as a discursively controlled agent one has to be prepared to accept praise or blame for one's actions insofar as they track or deviate from reason.[36]

There are two points of contact between the discourse model and the republican idea of freedom as nondomination. On the one hand, distorted communication is one of the primary effects of domination; as Pettit points out, "[i]t is a commonplace of received lore that [a dominated] person will not be able to speak out in a forthright and free way," and that this will "jeopardize the agent's discursive control as effectively as any act of outright coercion or manipulation."[37] It follows that the pursuit of republican freedom requires that every citizen be able to participate meaningfully in public discourse; that they are adequately educated and informed, that they have access to the material and social resources – adequate food, shelter, clothing, health care, means of communication and transportation, and so on – that are needed to maintain themselves as reliable and effective interlocutors, and that they are not subject to arbitrary power in the home, the workplace, the public sphere, or any other domain of their lives in a way that might deter them from candidly stating and defending their views.[38] Needless to say, it will be a matter of judgment – and ultimately of political contestation – what the necessary

---

[36] Pettit, *Theory of Freedom*, chapter 4, quoted at pp. 99, 70.
[37] Ibid., p. 78; cf. ibid. pp. 140–1.
[38] See, for example, Pettit, *Republicanism*, pp. 140–3 and 158–63, *On the People's Terms*, pp. 110–17, *Just Freedom*, pp. 84–93. Pettit often appeals in this context to the "capabilities approach" to measuring human welfare that is defended by Amartya Sen and Martha Nussbaum; see, for example, Amartya Sen, *Development as Freedom* (New York: Anchor

threshold is for meeting each of these conditions, and whether a particular shortfall is significant enough to pose a threat to republican freedom: when a person is entitled to say, for example, like Romeo's apothecary, that "my poverty, but not my will, consents." As a rough heuristic for determining when this standard has been met Pettit proposes what he calls the "eyeball test": that citizens "be so resourced and protected in the basic choices of life ... that they can look others in the eye without reason for fear or deference."[39]

The second connection between discursive control and republican freedom has to do with the outcomes rather than the preconditions of discourse. As we have seen, the enjoyment of freedom as discursive control requires not only that each person be able to participate effectively in discourse, but also that each person be influenced by others only in ways that he or she has discursively authorized. In political terms, this means that the various rules that a polity imposes on its citizens have to be discursively authorized – and discursively contestable – by those very citizens, and that each citizen must therefore have an equal chance to influence the processes through which those rules are made. In more traditional language, a republic has to be self-governing in the sense that its citizens are both the authors and the addressees of the laws that bind them. Crucially, this requirement applies not only to the various things that a polity does – via laws, executive actions, and so on – but also to the things that it *fails* to do: a government that allows discursively unauthorized and remediable social conditions to shape the behavior of its citizens poses no less of a threat to republican freedom than a government that creates such conditions itself. Here again it will be a matter of judgment and political contestation when a deviation from the ideal of discursive control is significant enough to pose a threat to republican freedom. As a rough heuristic for determining when this standard has been met Pettit proposes what he calls the "tough luck test": "that if a collective decision goes against you, then you have reason to view this as tough luck, even by the most demanding local criteria, and not as the sign of a malign will working against you or your kind."[40]

There are two questions that we might have about the relationship between republicanism so understood and the market. The first and most

---

Books, 1999), and Martha Nussbaum, *Creating Capabilities: The Human Development Approach* (Cambridge, MA: Harvard University Press, 2011).

[39] Pettit, *Just Freedom*, p. xxvi; cf. ibid., pp. 98–100 and *On the People's Terms*, pp. 84–7.

[40] Pettit, *Just Freedom*, p. xxvi; cf. ibid., pp. 142–4 and *On the People's Terms*, pp. 176–9.

obvious question is whether participation in or dependence on markets poses a threat to republican freedom. On the one hand, market *transactions* are typically discursively controlled: a contract is a paradigmatic example of a past commitment for which one can expect to be held responsible by other people, however one's will may have changed in the meantime. On the other hand, a market *economy* is a paradigmatic example of a decision-making process that has no coherent intentions and incurs no lasting commitments; whose behavior is neither discursively controlled nor contestable.[41] The second and more far-reaching question is whether the pursuit of republican freedom so understood poses a threat to a distinct kind of freedom that we also have reason to value: freedom understood as the *absence* of responsibility. As we have already seen, republicans have weighty reasons to disperse decision-making power away from the state, and markets are an essential tool for doing so. However, by treating the dispersal of power as the *only* reason that we might have for allowing markets to exist – by tolerating markets only up to the point at which they prevent more domination than they create – republicans fail to recognize the wide variety of other reasons that we might have for creating a domain of nonresponsible conduct; reasons that are, as we will now see, especially salient when republican freedom is defined in terms of discursive control.

2.4 DO MARKETS DOMINATE?

Pettit's discourse model yields a powerful and flexible theory of freedom – one that makes it possible to draw a connection, as he puts it, between the psychology and the politics of human agency.[42] It also offers a clear improvement over the two models of republican freedom that we examined in Section 2.2: unlike the interest model it operates in a reason-guided and contestable way and is thus procedurally nonarbitrary, and unlike the virtue model it offers freedom to all who are willing and able to take part in discourse, and is thus egalitarian.[43] Moreover, in contrast to

---

[41] Market outcomes can of course be controlled or contested in the sense that they can be reversed by the state or by sufficiently powerful private actors, but in such cases they are no longer *market* outcomes in the relevant sense.
[42] Here I paraphrase the subtitle of *A Theory of Freedom*.
[43] Political exclusion has sometimes been defended on the grounds that certain people lack the ability to engage in discourse; consider, for example, Aristotle's claim that "[t]he slave is wholly lacking the deliberative element [of the soul]; the female has it but it lacks authority": *Politics*, p. 22 (1260a12–14/book 1, chapter 13). Even Aristotle seems to

both of those models the appeal to public deliberation does not require that we stipulate which political ends count as substantively nonarbitrary: this is a matter to be worked out in politics, not settled in advance of it. However, by treating markets as neither anathema nor essential to the enjoyment of republican freedom – as do the virtue and interest models, respectively – the discourse model leaves the relationship between republicanism and the market unsettled. On the one hand, insofar as we value republican freedom because it ensures that the conditions under which we act are discursively authorized and contestable, then participation in or dependence on markets would seem to be incompatible with its enjoyment. On the other hand, because markets are nonagentic in the specific sense of being nondiscursive, they do not seem to implicate the part of our lives (our status as persons) that is relevant to our freedom – except to the extent that they empower others to interfere with us in nonreason-guided ways. As I have already indicated, Pettit focuses on the second of these considerations in his own treatment of markets; as I will now argue, the more consistent republican position is to focus on the first.

A notable challenge to this line of argument is found in the writings of Friedrich Hayek, who was one of the most sophisticated and influential defenders of markets in the twentieth century, and who follows the republican tradition in defining freedom as "independence of the arbitrary will of another," and echoes Pettit in holding that "[l]iberty and responsibility are inseparable."[44] Despite his opposition to arbitrary power Hayek paints a vivid picture of the "seemingly irrational forces of the market": "A complex civilization like ours," he argues,

is necessarily based on the individual's adjusting himself to changes whose cause and nature he cannot understand: why he should have more or less, why he should

---

doubt, however, that this is true of those who were actually enslaved in his day – see ibid., book 1, chapter 6 – and he makes no effort to defend the absurd claim that it is true of women. Moreover, to say that an agent is discursively controlled is *not* to say that he or she always acts in accordance with reason – a more demanding condition that Pettit calls "orthonomy" – but rather that in cases of failure he or she could have been brought to do so under the right counterfactual conditions. The appeal to discursive control therefore creates a much lower threshold for political inclusion than the appeal to autonomy or right reasoning that we examined in Chapter 1, although admittedly some people – most notably young children, but also those who suffer from severe cognitive impairment or mental illness – will nevertheless fail to meet it. See Philip Pettit and Michael Smith, "Freedom in Belief and Desire," *Journal of Philosophy* 93 (1996), pp. 429–49, and see also Pettit, "Joining the Dots," pp. 238–44.

[44] Friedrich Hayek, *The Constitution of Liberty* (Chicago: University of Chicago Press, 1960), pp. 12, 71.

Do Markets Dominate?

have to move to another occupation, why some things he wants should become more difficult to get than others, will always be connected with such a multitude of circumstances that no single mind will be able to grasp them.[45]

Hayek reconciles his allegiance to markets with his concern to minimize dependence by appealing to the impersonal nature of market outcomes. This allows him to treat even the most severe economic hardships as nonfreedom-reducing: "Even if the threat of starvation to me and perhaps to my family impels me to accept a distasteful job at a very low wage," he argues,

> even if I am "at the mercy" of the only man willing to employ me, I am not coerced by him or anybody else. So long as the act that has placed me in my predicament is not *aimed* at making me do or not do specific things, so long as the *intent* of the act that harms me is not to make me serve another person's ends, its effect on my freedom is not different from that of any natural calamity – a fire or a flood that destroys my house or an accident that harms my health.[46]

As we have seen, Pettit does not think that anyone should be "at the mercy" of anyone else to the extent that Hayek contemplates, no matter what the cause of their misfortune, and so he ties the enjoyment of republican freedom to the existence of a robust "safety net" that insulates people from economic hardship.[47] Nevertheless, he agrees with Hayek in thinking that power has to be exercised intentionally, or at least in culpable negligence, in order to count as arbitrary, and that the vulnerability of market actors to sudden misfortune – even if it is the misfortune, not of starvation, but of moving from gainful employment to social assistance – does not make them unfree from a republican point of view. More precisely, he argues that while market outcomes ("the aggregate consequences of independently motivated actions by others") may "vitiate" our freedom – that is, while they may diminish the opportunities that we have – they do not "invade" it in a way that constitutes domination, because they do not "reflect the will of another as to what [we] should do."[48] He concludes that the market, as long as it is free of force and fraud

---

[45] Hayek, *Road to Serfdom*, pp. 224, 223.
[46] Hayek, *Constitution of Liberty*, p. 137 (emphasis added).
[47] Even Hayek admits that "the preservation of competition [is not] incompatible with an extensive system of social services, so long as the organization of these services is not designed in such a way as to make competition ineffective over wide fields" (*Road to Serfdom*, p. 43), although he became more cautious on this point over time.
[48] Pettit, *On the People's Terms*, pp. 35–49, quoted at pp. 39, 40. Pettit previously used the terms "conditioning" and "compromising" to mark roughly the same distinction: Pettit, *Republicanism*, pp. 75–7.

and operates from a baseline that is not contaminated by arbitrary power (strong conditions, to be sure), may "reduce[] the range or the ease with which you enjoy freedom as non-domination, without itself being dominating."[49] In short Pettit, like Hayek, treats the fact that markets are impersonal – that no one in particular is responsible for what they do – as grounds for excluding them from the list of freedom-threatening institutions: again, as long as no one's freedom is "vitiated" to such an extent that they become subject to domination as a result.

Pettit appeals to two familiar distinctions to support this line of argument. The first is "the distinction between securing people against the natural effects of chance and incapacity and scarcity and securing them against the things that they may try to do to one another" – a distinction, he notes, that "is of the first importance in political philosophy."[50] This distinction, important as it is, excludes a salient third category: outcomes that are not the result of any human intention, but that are within the power of human beings to alter or avoid. This is of course the category that markets fall into: they do not intentionally inflict harms (or confer benefits) on anyone, but the decision to allow them to do so is nevertheless an intentional one. If human beings were able to control the weather then it would be appropriate to say that the people who were made vulnerable because of a failure to exercise that control in a given range of cases were dominated, even if we did not know in advance who would be harmed.[51] Similarly, we do not know in advance who will be harmed if we allow markets to operate in a given domain, but we do know that all things being equal transferring control over social outcomes from a republican state to a market increases the overall amount of vulnerability that exists, and thereby diminishes the fitness of the people in question to be held responsible for what they do. The choice that we face, in short, is not between being subject to the will of an identifiable agent or being subject to

---

[49] Pettit, "Freedom in the Market," p. 139. Pettit has not always been consistent on this point; in a discussion of harm to the environment he remarks that "[e]ven if the damage comes about inadvertently ... or as the aggregate outcome of individually innocent actions, it counts as a loss in the ledger-book of republican liberty" (*Republicanism*, p. 138) – a line of argument that would seem to apply equally well to economic harms arising from the operation of markets. Presumably this was just a slip.

[50] Pettit, *Republicanism*, pp. 52–3.

[51] This is not an entirely hypothetical case; for an argument that current generations are dominating future generations through their failure to adequately reduce carbon emissions see John Nolt, "Greenhouse Gas Emission and the Domination of Posterity," in Denis G. Arnold, ed., *The Ethics of Global Climate Change* (New York: Cambridge University Press, 2011), pp. 60–76.

impersonal forces, but rather between having the conditions under which we act defined in a way that is discursively authorized and contestable or having them defined in a way that is not.[52]

The second distinction that Pettit appeals to is "[the] psychologically resonant distinction between restrictions that exasperate and restrictions that may also outrage": "You may be frustrated and exasperated by hindrances that do not impose another's will," he points out, "[b]ut if you suffer will-imposed hindrances" then "you will also burn with resentment and indignation."[53] Here again Pettit's distinction, while important, excludes a salient third category: how should we be expected to feel about hindrances that are *indirectly* the product of human will; that is, that are imposed impersonally, but that are within the power of human beings to remove? The answer, of course, is that how we feel will depend on how aware we are that the hindrances in question are removable – and maybe on how likely we think it is that they might be removed. But feelings are not always a reliable guide in such cases. We often fail to recognize that familiar and seemingly fixed features of our social environment are nevertheless contingent, and that any harms that we suffer as a result are, in that indirect sense, "will-imposed": we are merely exasperated when we ought also to be outraged. This is especially likely to happen when, as in a market economy, the harms themselves are visited in an impersonal way; as the political philosopher G. A. Cohen points out, in such an economy "there is an ideologically valuable anonymity on both sides of the relationship."[54] Looked at in this way, Pettit's claim that a properly designed market system would be "akin to the natural environment" follows a long ideological tradition of insulating markets from criticism by naturalizing them.[55]

In short, Pettit's claim that markets do not pose a direct threat to republican freedom is hard to square with his person-centered conception

---

[52] Again, market outcomes can be reversed or controlled by the state or by sufficiently powerful private actors, but in such cases they are not *market* outcomes in the relevant sense.

[53] Pettit, *On the People's Terms*, pp. 44, 43.

[54] G. A. Cohen, "The Structure of Proletarian Unfreedom," *Philosophy and Public Affairs* 12 (1983), quoted at p. 13 (emphasis removed).

[55] Pettit, "Freedom in the Market," p. 139. The possibility of ideological blindness raises a broader worry about the "eyeball test." Pettit acknowledges that "[p]eople are liable to vary across societies in the different levels of vulnerability to which they have become inured," but insists that "it is clearly local standards that should provide the relevant benchmark for determining when fear or deference is irrational and when prudent": Pettit, *On the People's Terms*, p. 85; cf. Pettit, *Just Freedom*, pp. xxvi–xxvii.

of republican freedom as discursive control. After all, the question of whether a constraint is intentionally imposed swings freely of the question of whether the presence of that constraint diminishes the fitness of those who are subject to it to be held responsible for what they do. Markets profoundly shape our behavior in all kinds of implicit and explicit ways – where we live, how we spend our time, who we associate with, what we hope for and fear – but they cannot be reasoned with, and they do not behave predictably or consistently over time: as the saying goes, past results are no guarantee of future performance. The extent to which I have access to satisfying or remunerative economic opportunities, insofar as markets decide these things, is a product of countless independent decisions by people who are entirely unaccountable, and for the most part unknown, to me. Market actors are therefore in a position analogous to that of the victim of coercion that we considered earlier: when I accept a distasteful job at a very low wage in order to avoid starvation – and in a wide range of more mundane situations – I may be said to act rationally and even willingly without being fully responsible for the choices that I make. If republicans are committed to subjecting the conditions under which we act to discursive control – and thus to reducing the uncertainty and anxiety that we experience[56] – then they should be concerned not only about the role that market *outcomes* play in creating opportunities for the arbitrary exercise of power, but also and more fundamentally about the role that markets as a *mechanism* for achieving those outcomes play in the lives of those who participate in or depend upon them.

Hayek is able to avoid this conclusion because he rejects out of hand the idea that the citizens of a polity might collectively authorize the constraints that they face in such a way that those constraints become freedom-promoting rather than freedom-reducing: it is always a mistake, in his view, "to replace the impersonal and anonymous mechanism of the market by collective and 'conscious' direction of all social forces to deliberately chosen goals."[57] From this point of view (the *neoliberal* point of view, as we will see in Chapter 3) the social practice of holding

---

[56] As Pettit points out, "[t]o suffer the reality or expectation of arbitrary interference is to suffer an extra malaise over and above having your choices intentionally curtailed. It is to have to endure a high level of uncertainty, since the arbitrary basis on which the interference occurs means that there is no predicting when it will strike. Such uncertainty makes planning much more difficult than it would be under a corresponding prospect of non-arbitrary interference. And, of course, it is also likely to produce a high level of anxiety": Pettit, *Republicanism*, p. 85.
[57] Hayek, *Road to Serfdom*, p. 24.

people responsible for their choices does not commit us to any claim about the social conditions under which those choices are made – that they are volitionally or discursively controlled, for example – nor does it provide us with any grounds for trying to improve those conditions. Attributions of responsibility are simply a way to incentivize economically rational behavior: "The assigning of responsibility is based," Hayek insists, "not on what we know to be true in the particular case, but on what we believe will be the probable effects of encouraging people to behave rationally and considerately," and "[t]hough a man's conviction that all he achieves is due solely to his exertions, skill, and intelligence may be largely false, it is apt to have the most beneficial effects on his energy and circumspection." Thus, when Hayek says that subjection to arbitrary power is "bad because it prevents a person from using his mental powers to the full and consequently from making the greatest contribution that he is capable of to the community," he does not mean that it distorts communication and thereby undermines the conditions of discursive control, but simply that it prevents people from independently applying their abilities, energy, and knowledge to the competitive determination of prices.[58]

I propose to draw the line between freedom-reducing and freedom-neutral constraints in a way that is more consistent with the republican commitments of the discourse model: *a freedom-reducing constraint is any constraint whose presence tends to diminish a person's fitness to be held responsible for what they do, and that is within the power of other people to alter or remove.* The key claim that makes the first half of this definition tractable – a claim that I draw from Pettit, although as I have argued I do not think that he applies it consistently – is that discursively authorized constraints do not diminish our fitness to be held responsible for what we do: the paradigmatic personal example being a legally enforceable contract, and the paradigmatic political example being a democratically enacted system of law. The key concern that is raised by the second half of the definition is that the question of which discursively unauthorized constraints are within human power to remove is subject to dispute at any particular time, and to considerable change over time. To take only one example, many public health hazards that are uncontroversially matters of public concern today would have been prohibitively costly to remove one hundred years ago, and completely intractable two hundred years ago. It follows that the question of which constraints count as freedom-reducing will always be context-bound and

[58] Hayek, *Constitution of Liberty*, pp. 77, 82–3, 134.

contestable: like Pettit's "eyeball test," this is an irreducibly *political* conception of what republican freedom requires. Because it does not appeal to the intentions (or lack thereof) of freedom-threatening agents, or to feelings of fear or outrage (or lack thereof) on the part of those whose freedom is threatened, it leads us to conclude, as republicans traditionally have, that markets do in fact threaten the freedom of those who participate in or depend upon them.

The obvious objection to this line of argument is that it would be exceptionally cumbersome and costly to try to guide as many social outcomes as possible through the direct application of human reason via discourse: Hayek is right to insist that markets have an essential role to play in steering social outcomes in a complex society like ours. This is no doubt one reason why Pettit is eager to show that suitably regulated markets do not pose a direct threat to republican freedom. A natural response to this concern – one that has probably already occurred to many readers – would be to say that participation in or dependence on markets is compatible with the enjoyment of republican freedom if the decision to allow markets to operate in a given domain is itself discursively controlled – that is, if it is made in a way that is consistent with republican principles of self-government. On this view, the first-order vulnerability to harm that markets create is nondominating as long as it is authorized through a second-order process that is free of domination – and as long as that authorization can be contested and revisited over time. This line of argument abandons Pettit's claim that a properly designed market regime is "akin to the natural environment" – markets are politically created, not natural – but it is otherwise consistent with his view that markets are (or at least can be) nondominating. And as I have already pointed out, liberals do give priority to republican freedom in the sense that they insist that the trade-offs between republican and market freedom be made in publicly visible and contestable ways and for publicly avowable reasons. However, as I will now argue, the reasons that we have for making those trade-offs are often not only independent of, but inimical to, the pursuit of republican freedom.

2.5 DO MARKETS LIBERATE?

The strongest republican response to the claim that markets are dominating rests on the observation that any effort to bring the economy under direct political control would create a dominating power that was far more dangerous than the market itself: to use Pettit's terms, such a move would replace the *dominium* of a decentralized market economy with the *imperium* of a state-directed command economy. According to this line of argument, we should tolerate domination only when the effort to remove it would create the potential for even more domination; when relying on the state to combat private power would give it a degree or kind of power that is itself likely to become dominating. It follows that we should delegate decision-making power to market actors up to the point at which the marginal amount of domination that would be created by further delegation is equal to the amount of domination that would be created by retaining that power in the hands of the state – provided, again, that the decision to delegate (or not) is made in a discursively controlled way. Of course, the tipping point between public and private domination will be impossible to define precisely, and the question of what the optimal amount of delegation is will therefore be politically contested. Nevertheless, this line of argument provides a straightforward instrumental reason for republicans to tolerate, and indeed to celebrate, the existence of a market economy. It is a natural fallback position for any republican who is willing to grant that markets can be dominating, but who wants to defend them in republican terms.[59]

I wholeheartedly agree that a command economy would pose a grave threat to – indeed, would probably be incompatible with – the enjoyment of republican freedom, even if the motives of those who administered it were impeccably republican. I therefore agree that republicans have weighty reasons to decentralize economic decision-making – and decision-making in a wide variety of other domains – even when doing so creates opportunities for nonstate domination. The problem with this line of argument, simply put, is that it *reduces* the case for markets to the role that they play in dispersing power away from the state, ignoring the many other important values that markets can advance. This problem is compounded by the fact that republican freedom as defined by the discourse model is an unusually demanding political ideal. Because nearly all of our actions directly or indirectly affect other people, nearly all of our actions are subject in principle to the requirement that we stand ready to justify them; to assume the demands, not just of attributability, but also of accountability. To be free, on this view, is to give one's beliefs and desires an "avowable" shape; indeed, freedom so understood is most fully

---

[59] I am grateful to Christian List for pressing this line of argument in response to an early version of this chapter. On *dominium* versus *imperium* see Pettit, *Republicanism*, chapters 5–6 and *Theory of Freedom*, chapter 7.

realized in the "virtual" enjoyment of the status of being reason-responsive, since whenever we act the avowability of our commitments, and thus our status as persons, can be called into question.[60] It follows that arbitrariness is a feature not only of the position in which we may stand in relation to other people – when we have the capacity to interfere with them in nonreason-guided ways – but of our own beliefs and desires insofar as they depart from reason.

The omnipresent demands of discursive control stand in sharp contrast to the classical republican conception of free personhood, in which the privileged status of the free man presupposed the existence of a "private" domain within which he was not accountable to his fellow citizens. This private domain was defined above all by the secure possession of property – especially land and other real property – and by the dominion that the free man exercised there over his social "inferiors": women, children, servants, slaves, vassals, and so on. The enjoyment of this domain of nonresponsible conduct – tempered, more in theory than in practice, by the doctrine of *noblesse oblige* – was one of the defining features and chief attractions of free status. It is easy to misunderstand the classical sources on this point: Plato, Aristotle, and others criticize their more democratic contemporaries for holding the "childish" view that freedom means doing as one likes, not because they denied that the free man is better able to do as he likes than other people – and that this gives him good reason to value his freedom – but rather because they expected *hoi polloi* to abuse the privilege.[61] In other words, the free man was free in the double-barreled sense of being responsible to and along with his peers for the conduct of public affairs, and of being shielded from their scrutiny in the conduct of his private affairs, where he largely dealt with people over whom he was master. Although republican ideology gives clear priority to the former aspect of free status, it is reasonable to suppose not only that both were highly prized, but that for many if not most free men the order of priority was reversed.[62]

---

[60] Patchen Markell explores this feature of Pettit's position in his "The Insufficiency of Non-Domination," *Political Theory* 36 (2008), esp. pp. 22–3. On virtual versus active control see, for example, Pettit, *Theory of Freedom*, pp. 90–3 and "Joining the Dots," pp. 226–8.

[61] See, for example, Plato, *Republic* 557a–564a; Aristotle, *Politics* 1310a30–35 (book 5, chapter 9), 1317b12–15 (book 6, chapter 2); Plato associates this view with "women and children" at *Republic* 557c.

[62] On the relationship between public and private freedom in ancient Greece see, for example, Richard Mulgan, "Liberty in Ancient Greece," in Zbigniew Pelczynski and John Gray, eds., *Conceptions of Liberty in Political Philosophy* (London: Athlone Press,

Do Markets Liberate? 81

The obvious objection to this conception of freedom is that it was built on a massive amount of domination; domination that was justified, ideologically speaking, by the claim that the dominated groups were "naturally" unfit for free status. This claim, though it was by no means unique to republicans, provides the ideological underpinnings of the "virtue model" of republican citizenship that we examined earlier. It became untenable with (or its untenability was revealed by) the gradual collapse of traditional hierarchies in the modern period: the elimination of hereditary privileges, the removal of property qualifications for the suffrage, the abolition of slavery and serfdom, the extension of equal legal, political, and social status to women, and so on. We will examine the significance of these developments for the emergence of the liberal tradition more closely in Chapter 4. For now, we can simply note that the collapse of traditional hierarchies was accompanied, and in large part caused, by a transformation in the nature of the private sphere itself. Throughout most of European history the enjoyment of property rights, and the resulting immunity from scrutiny and interference within a given domain, coexisted with extensive legal and customary restraints on the conditions under which property could be used or alienated – sumptuary laws and laws of entail being only the most dramatic examples. These restraints were gradually lifted in the modern period, so that, as J. G. A. Pocock points out, by the end of the eighteenth century "defining something as property was becoming hard to distinguish from defining it as commodity."[63] As a result the domain of nonresponsible conduct was no longer confined to the free man's household, but extended into the much broader arena of the market, with correspondingly broad social and political consequences – among them being the fact that it now posed a more direct challenge to the power of the state. This fact provides the material underpinnings of the "interest model" of republican citizenship that we examined earlier.

The discourse model reverses the traditional republican story about the relationship between the public and private spheres: our identity as free

---

1984), pp. 7–26; for a similar treatment of ancient Rome see P. A. Brunt, "*Libertas* in the Republic," in *The Fall of the Roman Republic and Related Essays* (New York: Oxford University Press, 1988), pp. 281–350. Brunt observes that for the Romans "[t]he 'name of liberty was sweet', if only because men instinctively wish to live as they please": ibid., p. 297; the internal quotation is from 2 Peter 2:19.

[63] J. G. A. Pocock, "The Political Limits to Premodern Economics," in John Dunn, ed., *The Economic Limits to Modern Politics* (New York: Cambridge University Press, 1990), quoted at pp. 124–5.

persons is first secured in public, via discourse, and then carried back into the private realm. In other words, where republicans have traditionally held that there are private preconditions for public freedom, the discourse model holds that there are public preconditions for private freedom. This shift in perspective has the great advantage of extending the promise of republican freedom to all people: everyone, regardless of their station, has to be prepared (in both senses of the word) to take responsibility for their statements and actions, even when they would rather not. However, it fails to account for the demand – we might say the felt human need – for a domain of nonresponsible conduct; a demand whose satisfaction was, again, central to the enjoyment of free status in the premodern period. This demand is primarily met today (insofar as it is met at all) in the market, where people are free to do as they choose with their property. As we have seen, and as every market actor knows, the enjoyment of this kind of freedom – market freedom – does not mean that we can do as we please: our choices are constrained at any given time by the limits of our resources, and over time by the aggregate effects of everyone else's choices. It simply means that we do not have to justify our choices to other people. The democratization of this kind of nonresponsibility was at least as significant, historically speaking, as the corresponding democratization of republican freedom; indeed, by placing economic power in the hands of ordinary people it played a key role in helping to bring the latter kind of democratization about. The crucial difference is that unlike the free property holder of old, in a liberal polity the market actor's nonresponsible choices affect other people who also hold free status.

Why then should a liberal polity allow this kind of nonresponsibility to exist? We will examine the value of market freedom more closely in Chapter 3; for now I will simply outline three familiar ways in which the case for market freedom is insufficiently captured by the claim that power should be dispersed away from the state. First, our available choices are almost always more limited than our desires, and so we constantly have to make trade-offs in the face of material and temporal constraints. This raises the question: Who should have the authority to decide which trade-offs are made, and how? The view that this authority should be placed in the hands of the people whose interests are most directly affected – a position that Hayek (among many others) forcefully defends[64] – provides the most

---

[64] "So long as we can freely dispose over our income and all our possessions, economic loss will always deprive us only of what we regard as the least important of the desires we were able to satisfy. A 'merely' economic loss is thus one whose effect we can still make fall on

powerful moral argument in favor of markets. Second, we are typically able to bring about a more efficient allocation of productive resources, and thus a greater level of overall wealth, when we allow economic decisions to be made by those who are in the best position to bring the relevant knowledge to bear, not only about their own consumption preferences, but also about local conditions of production, distribution, and trade – information that is communicated by and to them via the price mechanism. Moreover, to increase the amount of wealth that exists is, all things being equal,[65] to reduce the severity of the material trade-offs that people have to make on the margin. Ever since Adam Smith pointed out that a common laborer in a "civilized" economy enjoys material comforts that are unknown to the wealthiest "savage," market economies have been associated with a vast expansion of the quality and variety of choices that are available to ordinary people.[66] This appeal to the superior efficiency of decentralized decision-making is of course the guiding theme of Hayek's work and provides the most powerful instrumental argument in favor of markets.[67]

A third, less purely economic case for market freedom can be drawn from the content of the discourse model itself; in particular from the distinction that it draws between "volitional control" – action in accordance with an agent's considered beliefs and desires – and "discursive control" – action in accordance with the publicly avowable commitments that the agent has assumed. As we have seen, it is possible to be held responsible as a "person" (a discursively controlled agent) for commitments with which one does not identify as a "self" (a volitionally controlled agent). It follows that under conditions of discursive control I will not necessarily be treated by others as the self who I take myself to be: there is often a gap between my publicly recognized identity and my own self-understanding, or to use Pettit's terms I am often a bystander, as a self, to my own person.[68] The discourse

---

our less important needs ... The question raised by economic planning is, therefore, not merely whether we shall be able to satisfy what we regard as our more or less important needs in the way we prefer. It is whether it shall be we who decide what is more, and what is less, important for us": Hayek, *Road to Serfdom*, pp. 99–100.

[65] Setting aside the question of distribution, which when considered along with the declining marginal utility of wealth complicates this claim without (I think) vitiating it entirely.

[66] See, for example, Smith, *Wealth of Nations*, I.i.11.

[67] For a seminal statement see Friedrich Hayek, "The Use of Knowledge in Society," *American Economic Review* 35 (1945), pp. 519–30; for a more popular account see chapter 1 of Milton Friedman and Rose Friedman, *Free to Choose: A Personal Statement* (New York: Harcourt Brace Jovanovich, 1980).

[68] As Pettit points out, "[a]s a person I can never be rid of anything done by agents – strictly, agent-slices – on my trajectory in time. As a self I can," and so "the same person may

model encourages us to associate our freedom in such cases with our personhood, but it is not clear that we should always be expected to do so. For example, I may hold myself to what I take to be a *higher* standard of conduct than society does, and view the efforts of others to hold me to the standards of (merely) discursive control with frustration or contempt: consider, for example, the avant-garde artist, the nonconformist, or the conscientious objector. Indeed, in cases like these we may reject the judgment not only of our discursive partners but also of the market: consider the implications of the phrase "selling out." In other words, someone who "owns" their actions without being willing or able to justify them to others is not necessarily less free (or less admirable) than someone who submits more completely to the discipline of discursive control.

To summarize, there is often a gap: (1) between what we want and what we can have, (2) between the choices that are available to us now and those that will be available in the future, and (3) between the commitments that we are held responsible for by our fellow citizens and those that we identify with on reflection. We might respond to these gaps: (1) by placing the authority to decide which material trade-offs to make in the hands of the people whose interests are most directly affected, (2) by promoting the development of decentralized decision-making mechanisms that expand opportunity on average and in the long run, but whose short-term effects no one can predict or control, and (3) by allowing people to substitute their own standards and expectations for those of society, and to abandon their past commitments for reasons that they, but not necessarily others, take to be good. In each case the kind of freedom that is at stake is freedom understood as nonresponsibility; the kind of freedom that is enjoyed paradigmatically – but not, as the third line of argument reminds us, exclusively – in commercial markets. Moreover, in each case extending this kind of freedom to individuals can be expected to promote the open-endedness and unpredictability – the special kind of vulnerability – that is associated with life in a liberal polity. The picture that starts to emerge here, and that we will explore more fully in the next chapter, is one of a plurality of qualitatively different kinds of values that the exercise of market freedom can promote, and that liberal polities have reason to pursue.

The republican case for markets as a tool for dispersing power away from the state fails to capture this kind of pluralism. Whatever the tipping

---

change their self: may be one self over one period, and a different self over another": Pettit, *Theory of Freedom*, pp. 84–5.

point between public and private domination might be, it is unlikely to coincide with the point at which economic efficiency, personal autonomy, or the wide variety of other values that markets can promote are also maximized – nor of course are those points likely to coincide with each other. A liberal theory of freedom, by contrast, embraces both republican and market-centered intuitions about freedom; that is, it not only holds that freedom can legitimately mean both of these things, but that we have reason to value and pursue them both, and that they can come into conflict with each other. While a liberal politics requires that markets be discursively authorized, and while it will sometimes authorize them in order to reduce the threat of state domination, it may also authorize them for other reasons and thereby allow more domination to exist than would otherwise be the case. In other words, from a liberal point of view republican freedom is an attractive but partial political value, and it may be legitimate to trade some republican freedom away for the sake of more market freedom – provided, again, that such trade-offs are authorized by republican means. The liberal conception of freedom therefore circumscribes, even as it incorporates, the republican one. Of course, it does not follow that we should adopt the liberal point of view. To get a sense of why we might do so we have to look more carefully at the meaning and value of market freedom itself – and as we will now see, in order to do *that* we have to broaden our definition of what a market is.

3

Market Freedom

> The liberal, or non-interference, principles of the classical (Smithian or Ricardian) economists were not, in the first place, economic principles; they were an application to economics of principles that were thought to apply to a much wider field. The contention that economic freedom made for economic efficiency was no more than a secondary support.
>
> John Hicks, "A Manifesto"

3.1 LIBERALISM AND MARKETS

Some of the most important political debates of the last fifty years have focused on the question of what role markets should play in a free society. On the one hand, the market-centered or "libertarian" school of thought that was developed in the postwar period by thinkers such as Ludwig von Mises, Friedrich Hayek, and Milton Friedman (each of whom played a key role in founding the influential Mont Pelerin Society) has grown into a sophisticated research program – one that now includes "right" and "left" variants.[1] Beginning with the Reagan – Thatcher revolution of the late 1970s and 1980s, and expanding to a global scale with the emergence

---

[1] On the origins and influence of the Mont Pelerin Society see, for example, R. M. Hartwell, *A History of the Mont Pelerin Society* (Indianapolis, IN: Liberty Fund, 1995); Philip Mirowski and Dieter Plehwe, eds., *The Road from Mont Pèlerin: The Making of the Neoliberal Thought Collective* (2nd ed., Cambridge, MA: Harvard University Press, 2015 [2009]); and Daniel Stedman Jones, *Masters of the Universe: Hayek, Friedman, and the Birth of Neoliberal Politics* (Princeton, NJ: Princeton University Press, 2012). Two useful sources on left-libertarianism are Peter Vallentyne and Hillel Steiner, eds., *The Origins of Left-Libertarianism: An Anthology of Historical Writings* (New York:

of the so-called Washington Consensus in the 1980s and 1990s, the appeal to markets and market freedom that these thinkers championed has come to play a leading, though by no means uncontested, role in public life. On the other hand, many critical theorists, activists, and ordinary citizens have raised fundamental concerns about the social and political consequences of "market-friendly" policies, and about the extension of market norms and practices into domains – such as education, health care, criminal justice, and environmental stewardship – that were once considered non- or extra-economic. This line of criticism has made "neoliberalism" the watchword for a social order in which the behavior of individuals, associations, and states is regimented and disciplined by increasingly globalized markets, and in which the prospects for personal autonomy and democratic self-government are correspondingly diminished.[2] In other words, markets have come to play a central role in defining – for better or worse – the social and political possibilities that are available to us in the twenty-first century.

One of the most striking features of these debates is that the two sides disagree not only about what markets should do, but also about what a market is and what kind of freedom markets offer. These disagreements can be attributed, I think, to two more fundamental points on which proponents and critics of market freedom *do* agree, each of which has given rise to confusion. First, they agree in thinking that markets are necessarily embedded in a social and legal framework that limits their scope and shapes their behavior. Since this framework can of course take many forms, this way of approaching the issue makes it hard to see what the distinguishing features of a market actually are, or how we should

---

Palgrave, 2001), and *Left-Libertarianism and Its Critics: The Contemporary Debate* (New York: Palgrave, 2001).

[2] The critical literature on neoliberalism is vast and rather diffuse; notable contributions that focus specifically on its political dimensions include David Harvey, *A Brief History of Neoliberalism* (New York: Oxford University Press, 2005); Jamie Peck, *Constructions of Neoliberal Reason* (New York: Oxford University Press, 2010); Wendy Brown, *Undoing the Demos: Neoliberalism's Stealth Revolution* (New York: Zone Books, 2015), and *In the Ruins of Neoliberalism: The Rise of Antidemocratic Politics in the West* (New York: Columbia University Press, 2019); and Benjamin L. McKean, *Disorienting Neoliberalism: Global Justice and the Outer Limit of Freedom* (New York: Oxford University Press, 2020). An important touchstone for this literature is Michel Foucault, *The Birth of Biopolitics: Lectures at the Collège de France, 1978–1979*, trans. Graham Burchell (New York: Palgrave, 2008 [2004]), although Foucault offers a different definition and a more nuanced appraisal of neoliberalism than most of its contemporary critics. For useful discussion on this point see Daniel Zamora and Michael C. Behrent, eds., *Foucault and Neoliberalism* (Malden, MA: Polity Press, 2016).

think about the relationship between markets themselves and the formal and informal rules by which they are constituted and governed. Second, proponents and critics of market freedom agree in treating commercial markets as the focal or paradigm case, even though they also agree in thinking that market-like behavior can be found (or induced) in many other domains of conduct. This emphasis on commercial exchange, and thus on the tenets of neoclassical economics, makes it harder to identify the distinct aims that we might have in allowing markets understood more broadly to determine social outcomes, and the distinct concerns that we might have about doing so. In order to properly consider the question of whether, how, and to what extent we should promote market freedom we have to provide a clearer – and broader – definition of what a market is.

In this chapter I argue that market freedom is best understood as a person-centered conception of freedom which consists in holding the privileged status of being a nonresponsible social actor; that is, someone who can impose certain costs on other people without being publicly accountable to them for doing so. A market, then, is just a domain of conduct in which people who hold this status interact with each other. As we will see, this understanding of markets and market freedom allows us to avoid each of the sources of confusion that I have just identified. On the one hand, it allows us to draw a clear distinction between markets themselves and the social and legal framework in which they are embedded. In a liberal polity this framework – consisting for example of well-defined rights, reliably enforced rules governing association and exchange, systems of incentives, efforts to promote, preserve, or limit competition, and so on – falls on the republican rather than the market side of the equation: it defines the background conditions of action that the citizens of that polity have collectively authorized, and thus marks the extent to which they can properly be held responsible for what they do. More precisely, it allows us to distinguish between costs to others that market actors can be held publicly accountable for imposing (for example, defrauding a customer or manipulating prices), and costs for which they cannot (for example, firing an employee or putting a competitor out of business).[3]

---

[3] Recall the distinction drawn in Chapter 1 between attributability and accountability: in an at-will employment regime employers may be responsible for their actions in the sense that those actions are *attributable* to them ("She's the one who fired me!") without being responsible in the sense of being *accountable* to anyone else for what they do – even when the affected parties are significantly harmed. Of course, attributability is not always a straightforward matter: for example, it may be hard to say who exactly is responsible for job losses that occur during a general economic downturn.

A polity in which distinctions like this are not collectively authorized lacks republican freedom and is thus, whatever else we might say about it, not a *liberal* polity.

On the other hand, the association of market freedom with nonresponsibility allows us to broaden our understanding of what a market is beyond the realm of commercial exchange and into the various other domains of conduct that make up the texture of daily life. This may sound at first like an endorsement of the neoliberal doctrine of "markets everywhere." However, to say that a market is a domain of nonresponsible conduct is not necessarily to say (as a neoliberal would) that it is a domain of competition, or that it is intended to achieve the aims that are often associated with competition: entrepreneurship, industriousness, self-discipline, and so on. After all, it is not clear how an appeal to these values could be used to justify the extension of the privilege of nonresponsibility into areas like culture, expression, and personal ethics. If markets are associated with nonresponsibility, and thus with the open-ended and unpredictable outcomes to which nonresponsible behavior gives rise, then the justification of markets and the definition of their proper limits has to be similarly open-ended: we not only have to broaden our understanding of what a market is, we also have to broaden our understanding of what makes market freedom valuable. As we will see, this line of argument highlights another key distinction between *liberalism*, which recognizes distinct noneconomic aims that a free society should pursue, and *neo*liberalism, which seeks to promote economic competition in as many domains of conduct as possible. It also makes it easier to see how the enjoyment of market freedom both depends upon and undermines the enjoyment of republican freedom.

I begin (Section 3.2) by distinguishing the association of market freedom with nonresponsibility from the libertarian and neoliberal alternatives. The libertarian defense of markets as sites of voluntary exchange holds that we should maximize the extent to which social outcomes are determined by individual choices rather than by the dictates of a central authority. The appeal to voluntariness is undercut, however, by the fact that market choices are made in response to the pattern of outcomes that is generated by everyone else's choices; a pattern that (in a properly functioning market) no market actor can influence or control, and thus that no market actor can be said to have chosen. In other words, there is a fundamental tension between the claim that markets allow people to determine the shape of their own lives and the claim that they minimize the influence that any particular person has over social outcomes. The neoliberal approach, which conceives of the market actor as an entrepreneur and of the market as a site of competition among entrepreneurs, is not inconsistent in this way. However, it suffers from a worrying ambiguity about the purposes that competition is meant to serve, and an equally worrying tendency to promote competition without regard for the desires or interests of those who are subject to it. As we will see, neoliberals sometimes justify their enthusiasm for competition by arguing that it is a "natural" feature of human behavior – that *homo sapiens* is in fact *homo economicus* – and sometimes by arguing that competition benefits those who are subject to it, at least on average, whether they realize it or not. Each of these appeals ignores or dismisses the value of republican freedom and is therefore fundamentally illiberal.

The rest of the chapter explores three implications of defining market freedom in terms of nonresponsibility. I first explore the implications for our understanding of the *scope* of market freedom, with particular attention to the role that nonresponsible choice plays in noneconomic domains of conduct, and to the role that noneconomic considerations play in shaping the structure and behavior of commercial markets. Because responsibility is not a binary variable – because we always have to consider the *extent* to which we are accountable to other people for our choices in a given domain – we find that market and nonmarket behavior are not entirely distinct categories, and that the line between them is contested and permeable (Section 3.3). Next, I explore the implications of this line of argument for our understanding of the *value* of market freedom. The key finding here is that its value is heterogeneous: there are a number of distinct reasons (I identify sixteen, and there are probably more) that we might have for permitting market freedom in a given domain, many of which complement each other in familiar ways. The association of market freedom with nonresponsibility therefore allows us to develop a richer and more nuanced appreciation of its value than the libertarian and neoliberal alternatives. It also helps us to develop a useful taxonomy of "genres" of liberal thought and practice (Section 3.4). I turn, finally, to the question of how we should think about the *limits* of market freedom. The key claim here, as we have already seen, is that in a liberal polity markets have to be authorized through a republican system of self-government and constrained by various republican (responsibility-promoting) mechanisms. It follows that the amount and kind of market freedom that individuals enjoy will vary significantly from time to time and from place to place, and that a wide variety of regimes, from "classically" liberal to social democratic, can properly be described as "liberal" (Section 3.5).

To summarize, the association of market freedom with nonresponsibility has three important advantages: (1) it allows us to clarify and broaden our understanding of what a market is; (2) it allows us to clarify and broaden our understanding of what the value of market freedom consists in; and (3) it allows us to clarify our understanding of the limits of market freedom, to appreciate the fact that market freedom is a partial political value, and that the appeal to a free-standing or self-regulating market is not only unattractive but illiberal. The argument of this chapter is therefore a mirror image of the argument of Chapter 2: just as republican freedom needs to be complemented by market freedom, so too does market freedom need to be complemented by republican freedom. A liberal polity is one in which each kind of freedom plays an essential but limited role. I examine the emergence, development, and contemporary importance of the idea of liberal freedom in the following chapters. The aim of this chapter is simply to reveal something of its shape by considering the limitations of two of its ideological competitors, each of which treats the enjoyment of market freedom as not only a necessary but also a sufficient condition for counting a polity as "free." In exposing the shortcomings of these approaches, I hope to clear the way for a more constructive and less utopian debate about whether, how, and to what extent we should promote market freedom.

3.2 FROM EXCHANGE TO COMPETITION

Since at least the time of Adam Smith economists have defined "the market" in local terms as a site of voluntary exchange, and in global terms as a decentralized mechanism for setting the terms under which exchange takes place – for determining (or revealing) the prices at which goods and services can be offered. This definition has two contrasting sets of implications. First, the emphasis on voluntary exchange highlights the importance of property rights, the possession of which is a necessary condition for being in a position to legitimately exchange something in the first place, and of consent, the granting of which is a necessary condition for an exchange of property rights (as opposed to an exchange simply of property) to occur. The emphasis on consent gives rise in turn to the expectation that market exchanges be bilaterally informed and (more controversially) that the parties be on relatively equal footing; that neither party be so weak or desperate that they are not able to offer genuine consent. Second, the emphasis on the determination (or revelation) of prices highlights the impersonal nature of market exchange: in a properly functioning market prices are not set by individual market actors but rather by the market itself; they are a function of the choices of all market actors taken together. This appeal to impersonality provides the basis for Smith's pioneering insight that markets provide an efficient means of allocating scarce productive resources and distributing scarce goods; a claim that was later formalized as the first theorem of welfare economics: that under ideal conditions market exchange will yield a Pareto-efficient distribution of resources in equilibrium. For convenience I will refer to the appeal to the voluntary exchange of property rights as the *consent argument*, and to the appeal to the impersonal and efficient determination of prices as the *efficiency argument*.

Taken together, these two lines of argument make up the core of the traditional economic case for allowing markets to determine a wide range of social outcomes. They also account, albeit in different ways, for the libertarian claim that participation in markets is essential to, and even constitutive of, the enjoyment of individual freedom. The consent argument focuses on the freedom of the individual "from" the state or collectivity and contrasts a social order that is brought about by individual choices with one that is brought about by the dictates of a central authority. As Friedman puts it, "there are only two ways of co-ordinating the economic activities of millions. One is central direction involving the use of coercion – the technique of the army and of the modern totalitarian state. The other is voluntary co-operation of individuals – the technique of the market place." To endorse "central direction" is to be committed, it would seem almost necessarily, to paternalism: a "free economy," Friedman argues, "gives people what they want instead of what a particular group thinks they ought to want," and so "[u]nderlying most arguments against the free market is a lack of belief in freedom itself."[4] The philosopher Robert Nozick summarizes this point with the cheeky observation that to regulate market exchanges is "to forbid capitalist acts between consenting adults."[5] The efficiency argument, by contrast, focuses on the freedom "to" satisfy as many of one's desires – or, more precisely, as many of the desires of the population taken as a whole – as possible. It contrasts a social order in which productive

---

[4] Milton Friedman, *Capitalism and Freedom* (Chicago: University of Chicago Press, 1962), pp. 13, 12, 15.
[5] Robert Nozick, *Anarchy, State, and Utopia* (New York: Basic Books, 1974), p. 163.

From Exchange to Competition

resources are developed to their fullest extent (at least in equilibrium) with one in which some productive potential is sacrificed for the sake of other values like social stability or distributive justice. In the latter case it would seem to follow that the effective ability of the population to do as it wishes has been reduced, and its freedom correspondingly diminished.

These two lines of argument – each of which appeals, as we can see, to an action-centered conception of freedom – can be made to work together in a familiar way: the efficiency gains that markets offer provide a justification for the rights to property and exchange on which they depend. However, on closer inspection the consent and efficiency arguments pull apart. The most attractive form of the consent argument associates freedom with personal responsibility; with being in a position to shape the direction of one's own life and with being allowed to enjoy (or obliged to endure) the consequences of one's own decisions and luck. The political theorist John Tomasi refers to this as the value of "responsible self-authorship," and treats it as the guiding moral principle of a free society: "possessing some bundle of material goods," he writes, "is not nearly so important as possessing those goods because of one's own actions and choices. When we are free, we are aware of ourselves as central causes of the lives that we lead."[6] Hayek and the other partisans of the efficiency argument hold a very different view: that what makes markets morally attractive, apart from their efficiency, is the fact that no one is responsible (either in the sense of accountability or of attributability) for what they do. We should prefer the "impersonal and seemingly irrational forces of the market," Hayek argues, to the "equally uncontrollable and therefore arbitrary power of other men" because "inequality is undoubtedly more readily borne, and affects the dignity of a person much less, if it is determined by impersonal forces than when it is due to design."[7] What is true of market outcomes is also true of market actors, who are led, as Smith famously put it, by an invisible hand to promote ends that are no part of their intention. Here freedom is a property of prices rather than of people: in an ideal market no one, by hypothesis, is able to influence prices unilaterally; rather everyone adjusts their behavior in response to the overall pattern of prices that the market yields. Thus, Smith concludes, "by pursuing his own interest" the market actor

---

[6] John Tomasi, *Free Market Fairness* (Princeton, NJ: Princeton University Press, 2012), p. xi.
[7] Friedrich Hayek, *The Road to Serfdom* (Chicago: University of Chicago Press, 1944), pp. 224, 117.

"frequently promotes that of the society more effectually than when he really intends to promote it."[8]

The idea of submitting to impersonal forces is not entirely unattractive: not only does the efficiency argument suggest that we do better, economically speaking, if we each tend our own garden, but it is often good – liberating, even – not to have to think about the broader social consequences of our actions. However, the impersonality of market outcomes calls the idea of "responsible self-authorship" seriously into question. Insofar as the efficiency argument presupposes that markets generate outcomes that no one in particular has chosen – that market actors are price-takers and not price-makers – the consent argument loses much of its force. Conversely, insofar as we try to shore up the ability of market actors to be authors of their own lives – insofar as we provide them with market power – we undermine the flexibility and spontaneity on which the efficiency argument depends. As Hayek points out, "[m]en can be allowed to act on their own knowledge and for their own purposes only if the reward they obtain is dependent in part on circumstances which they can neither control nor foresee," and so "freedom is inseparable from rewards which often have no connection with merit."[9] Indeed, as we saw in Chapter 2, Hayek suggests that the appeal to personal responsibility in a market society is often little more than a useful fiction, intended to focus the mind of the market actor without necessarily reflecting the contribution that he or she makes to the outcomes that are realized. In short, the libertarian case for markets rests on two contradictory claims: first, that markets promote personal responsibility via the mechanism of voluntary exchange, and second, that markets promote economic efficiency under conditions of personal nonresponsibility.

The neoliberal case for markets does not suffer from this kind of inconsistency, because it largely abandons the appeal to responsible self-authorship.[10] Of course, the word "neoliberal" is now almost universally used – often rather loosely – as a term of abuse, and Hayek and Friedman, who are widely regarded as the two leading theorists of neoliberalism,

---

[8] Adam Smith, *An Inquiry into the Nature and Causes of the Wealth of Nations* (Oxford: Clarendon Press, 1979 [1776]), IV.ii.9; on the behavior of market prices under conditions of "perfect liberty" see especially ibid., I.vii.

[9] Friedrich Hayek, *Law, Legislation and Liberty*, vol. 2: *The Mirage of Social Justice* (Chicago: University of Chicago Press, 1976), p. 120 (emphasis removed).

[10] The absence of a moralized conception of responsibility is what Foucault found attractive, or at least tempting, about neoliberalism: see especially Foucault, *Birth of Biopolitics*, lecture 10.

generally preferred simply to call themselves liberals, and are often treated (as I have treated them so far) as defenders of the traditional libertarian view. Nevertheless, when properly understood "neoliberalism" provides a useful shorthand for marking a genuine departure from the liberal tradition of thinking about markets that stretches back to Smith. According to this new way of thinking, the defining feature of a market is not exchange but rather competition,[11] where competition is constituted on the one hand by a system of implicit or explicit incentives, and on the other hand by the presence within that system of a population of rational actors who respond to the incentives in a way that seeks to maximize the satisfaction of their preferences – which are generally taken, for the purposes of analysis, as given.[12] The neoliberal approach breaks from traditional libertarianism in assigning a positive role to the state in creating and maintaining the competitive system; as Hayek puts it, "where effective competition can be created, it is a better way of guiding individual efforts than any other," and "in order that competition should work beneficially, a carefully thought-out legal framework is required." Friedman, in an early statement of the neoliberal agenda, agrees that policymakers should "substitute for the nineteenth century goal of laissez-faire ... the goal of the competitive order," and emphasizes that it is up to the state to "provid[e] a framework within which free competition could flourish" – and no more than that.[13]

By abandoning the definition of markets as sites of exchange – and thus, *a fortiori*, of voluntary exchange – neoliberalism offers a fundamentally

---

[11] Scholars of neoliberalism largely agree in treating the emphasis on competition as its defining feature: Wendy Brown argues, for example, that "[i]n neoliberal reason and in domains governed by it, we are only and everywhere *homo oeconomicus* ... an intensely constructed and governed bit of human capital tasked with improving and leveraging its competitive positioning and with enhancing its (monetary and nonmonetary) portfolio value across all of its endeavors and venues" (*Undoing the Demos*, p. 10), and Daniel Stedman Jones defines neoliberalism as a "free market ideology based on individual liberty and limited government that connect[s] human freedom to the actions of the rational, self-interested actor in the competitive marketplace" (*Masters of the Universe*, p. 2). Foucault, in his pioneering analysis, observes that "for the neo-liberals, the most important thing about the market is not exchange, that kind of original and fictional situation imagined by eighteenth century liberal economists. The essential thing of the market is elsewhere; it is competition": Foucault, *Birth of Biopolitics*, p. 118.

[12] For a succinct and influential statement of the methodological assumptions behind this view see Gary S. Becker, *The Economic Approach to Human Behavior* (Chicago: University of Chicago Press, 1976), chapter 1.

[13] Hayek, *Road to Serfdom*, p. 41; Milton Friedman, "Neo-Liberalism and Its Prospects" (1951), reprinted in Lanny Ebenstein, ed., *The Indispensable Milton Friedman: Essays on Politics and Economics* (Washington, DC: Regnery Publishing, 2012), quoted at p. 7.

new way of thinking about the relationship between markets and freedom. In particular, the key freedom-relevant distinction that neoliberals appeal to is not the distinction between interference and noninterference, but rather between coercion and noncoercion, where coercion means, as Hayek puts it, that "one man's actions are made to serve another man's will, not for his own but for the other's purpose." Market freedom so understood is not concerned with expanding the number of choices that a person has; Hayek holds that "though the alternatives before me may be distressingly few and uncertain," if "it is not some other will that guides my action" then "I may have to act under great pressure, but I cannot be said to act under coercion." Nor is freedom so understood concerned with giving a person control over the social environment in which he or she acts: Hayek emphasizes that "the price system will fulfill [its] function only if competition prevails, that is, if the individual producer has to adapt himself to price changes and cannot control them," and Friedman agrees that "[t]he participant in a competitive market has no appreciable power to alter the terms of exchange," and indeed "is hardly visible as a separate entity."[14] Rather, freedom for the neoliberal consists in the ability to respond to the overall system of incentives – of potential costs and benefits – as one sees fit: it is, as Hayek puts it, "[f]reedom to order our own conduct in the sphere where material circumstances force a choice upon us."[15] A free society is one in which social outcomes are determined, as far as possible, by the choices of free persons so defined; in which no one is able to replace competition with coercion by substituting their own will for the "will" of the market. The proper role of the state is to keep the field of competition open by preventing any market actor from acquiring that kind of power.

By replacing exchange with competition as the defining feature of a market neoliberals made it possible to extend the tools of economic analysis into a wide range of areas in which the consent and efficiency arguments have little if any role to play. Hayek, for example, saw commercial markets as part of a broader class of "spontaneous orders" that emerge without the direction of an organizing plan or central authority; a class that also includes "law and morals ... language ... money, and ... the growth of technological knowledge."[16] Friedman similarly identified

---

[14] Friedrich Hayek, *The Constitution of Liberty* (Chicago: University of Chicago Press, 1960), pp. 133, 137; Hayek, *Road to Serfdom*, p. 56; Friedman, *Capitalism and Freedom*, p. 120.

[15] Hayek, *Road to Serfdom*, p. 231.

[16] Friedrich Hayek, "Dr. Bernard Mandeville," *Proceedings of the British Academy* 53 (1967), p. 129.

language, scientific knowledge, and "a society's values, its culture, [and] its social conventions" as examples of cases in which "a complex and sophisticated structure arises as an unintended consequence of a large number of individuals cooperating while each pursues his own interests."[17] The economist Gary Becker, who was perhaps the most ingenious and influential proponent of extending the market metaphor in this way, pioneered the use of "rational actor" models to explain behavior in domains as diverse as crime, marriage and reproduction, and racial discrimination, and went so far as to suggest that "the economic approach is a comprehensive one that is applicable to all human behavior."[18] The consent and efficiency arguments do more to confuse than to illuminate these kinds of cases: to suggest that language, culture, and morality develop not just spontaneously, but voluntarily and optimally, when they are free of centralized control would be either incoherent or extraordinarily Whiggish. The neoliberal defense of markets rests instead on the claim that the competitive pursuit of individual self-interest is a basic feature of human nature – that, as I have said, *homo sapiens* is *homo economicus* – and that to ignore this fact is delusional and counterproductive.

The language of "spontaneity" is misleading, however, if it is taken to mean that a competitive system of the kind that neoliberals envision could exist without a coercively enforced set of rules which ensures that competition unfolds in an orderly and constructive way. As Hayek emphasizes, "[t]he functioning of competition ... depends, above all, on the existence of an appropriate legal system, a legal system designed both to preserve competition and to make it operate as beneficially as possible."[19] This raises the questions of what form this system should take, and of who decides whether it is operating beneficially. Neoliberals tend to be notably – and troublingly – silent on both of these questions. On the one hand, Hayek holds that it is more important that the terms of competition be fixed in advance than that they take a particular form: government coercion "is reduced to a minimum and made as innocuous as possible," he argues, "by restraining it through known general rules, so that in most instances the individual need never be coerced unless he has placed himself in a position where he knows he will be coerced." Under these conditions,

---

[17] Milton Friedman and Rose D. Friedman, *Free to Choose: A Personal Statement* (New York: Harcourt Brace Jovanovich, 1979), pp. 25–6.
[18] Becker, *Economic Approach to Human Behavior*, p. 8.
[19] Hayek, *Road to Serfdom*, p. 43.

"the laws of the state have the same significance for me as the laws of nature; and I can use my knowledge of the laws of the state to achieve my own aims as I use my knowledge of the laws of nature."[20] On the other hand, neoliberals – like the theorists of negative liberty that we discussed in Chapter 1 – deny that there is a necessary connection between freedom and self-government: Hayek acknowledges that there is a tradition of thought which identifies freedom with "participation of men in the choice of their government," but insists that "a free people in this sense is not necessarily a people of free men, nor need one share in this collective freedom to be free as an individual."[21]

The emphasis on "spontaneous" choice within a system of incentives that the people concerned did not necessarily choose and whose consequences they cannot control or predict sets the neoliberal conception of freedom apart from the traditional liberal view in three important ways. First, it drastically lowers the bar for what counts as a free choice: although market transactions have to be bilaterally informed (because fraud and deception diminish a market's information-aggregating abilities), the presence of power asymmetries between market actors does not diminish the freedom of the weaker parties – as long, again, as no one is in a position to unilaterally set the terms of exchange. Inequalities of wealth and income are therefore a matter of indifference from a neoliberal point of view. This way of thinking stretches the idea of consent to the breaking point; as we saw in Chapter 2, Hayek goes so far as to suggest that "[e]ven if the threat of starvation to me and perhaps to my family impels me to accept a distasteful job at a very low wage, even if I am 'at the mercy' of the only man willing to employ me, I am not coerced by him or anybody else" as long as "the act that has placed me in my predicament is not aimed at making me do or not do specific

---

[20] Hayek, *Constitution of Liberty*, pp. 21, 142. Hayek goes on to argue that "[l]aw in its ideal form might be described as a 'once-and-for-all' command that is directed to unknown people and that is abstracted from all particular circumstances of time and place and refers only to such conditions as may occur anywhere and at any time": ibid., pp. 149–50.

[21] Ibid., p. 13. Hayek later remarked more darkly that "the predominant model of liberal democratic institutions, in which the same representative body lays down the rules of just conduct and directs government, necessarily leads to a gradual transformation of the spontaneous order of a free society into a totalitarian system conducted in the service of some coalition of organized interests": Friedrich Hayek, *Law, Legislation and Liberty*, vol. 1: *Rules and Order* (Chicago: University of Chicago Press, 1973), p. 2. This is of course the thought that lies behind the title of his most famous book, *The Road to Serfdom*.

things."[22] In short, where freedom has traditionally been associated in liberal political thought with the ability to shape the course of one's life by one's own lights – with Tomasi's ideal of responsible self-authorship, or with John Stuart Mill's ideal of "pursuing our own good in our own way"[23] – for neoliberals it stands for the mere fact of not having been coerced in the narrow sense described above.

Second, the emphasis on fixed rules and the suspicion toward the collective determination of public ends has fundamentally conservative implications, not only for the making of public policy (which is obvious enough), but also for the distribution of social power. Neoliberals often obscure this feature of their position by portraying the emergence of "spontaneous order" as an event that took place, or that could have taken place, in a distant past, or that might take place in a hypothetical future. When neoliberal policies are implemented in actually existing polities – when public regulation is replaced with "free" competition within a framework of fixed rules – the practical effect is to "lock in" the competitive advantages of the already-powerful, and then to give those advantages an open field of play. This is one reason why the implementation of neoliberal policies is typically associated with sharp increases in material inequality and sharp declines in class mobility – another important reason being that powerful actors play a disproportionate role in designing the rules that govern competition, especially (but not only) when those rules are externally imposed.[24] In short, where freedom has traditionally been associated in liberal political thought with the equal opportunity of each person to improve his or her station, for neoliberals it stands for the mere fact of being a player in a competitive game, no matter how disadvantageous one's starting position might be.

Third and most importantly, the suspicion toward "public choice" means that neoliberal policies can be – as indeed they often have been – paternalistically imposed on people without their having any say in the matter. This phenomenon is familiar from the era of the so-called

---

[22] Hayek, *Constitution of Liberty*, p. 137. The reference to "the only man willing to employ me" seems to overlook the fact that monopsony is a paradigmatic case of market failure. The context suggests that Hayek thinks that the impersonal motivations of the potential employer suffice to make his behavior noncoercive, despite his obvious market power. Or maybe this is just a slip.

[23] John Stuart Mill, *On Liberty*, in *Collected Works*, ed. J. M. Robson (Toronto: University of Toronto Press, 1963–91), vol. 18, p. 226.

[24] Of course, as defenders of neoliberalism (and others) will be quick to point out, the powerful also play a disproportionate role in shaping the regulatory regimes that exist in traditional liberal polities.

Washington Consensus, running from roughly 1980 to 2008, when a suite of macroeconomic "structural adjustments," consisting most notably of economic deregulation, fiscal austerity, unilateral removal of barriers to foreign trade and investment, and privatization of state-owned enterprises, were imposed on developing countries as a condition of receiving aid from international agencies like the International Monetary Fund and the World Bank – often with disastrous economic results.[25] In these cases the orders within which market actors were obliged to make their choices were very far from being "spontaneous," however spontaneous the choices themselves may have been. Whether such "adjustments" are defended as a necessary condition of participation in a globalized economy[26] or condemned as the sinister imposition of a hegemonic political will,[27] the prospects for self-government within a neoliberal framework are equally dim. In short, where freedom has traditionally been associated in liberal political thought with the existence of a political order that is constituted by and responsive to the will of its members, in a neoliberal regime individuals make "rational" choices within a system of rules that they cannot contest and that they may or may not have played a role in making.

Taken together, these features of the neoliberal position have led many critics to conclude that its practical impact has been, as the political theorist Wendy Brown puts it, "to attenuate radically the exercise of freedom in the social and political spheres."[28] I will take a different line: that neoliberalism contains a powerful but limited insight about the

---

[25] The economist Joseph Stiglitz is probably the most prominent critic of the economic legacy of the Washington Consensus: see, for example, his *Globalization and Its Discontents Revisited: Anti-Globalization in the Era of Trump* (New York: W. W. Norton, 2018 [2002]). For a more sympathetic appraisal see Jagdish Bhagwati, *In Defense of Globalization* (New York: Oxford University Press, 2007).

[26] The claim that neoliberal reforms are an inevitable byproduct of the development of global capitalism has often been invoked in its defense, as for example in Margaret Thatcher's famous declaration that "there is no alternative." It plays an equally prominent role in Marxian criticism, which holds that neoliberalism is simply the latest stage in the unfolding of capitalism's internal contradictions. This is the central argument of Harvey's *Brief History of Neoliberalism*, which dismisses neoliberal ideas about freedom as ideological window-dressing intended to justify the (further) accumulation of power by economic elites.

[27] For the argument that neoliberal reforms were imposed on developing countries with the intention of cementing their subordinate position in the global economy see, for example, Ha-Joon Chang, *Kicking Away the Ladder: Development Strategy in Historical Perspective* (New York: Anthem Press, 2003).

[28] Brown, *Undoing the Demos*, p. 108.

nature of freedom, and that its shortcomings arise from a failure to recognize those limits; a failure to recognize above all that in a liberal polity market freedom has to be complemented and qualified by republican freedom. The first step in advancing this line of argument is to develop a conception of market freedom that swings freely of the social and legal framework within which it is enjoyed; one that captures the distinct social status of the market actor, and the distinct set of values that are promoted by granting people that status in a given domain. As I have already indicated and as I will now argue, the defining feature of market freedom, and thus of markets themselves, is not competition but rather nonresponsibility. Conceiving of markets and market freedom in this way allows us to more clearly identify the variety of forms that market behavior can take, the variety of reasons that we might have for giving markets an important, but limited, role to play in a liberal polity, and the variety of considerations that we should take into account when deciding what the scope of market freedom should be.

3.3 FROM COMPETITION TO NONRESPONSIBILITY

I have argued that market freedom does not consist in the ability to enter into voluntary exchanges or to pursue one's interests within a competitive system, but rather in the ability to impose certain costs on other people without being publicly accountable to them for doing so. This is not to say that market actors always or even usually act "selfishly" – they may try to make (what they see as) "socially responsible" choices – it is simply to say that this kind of self-regulation is, from a public point of view, supererogatory. Like republican freedom, market freedom so understood is a person-centered rather than an action-centered conception of freedom: it consists in holding the privileged status of being a nonresponsible social actor. A market is a domain of conduct in which people who hold this status interact with each other. Commercial markets can be thought of as a proper subset of "markets" so defined, but a wide range of relatively unregulated domains of conduct, from traffic patterns to child-rearing practices to the "marketplace" of ideas, can also qualify. Because this definition of markets and of market freedom takes an agnostic position on the question of whether market transactions are voluntary, it avoids the tension between the consent and efficiency arguments that I have associated with the libertarian defense of markets. Because it allows us to use the word "market" to describe a wide range of social spaces that have little if anything to do with buying and selling, it can comfortably accommodate the broadening of the market metaphor that we find in neoliberal thinkers like Hayek, Friedman, and Becker. And because it treats nonresponsibility as an important but partial political value, it is not subject to the charge that it promotes market freedom at the expense of other important values like personal autonomy, equal opportunity, and self-government.

Needless to say, the scope of market freedom so defined is never unlimited: it is never the case – except in cases of complete social breakdown – that we are not publicly accountable for at least some of the consequences of our actions. It follows that market freedom, like republican freedom, is an ideal that can only be realized in degrees; we can only talk about the *extent* to which a given domain of conduct counts as a market, or a given kind of behavior as market behavior. Nonresponsibility is in this sense a dimension or aspect, and not simply a property, of behavior in a given domain. Indeed, as neoliberals emphasize, the attractive features of markets depend on the imposition of coercively enforced rules in otherwise unregulated domains of conduct. Consider, for example, the contract, the primary vehicle of exchange in commercial markets. Contracts, as legally enforceable agreements, create islands of responsibility, and thus of predictability and control, in the broader domain of nonresponsibility within which market actors are allowed to pursue their interests as they see fit: their purpose is to make clear to the contracting parties what responsibilities they are undertaking, and to provide a publicly enforceable guarantee that those responsibilities will be met. Moreover, because all contracts have unchosen effects on people who are not party to them – externalities, as economists call them – the question of which contracts should be enforced, and how, is a matter of public concern: as I pointed out in Chapter 1, we currently regulate the sale of alcohol, tobacco, and firearms, and prohibit the sale of leaded gasoline, narcotics, and people. The shape of market freedom therefore depends on the criteria that we use to decide which rules should apply in a given domain, and this depends in turn on what aims we have in permitting nonresponsible choice in the first place. Markets can take any number of forms depending on how these rules are structured.

From this point of view the competitive market of neoclassical and neoliberal economic theory is a special case, not in the familiar sense that it is a regulative ideal that we can use to evaluate the actual commercial markets that we find in the world, but in the more radical sense that its definition of what counts as "ideal" rests on a distinct and partial set of criteria. As we have seen, an ideal commercial market is one that is sufficiently competitive that no one is able unilaterally to determine or even measurably to influence its behavior – in which, as Friedman puts it, "[t]he participant ... has no appreciable power to alter the terms of exchange."[29] The salient feature of such a market is the fact that no one is responsible for the system of prices, or for the resulting distribution of wealth and income, that it yields. Nevertheless, as we have seen, commercial markets depend on the public enforcement of certain kinds of responsibility; in particular on the enforcement of contracts, which depends in turn on the existence of well-defined property rights and of publicly enforced guarantees against theft, force, and fraud. They depend further – though here the details are more controversial – on ongoing public regulation to prevent the emergence of monopolistic or oligopolistic "market power," to punish price-fixing and other forms of collusion (which can be either a cause or an effect of market power), and so on. The aim of this kind of regulation is to ensure that each market actor sends a genuinely independent signal about the conditions of production, consumption, and exchange in a given domain, allowing for the emergence of a system of prices that accurately reflects the relative supply of and demand for various goods and services, and thereby making possible a Pareto-efficient distribution of resources.

The appeal to Pareto efficiency highlights what is perhaps the most fundamental difference between an exchange- or competition-centered and a nonresponsibility-centered conception of markets. From the latter point of view *market prices themselves are externalities*: that is, they impose costs and confer benefits on third parties in ways that no one – least of all the affected people themselves – can predict or control. The imposition of these costs, as the market price of goods that one wants or needs goes up, or the market price of goods that one owns (including one's own skills and labor) goes down, is publicly tolerated because and to the extent that the cost of regulating them is thought to exceed the cost of not doing so – a calculation that will of course vary from case to case. According to standard economic theory "pecuniary" externalities of this kind do not count as "real" externalities because in a complete market gains and losses resulting from changes in relative prices cancel out (recall that Pareto efficiency is indifferent to questions of distribution).[30] However, if we

---

[29] Friedman, *Capitalism and Freedom*, p. 120.
[30] Of course, actually existing markets are not "complete" in the relevant sense; for an influential discussion see Bruce C. Greenwald and Joseph E. Stiglitz, "Externalities in Economies with Imperfect Information and Incomplete Markets," *Quarterly Journal of Economics* 101 (1986), pp. 229–64.

define an externality in strict terms as an unchosen effect of a market transaction on a third party then we cannot ignore allocative and distributive effects in this way. As we saw in Chapter 2, the salient question from the standpoint of republican freedom, and thus from the standpoint of a liberal polity, is whether a given constraint diminishes a person's fitness to be held responsible for what they do and is within the power of other people to remove – not whether the imposition of that constraint is balanced out (in theory) by the removal of an equivalent constraint on someone else. As we also saw, market outcomes clearly impose such constraints. The association of market freedom with nonresponsibility therefore exposes the limits of the traditional economic defense of commercial markets.

It does not follow of course that the economic defense of commercial markets is invalid. It does follow, however, that it cannot readily be applied to other domains of conduct. Consider, for example, the so-called marketplace of ideas, in which people are free to share information and to express beliefs and opinions (within certain limits[31]) without being accountable to others either for their accuracy or for the social effects that they have. There is of course considerable disagreement about what values are advanced by allowing people to express themselves freely in this way, but whatever position we take on that question its practical implications are likely to be very different from those that apply in the commercial case. According to the familiar Millian account, for example, liberty of thought and discussion is a necessary condition for the acquisition of true (or reliable) beliefs. Here society may have a legitimate interest in preventing collusion, if by this we mean a conspiracy to suppress certain points of view, but it can hardly be said to have an interest in preventing close collaboration or even monopoly as long as it is achieved through genuine persuasion: reaching agreement through deliberation is, after all, the aim of the whole exercise.[32] Or consider a situation in which people are free to choose what route to take when traveling to a given destination. Here, providing the kind of information that would count as collusive in a commercial market allows the system to perform more efficiently, not less so: this is why we have traffic reports, for example.

---

[31] Defined, for example, by laws against libel and slander, incitement and "hate speech," false advertising, obscenity, the disclosure of state secrets and of certain kinds of personal information, and so on.

[32] As Mill puts it, "the well-being of mankind may almost be measured by the number and gravity of the truths which have reached the point of being uncontested": Mill, *On Liberty*, p. 250.

When we consider the wide variety of other domains of conduct in which the privilege of nonresponsibility is or might be enjoyed, we can see that there is an equally wide variety of ends that markets can be used to pursue, and a correspondingly wide range of conditions under which they can be said to be operating efficiently.

It is important to emphasize, finally, that just because we enjoy the privilege of nonresponsible choice in a given domain it does not follow that our actions are unconstrained to that extent, or even that they are necessarily less constrained than in domains where our conduct is more closely regulated. All social relationships give rise to mutual expectations and can involve the imposition of implicit or explicit penalties when those expectations are violated. So far we have focused on penalties that are collectively authorized and backed by the coercive power of the state, but the costs that we impose on each other without the direct involvement of the state – ranging from local expressions of disapproval to large-scale protests – are of course some of the most powerful factors that shape our behavior.[33] Indeed, Mill points out that the "tyranny of the prevailing opinion and feeling" is often *more* powerful than the "tyranny of the magistrate," because it "penetrat[es] much more deeply into the details of life ... enslaving the soul itself."[34] What makes these "private" penalties different from legal sanctions is not the extent to which they influence our choices, but rather the fact that no publicly coordinated effort is made to control their effects. In a polity that seeks to promote religious freedom, for example, people may face enormous social pressures when making decisions about their manner of observance or nonobservance, but from a public point of view the overall pattern of behavior is a matter of indifference, whatever intelligible patterns we may see at a given time or over time. In a polity that seeks to promote gender and racial equality, by contrast, the overall pattern of behavior is *not* a matter of public indifference; rather the tools of law and public policy are used to try to ensure that individual actions do not create or exacerbate gender or racial hierarchies – although those efforts will of course be aided or frustrated by the corresponding attitudes of support, opposition, or indifference on the part of "private" actors.

As these two examples suggest, the boundary between responsible and nonresponsible choice in a given domain is often contested and permeable.

---

[33] For an acute analysis of how the "social uptake" of our actions affects our ability to take responsibility for what we do see Sharon R. Krause, *Freedom Beyond Sovereignty: Reconstructing Liberal Individualism* (Chicago: University of Chicago Press, 2015).

[34] Mill, *On Liberty*, p. 220.

On the one hand, some "private" practices of praise and blame seek to change public policy in such a way that people are held publicly accountable for their (currently) nonresponsible choices: this was one of the primary aims of the civil rights movement, for example, and it is also the aim of the ongoing campaign against sexual misconduct in the workplace and elsewhere. On the other hand, some policy debates hinge on the question of whether people should be released or shielded from the consequences of the nonresponsible choices that are available to them. For example, the question of whether and to what extent employment contracts should be regulated hinges in part on the question of whether such contracts should be considered legitimate simply by virtue of the fact that they were entered into ("freely"), or whether on the contrary the power asymmetry between employers and employees casts doubt on the claim that employees should be made to endure the adverse conditions under which they have nominally agreed to work.[35] A similar line of argument can be used to support the regulation of "vices" like drinking, gambling, pornography, and prostitution: here again the question is whether the availability of certain alternatives will lead some people to make choices for which they cannot properly be held responsible, whether because of adverse features of their psychology (for example, a propensity to addiction or a lack of impulse control), unfavorable material circumstances (for example, poverty or other kinds of vulnerability), or some other factor.[36] As in the case of employment contracts, a standing objection to the regulation of such choices is that it is paternalistic; it fails to treat people as the responsible actors that they are or could become.

Typically, though, the aim of "private" practices of praise and blame is simply to change the "private" behavior of other people; to improve, if you like, the "market share" of certain beliefs and practices. Social expectations play a central role in shaping behavior in areas as trivial as personal etiquette, as intimate as child-rearing, and as momentous as religious observance. They can be imposed actively – for example, through

---

[35] On the various ways in which an at-will employment regime can jeopardize the republican freedom of workers see Elizabeth Anderson, *Private Government: How Employers Rule Our Lives (and Why We Don't Talk about It)* (Princeton, NJ: Princeton University Press, 2017); for an historical account see Alex Gourevitch, *From Slavery to the Cooperative Commonwealth: Labor and Republican Liberty in the Nineteenth Century* (New York: Cambridge University Press, 2015).

[36] On the question of when and how markets undermine the conditions of responsible agency see Debra Satz, *Why Some Things Should Not Be for Sale: The Moral Limits of Markets* (New York: Oxford University Press, 2010).

expressions of approval and disapproval, or acts of persuasion and protest – or passively – for example, simply by doing what everyone else is doing, or by trying to lead an exemplary life by one's own lights. Indeed, so widespread and pervasive are the ways that we influence each other's behavior without centralized coordination that it is easy to overlook or undervalue the kind of freedom on which they depend. As we have seen, the salient feature of this kind of freedom – market freedom – is not exchange or competition but rather nonresponsibility; the fact that we are allowed, and even encouraged, to interact with each other under conditions in which no one is publicly accountable for the broader consequences of those interactions, and in which social outcomes are therefore fundamentally open-ended and unpredictable. Again, this kind of freedom is necessarily limited: our ability to participate effectively in any domain of conduct requires that we have certain guarantees regarding, at a minimum, our physical safety and the reliability of our potential partners. Nevertheless, the existence of a domain of nonresponsibility, when it is granted as a matter of principle and recognized as a matter of law, distinguishes liberal polities from illiberal ones. We turn now to the question of what reasons we might have for treating freedom so understood as a fundamental political value.

3.4 THE VALUE OF MARKET FREEDOM

It may seem that the upshot of the discussion so far is to encourage us to be skeptical about the value of market freedom: I have found fault with the standard libertarian and neoliberal defenses of markets, and I have argued that the enjoyment of nonresponsibility is always limited and context dependent. Given the close association between *non*responsibility and *ir*responsibility, it may seem – as indeed it has seemed to many antiliberals – that market freedom is a singularly unattractive kind of privilege for people to enjoy; one that could only be granted as a concession to human weakness or out of a failure of nerve on the part of public officials. What grounds, then, do liberals have for treating market freedom as a fundamental political value? Why should we not always hold people publicly accountable for their choices, at least in principle, if those choices impose costs on other people without their consent? Why, for example, should we allow people to consume wastefully, say hurtful things, neglect their health, or spoil their children? The great advantage of associating market freedom with nonresponsibility is that it provides us with a broader and richer set of resources for answering questions like these than other approaches. I will now briefly describe four distinct – though often complementary – sets of reasons that we might have for permitting market freedom in a given domain, most of them quite familiar. The first set of reasons (##1–4) has to do with the background conditions that obtain in a given society, and might hold weight in any polity, liberal or otherwise. The other three sets of reasons are more distinctively liberal: the second (##5–8) has to do with preventing the abuse or harmful exercise of political power; the third (##9–12) with the social benefits that the enjoyment of market freedom can yield; and the fourth (##13–16) with the interests of the people to whom it is extended. Despite its breadth, this list is almost certainly not exhaustive.

(a) Background Conditions

(1) *Indifference.* Perhaps the most common and least remarked-upon reason for permitting market freedom is that most choices are deemed too unimportant, or their effects on other people too insignificant, to be worth regulating. Many choices seem to have no public effects at all: for example, whether I put my pants on left leg first or right leg first, or whether I twiddle my thumbs forwards or backwards. For many other choices the public effects, while discernible, can safely be assumed to be trivial: for example, what color shirt I wear, or how I pronounce the word "potato." Any effort to regulate choice in cases like these would likely be met with bewilderment, and then with resentment or resistance. The fact that the vast majority of choices fall into this category explains why the "pure" conception of negative liberty – the view that the extent of one's freedom should be measured by the number of things that one is physically able to do – is so unwieldy and leads to such counterintuitive results in practice. More importantly, the fact that most nonresponsible choices are seen as insignificant probably accounts for the widely held view that noninterference should be the "default" expectation in any domain of conduct: after all, when someone tries to stop us from doing something our natural response is (quite properly) to ask why. Of course, *pro tanto* reasons often exist to justify the regulation of even seemingly trivial choices: for example, if wearing a shirt of a certain color has special public significance, or if the materials needed to produce it might be used for some public purpose. If we want to continue to assert the privilege of nonresponsibility in the face of such reasons,

then we have to appeal to something weightier than mere indifference.

(2) *Tradition.* Often market freedom is permitted simply because there is a longstanding practice of letting people make their own decisions in a given domain. To some extent this rationale overlaps with the preceding one: nonresponsible choice may be traditional in a given domain because it has not occurred to anyone to regulate it, and this may be because choices in that domain are not thought to be publicly significant. However, the appeal to tradition often carries weight even when nonresponsible choices are understood to have significant public effects. Habit and custom are important stabilizers of individual identity and powerful guarantors of social order. The attempt to regulate choice in domains where there is an established tradition of nonresponsibility may therefore lead at the individual level to confusion and anomie, and at the social level to dislocation and disorder. Public officials may therefore be reluctant to disrupt existing practices of nonresponsible choice even when significant public benefits might in principle be realized by doing so. Needless to say, the same consideration may speak against the idea of extending market freedom into domains of conduct where choice is currently regulated. In either case, the weight of tradition may sometimes lead us to go with the markets that we have, not the markets that we wish we had.

(3) *Conservatism.* This line of argument takes a small but important step beyond the bare appeal to tradition: instead of deferring to longstanding practices of nonresponsible choice because of the harm that might be done if they were to be disrupted, we might defer because we believe that there must be a good reason why those practices have endured, even if we cannot immediately discover or articulate what that reason is. In other words, we might attribute positive effects to existing patterns of nonresponsible choice, rather than (or in addition to) simply anticipating negative effects from their disruption. This familiar Burkean brand of conservatism – which, like its tradition-based counterpart, can also cut in the other direction – has equally familiar limitations: the inarticulate appeal to the weight of the past, while it can provide a useful rejoinder to overly hasty or ambitious efforts to improve on the status quo, cannot provide a satisfying response to a persistent claim that the existing line between responsible and nonresponsible choice should be redrawn. The conservative case

for (or against) market freedom therefore occupies an uneasy middle ground between the negative appeal to tradition and the assertion of distinct positive reasons for permitting (or restricting) market freedom in a given domain.

(4) *Infeasibility.* The most straightforward positive reason for permitting market freedom in a given domain is that public officials do not have the capacity to regulate it effectively, or that it would be too costly to develop and exercise such a capacity. The limitations in question may be technical; for example, effective regulation might require a combination of comprehensive surveillance, swift communication, and accurate record-keeping that is beyond the scope of what a given society can provide. Or the limitations may be administrative; that is, public officials may be unable to project the level of coercive force that would be needed to enforce regulation in a given domain, even if they have access to the necessary information. Needless to say, the word "infeasible" is equivocal; things that are technically or administratively feasible in principle might be so costly that they are infeasible in practice, and the question of what costs are worth bearing is often a matter of dispute. Moreover, the boundaries of infeasibility can change over time as technical and administrative capacities develop or decay. The appeal to infeasibility is thus an especially flexible criterion for determining the boundaries of market freedom. Nevertheless, the existence of relatively stable limits on public capacity – especially in the premodern period, when technical and administrative advances were generally slow and halting – often accounts for the "traditional" enjoyment of nonresponsibility in a given domain – and as we have seen, tradition can acquire independent weight as a ground for permitting market freedom.

(b) Political Considerations

(5) *Epistemic modesty.* Distinct from the question of whether public officials have the technical and administrative capacity to regulate a given domain of conduct is the question of whether they have the judgment and foresight that are needed to do so effectively. All efforts to regulate human conduct have unforeseen consequences, and even well-meaning interventions sometimes make things

worse. Public officials might therefore allow nonresponsible choice in a given domain, even when they have the capacity to regulate it in principle, because they have a healthy appreciation of their own fallibility. The limits of human judgment and foresight, while not invariable, are more stable than the technical and administrative capacities that societies can bring to bear, and as the latter capacities expand – and as the social world becomes correspondingly more complex – the potential for overreach expands as well. Needless to say, it requires an unusual amount of forbearance on the part of public officials to refrain from using the tools that they have at their disposal when they are faced with significant public problems or strong public demands for action. Nevertheless, there are some problems, according to this line of argument, that we should not try collectively to solve: "First, do no harm" is the watchword of this rationale for permitting market freedom.

(6) *Prudence.* In addition to asking whether public officials have the foresight and judgment that would be needed to regulate conduct effectively, we might also ask whether they or their successors can be trusted to use their authority for its intended purposes. Even well-designed and properly functioning political institutions place a lot of discretionary power in the hands of those who are called upon to administer public policy – most notably executive agencies and the police – and human beings have a well-documented tendency to abuse power when given the chance. A standing argument in favor of permitting market freedom is thus that the regulation of conduct in a given domain would require that more power be given to public officials; power that can and at least occasionally will be abused. Even if we believe that the benefits of regulation outweigh the risk of abuse in a given case, we might nevertheless worry that granting public officials the power to regulate that domain of conduct would set a dangerous precedent for other cases, or that it would put resources in their hands that could later be used for less benign purposes. Market freedom can therefore be an important guarantor of limited government.

(7) *Stability.* Another reason to permit market freedom in a given domain is that there may be deep disagreement about what form public regulation should take. In such cases public officials may decide to let individuals and groups go their own way because they fear that trying to impose a common rule of conduct would pose a threat to social order. This line of argument is likely to be

especially salient in cases where there is a rough balance of power between factions on a given issue, or when some people care deeply enough about the issue that any effort to regulate conduct would be likely to inspire resistance. Regimes of religious toleration often arise from and depend upon a *modus vivendi* of this kind, as the adherents of each (sufficiently powerful) sect understand – often from hard experience – that any effort to impose their beliefs and practices on the whole would lead to unrest or violence. Needless to say, the space that is thereby created for nonresponsible choice is inherently fragile: as with all *modus vivendi* arrangements, if the balance of power between factions shifts or the intensity of feeling on a given issue changes then we should expect the boundaries of market freedom to change as well. However, a *modus vivendi* can sometimes prepare the way for a more principled defense of market freedom – as has arguably happened in the religious case.

(8) *Dispersion of power*. The two preceding reasons for permitting market freedom can be made to work together in a familiar way. Often the foreseeable result of giving public officials the power to regulate behavior in a given domain is that the power in question will be exercised by a particular group or faction, which may be bound together by wealth, hereditary privilege, racial, ethnic, or gender identity, religious affiliation, or any other form of actual or perceived shared interest. As we have seen, placing the power to regulate in the hands of such a faction not only means that choices in a given domain may be regulated for its own benefit, but that it may also be able to use (or abuse) that power for other purposes. Allowing nonresponsible choice in a given domain can therefore be an effective way to disperse power and diminish the threat of factional domination. Here again market freedom can be an important guarantor of limited government.

(c) Social Considerations

(9) *Diversity*. A third set of reasons for permitting market freedom has to do with the social benefits that its enjoyment can yield. The most obvious benefit is that letting people choose nonresponsibly in a given domain often allows for a more diverse set of outcomes to be realized than a centralized, "one size fits all" regulatory

regime. Diversity can of course be instrumental to the achievement of a number of other social ends, some of which we will consider below, but it is also a distinct kind of value taken in itself. On the one hand, because individual tastes, preferences, experiences, and interests differ, a social arrangement that yields a wide variety of outcomes is more likely to offer a range of choices that appeals to each person. On the other hand, many people find diversity to be a desirable feature of social life even when many of the possibilities on offer are not ones that they would choose for themselves, simply because it makes life more colorful, more interesting, and more stimulating. A world in which there was only one language, one cuisine, one style of dress, one form of recreation, one kind of music, one literature, one system of speculative philosophy – even, the more liberal-minded may add, in which there was only one political ideology or one religion – would be a poorer world to that extent.

(10) *Experimentalism.* In addition to its intrinsic value, the diversity of outcomes that the enjoyment of market freedom yields can also make it possible to test alternatives and identify best practices in various domains of conduct, and thus to improve the quality of knowledge, technique, and decision-making over time. This line of argument is often associated with Mill's defense of liberty of thought and discussion, which focuses on the pursuit and acquisition of truth. However, it can be applied more broadly to any domain of conduct in which discovery and innovation have an important role to play, from the elaboration of cultural forms to the development of new technologies to the reform of institutions. The experimentation that goes on in these domains may be organized and systematic, as in the case of scientific inquiry, or haphazard and informal, as in the case of economic competition or the so-called marketplace of ideas. In either case, nonresponsible choice is a key driver of the creativity and dynamism that are characteristic of liberal polities.

(11) *Serendipity.* Where experimentation aims at developing or improving upon existing practices, market freedom might also be permitted in a given domain simply because it allows for the unexpected and fortuitous to happen. That is, nonresponsible choices often yield outcomes that could not have been foreseen, but that are retrospectively found to be valuable. As in the case of diversity, we might value this kind of serendipity for its own

sake – variety is, after all, the spice of life – or because we know from experience that useful things often have unexpected origins. Technological advances such as the microwave and the X-ray, and medical advances such as penicillin and the pacemaker, came about in this largely fortuitous way. Some corporations – 3M and Google are notable examples – have tried to promote happy accidents like this by allowing their employees to devote a substantial portion of their working hours to "unstructured time" in which they can pursue ideas and projects that lie outside their official duties. Countless cultural innovations have resulted from improvisatory or aleatory practices in music, literature, dance, and the visual arts. Much of the characteristically open texture of life in a liberal polity depends on its willingness to leave room for the unexpected.

(12) *Efficiency.* A more systemic rationale for permitting market freedom arises in cases when uncoordinated choice can be expected to bring about an efficient distribution of scarce resources. This line of argument is most familiar from its application to commercial markets, where it has been worked out in considerable technical detail. The basic idea is that market prices provide a clear and reliable signal of changes in the supply of and demand for various resources; changes which are the product of innumerable changes in local conditions of production, consumption, and exchange. Changes in prices have a reciprocal effect in turn on market behavior, creating an incentive to shift consumption from more to less costly goods, and to shift productive resources from less to more profitable uses. Because (or insofar as) markets are self-equilibrating in this way, the outcomes that they yield are more efficient – they exploit productive resources and satisfy consumption preferences more fully – than the decisions of any centralized authority, no matter how well-informed or well-intentioned it might be. Of course, the efficiency case for market freedom rests on a number of assumptions – for example, perfect information about prices and commodities, no barriers to entry or exit, and no transaction costs – that are never fully realized, and often not sufficiently approximated, in practice. Moreover, this line of argument is hard to generalize into noncommercial domains of conduct. Nevertheless, it is often a good rule of thumb that decision-making power should be

placed in the hands of the people who are closest to the scene of action, and who can therefore be expected to have a finer-grained understanding of the context in which decisions are made. In this sense the appeal to efficiency provides a positive counterpart to the negative appeal to epistemic modesty that we considered earlier.

(d) Individual Considerations

(13) *Anti-paternalism.* A fourth and final set of reasons for permitting market freedom appeals to the interests of the people to whom it is extended. Here the most straightforward argument is that denying people the ability to choose for themselves sends the implicit or explicit message that they are incapable of making, or that they cannot be trusted to make, good choices in that domain. There are two kinds of objections that we might have to this kind of paternalism. The first is instrumental: it is often reasonable to suppose that people know more about their own circumstances, and have a greater regard for their own interests, than any central authority. A centralized regulatory regime runs roughshod over this kind of situated knowledge, often with predictably bad results. A more fundamental objection to paternalism is that it is disrespectful to the people on whom it is practiced. This kind of disrespect will tend to breed resentment under any circumstances, but it is especially pernicious when it reinforces existing patterns of inequality: for example, when the choices of women, the poor and working class, or of ethnic, racial, or religious minorities are disproportionately subject to supervision and regulation. Enjoying the privilege of nonresponsible choice can therefore be an important marker of equal status in a liberal polity.

(14) *Perfectionism.* A second individual-level reason that we might have for permitting market freedom in a given domain is that allowing people to make their own choices can promote self-discipline and self-reliance. That is, even when we have reason to expect that people will occasionally or systematically make poor choices, or that their choices will create significant negative externalities, we might nevertheless allow them to act nonresponsibly because we think that only if they are enabled (or compelled)

to choose for themselves will they be able to learn from their mistakes and make better decisions over time. Moreover, the good habits and qualities of character that are thereby developed will often spill over into other domains where choice is more closely regulated. Conversely, taking choices out of people's hands can cultivate habits of passivity and dependence in them, even when the regulatory regime that is imposed achieves its intended aims.

(15) *Privacy.* A diametrically opposed reason for permitting market freedom is that it provides a necessary release from the burdens of public responsibility and self-improvement. We all need at least occasionally to take "moral holidays" in which we can pursue whims, indulge in vices, do things just for fun, or simply waste time, even when this prevents us from realizing our full potential or from making our fullest contribution to society. Drawing the bonds of public supervision and accountability too tightly can give rise to anxiety, depression, and exhaustion, which can lead in turn to self-destructive or socially harmful behavior. The existence of a "private" sphere of nonresponsible choice is to this extent an essential element of individual well-being.

(16) *Sovereignty.* A final reason for permitting market freedom – which some will see as the most fundamental reason of all – is that people simply have a right to make their own decisions in a given domain. The list of rights that have been derived from this appeal to individual sovereignty – rights to privacy, property, and bodily integrity; to belief, thought, and expression; to assembly, association, and movement; and so on – is both extensive and subject to dispute, as is the list of caveats that have been attached to them: few would argue on reflection that any of the aforementioned rights is absolute. Some of the grounds on which individual rights have been claimed – for example, out of a concern to limit the powers of government, to maintain social stability, to prevent paternalism, or to promote self-improvement – have already been discussed. Nevertheless, liberals have often given independent weight to certain rights over and above these considerations, and have been willing to bear substantial social, political, and economic costs in order to ensure that they are not violated.

Needless to say, countervailing considerations can be invoked against each of these reasons for permitting market freedom, and many of them are in tension with each other: it is hard (though not impossible), for example, to value both social stability and experimentalism, and we have already examined the tension between the claims of social efficiency and individual sovereignty. More importantly, the force of each reason will vary substantially across cases and over time. Which decisions seem insignificant; which traditions seem worth respecting; what it is feasible or prudent to regulate; what we are willing to fight about; how important we think diversity, efficiency, and self-reliance are; how well we think people know their own interests; even what rights we think people have: we disagree about each of these issues now, and our views about them have changed significantly over time and will continue to change going forward. These kinds of disagreements make up much of the substance of a liberal politics and help to explain why liberalism is such a flexible and mutable political ideology.

Nevertheless, the various reasons that we have identified for permitting market freedom, while conceptually distinct, cluster together in intelligible ways, and allow us to identify several broad schools or "genres" of liberal political thought. One school of thought places an emphasis on human fallibility, myopia, and cruelty; on the fragility of social and political order; on the tendency of those in power to abuse their trust; and on the tragic nature of political choices (##5–8). Liberals who think along these lines – figures like Alexis de Tocqueville, Max Weber, Isaiah Berlin, and Judith Shklar – see market freedom as an essential means of checking what would otherwise be the overweening and dominating power of state and society. A second school of thought places an emphasis on human creativity and ingenuity, and on the material prosperity, cultural flourishing, and moral improvement that their application makes possible (##9–12). Liberals who think along these lines – figures like Wilhelm von Humboldt, John Stuart Mill, John Dewey, and Elizabeth Anderson – see market freedom as an essential means of unleashing human potential for the sake of social progress. A third school of thought places an emphasis on individual autonomy, self-reliance, and personal development (##13–16). Liberals who think along these lines – figures like Benjamin Constant, T. H. Green, L. T. Hobhouse, and Sharon Krause – see market freedom as an essential means of releasing people from the distorting influence of social expectations, thereby allowing them to discover and realize their own distinctive way of being in the world. Each of these schools of liberal thought – tragic, progressive, and individualist – is of course further shaped by the weight that its adherents place on the value of tradition, what they believe to be the appropriate rate of social change, and what they take to be the limits of public capacity (##2–4).

There are of course other ways of carving up the terrain of liberal thought, and other ways of categorizing the thinkers that I have just named – some of whom will seem to some readers like strange bedfellows. The essential point for present purposes is that liberalism is both a broad church and a vital tradition, and that its breadth and vitality arise above all from its appreciation of the political, social, and personal importance of nonresponsible choice in all of its various dimensions. Having established market freedom's place at the center of the liberal scheme of values, we turn now to the question of how its limits should be defined, and thus of its relationship to republican freedom.

3.5 THE LIMITS OF MARKET FREEDOM

I began this chapter by calling attention to the central role that markets play in defining the social and political possibilities that are available to us today. In the intervening discussion I have argued that market freedom is not defined by consent: none of us can be said to have consented to the menu of market choices that is available to us, or to the pattern of potential costs and benefits that is attached to them. Nor is market freedom defined by competition, since all competition is structured by a system of rules that is either externally imposed or collectively agreed upon. Instead, I have identified market freedom with the ability to decide for oneself how to respond to the menu of choices that one faces without being publicly accountable for the consequences of those decisions, and thus with the ability to impose certain costs on other people without their consent. Market freedom so understood is a fundamental but partial political value: the nonresponsibility that market actors enjoy is necessarily embedded in a social and legal framework that qualifies and limits that freedom, and we therefore have to speak of the *extent* to which we enjoy market freedom in a given domain. Moreover, as we saw in Chapter 2, the enjoyment of market freedom poses a standing threat to the enjoyment of republican freedom, because our nonresponsible choices affect other people in ways that they do not choose or control.

It follows that in a liberal polity the transfer of decision-making authority from state to market does not result in an increase in freedom as such. Rather, one kind of freedom is lost – republican freedom; the freedom not to be subject to nonresponsible or arbitrary power – and another kind of freedom is gained – market freedom; the freedom to make choices without being publicly accountable for (some of) the effects that they have on other people. Conversely, to expand the scope of republican freedom is to declare a given domain of conduct to be of sufficient public concern that we take collective responsibility for the outcomes that are realized within it. We have decided as a society that we have a shared interest in how children are educated, wars prosecuted, and criminals punished, even if we are not parents, soldiers, or victims of crime ourselves. When these functions are performed by "private" actors whose actions we do not control, in pursuit of ends that we have not approved, then we cannot properly be held responsible for the consequences that result and are in that straightforward sense unfree. As we have seen, and as any citizen of a liberal polity knows, liberals do not agree about how the trade-offs between these two kinds of freedom should be made – this, again, is what a liberal politics is about. However, as we have also seen, liberals do agree that republican freedom has priority over market freedom in the procedural sense that the trade-offs have to be made in publicly visible and contestable ways and for publicly avowable reasons. In other words, the rules that establish the limits of market freedom have to be created and enforced in a way that is consistent with the demands of republican freedom: this, again, is the crucial difference between a *liberal* polity and a *neoliberal* polity.

Strictly speaking every domain of social interaction is of public concern in at least the limited sense that the state is ultimately responsible for guaranteeing the physical safety of those who engage in it. Beyond that point it is a matter of public debate when and how people should be allowed to impose costs on others without their consent. Some liberals – today they are often called "classical" liberals – hold that the considerations that speak in favor of market freedom are weighty enough that the state's role should be strictly limited to its security-preserving and property-protecting functions. I have significant reservations about that view, but there is nothing in the freedom-centered conception of liberalism that I have defended that prevents us from acknowledging it as a liberal view in good standing.[37] The only caveat (which "classical" liberals are typically happy to grant) is that we cannot rest content with the mere

---

[37] A standard critique of "classical" liberalism is that an unregulated system of exchange will lead over time to inequalities among citizens that are substantial enough to undermine the very possibility of republican government. For an especially strong version of this critique see Samuel Freeman, "Illiberal Libertarians: Why Libertarianism Is Not a Liberal View," *Philosophy and Public Affairs* 30 (2002), pp. 105–51. While I feel the force of Freeman's argument (thus some of the reservations alluded to above), I think that it is best read as

provision of security; we have to enjoy the kinds of procedural protections – democratically accountable public officials, an independent judiciary, freedoms of speech and press, rights to petition and assembly, and so on – that make our lives and property robust against arbitrary interference, whether by the state or by private actors. Our security has to be underwritten, in other words, by a republican form of government.

Few contemporary liberals, and no contemporary liberal polities, toe the pure "classical" line; "classical" liberalism lies at one end of a continuum the other end of which is occupied by "social democratic" liberalism, which takes a less permissive stance on the scope of market freedom, and which is of course subject to the same republican caveat. We have decided (not without controversy and struggle) that people should be held publicly accountable for imposing certain kinds of costs on others: for example, through minimum wage and maximum hours laws, workplace and product safety laws, anti-discrimination and "hate speech" laws, environmental and public health regulations, and so on. I am free to decide what to spend my money on, but I am not allowed to buy something that is not publicly recognized as a legal commodity. I am free to decide what route to take to work, but I have to stay on public thoroughfares and observe the relevant traffic laws. I am free to decide whom to associate with and which social norms to observe, but I am not allowed to join (what society has defined as) a subversive organization, or to engage in (what society has defined as) discriminatory or indecent behavior. As we have seen – and as we all know – there is plenty of disagreement about where and how the boundaries of market freedom should be drawn: many liberals think that more should be done to protect workers, consumers, and the environment, and to prevent or punish (what they regard as) subversive, discriminatory, or indecent behavior, and many liberals think that existing regulations go too far along one or more of these dimensions. There is no way to resolve disagreements like these once and for all without stepping outside the nonutopian bounds of a liberal politics.

The picture of liberalism that emerges from this discussion may seem unfamiliar to some readers, because unlike the academic liberalism of the last few decades (post-Rawls) it treats freedom rather than justice as the "first virtue" of social institutions.[38] This sense of unfamiliarity is

---

a defense of a particular position along the liberal continuum and not as a demarcation of the boundaries of liberalism itself.

[38] Rawls declares justice to be the "first virtue of social institutions" in the opening lines of *A Theory of Justice*.

no accident: one of the central arguments of this book is that contemporary academic liberalism rests on a flawed and idiosyncratic understanding of what liberalism is, and that it has therefore failed to make use of the full range of normative and practical resources that the liberal tradition provides. I hope that the preceding three chapters have succeeded in portraying a freedom-centered liberalism as an intelligible and attractive – though not of course incontestable – political ideology. The burden of the following two chapters is to show that this freedom-centered view has a better claim to the title "liberal" than its justice-centered counterpart: first, by showing that it does a better job of accounting for the emergence and development of the liberal tradition in the modern period (Chapter 4); and second, by showing that it does a better job of responding to the problem of polarization that faces liberal polities – and liberalism itself – today (Chapter 5).

4

The Liberal Tradition

[T]his affable and kind little widow was no great dame, but a dependant like myself. I did not like her the worse for that; on the contrary, I felt better pleased than ever. The equality between her and me was real; not the mere result of condescension on her part: so much the better – my position was all the freer.

                        Charlotte Brontë, *Jane Eyre*

4.1 THE LIBERAL PROBLEM

"A new chapter in a novel is something like a new scene in a play." So begins the pivotal eleventh chapter of *Jane Eyre*, in which the eponymous heroine finally escapes the orbit of family and school and embarks on her adult life. Brontë paints a vivid picture of what it is like to be a young person experiencing this kind of freedom for the first time: "It is a very strange sensation to inexperienced youth," she writes, "to feel itself quite alone in the world, cut adrift from every connection, uncertain whether the port to which it is bound can be reached, and prevented by many impediments from returning to that it has quitted. The charm of adventure sweetens that sensation, the glow of pride warms it; but then the throb of fear disturbs it." Upon her arrival at Thornfield, the "new scene" where the main action of the novel takes place, Jane's feelings are less mixed: "My faculties, roused by the change of scene, the new field offered to hope, seemed all astir. I cannot precisely define what they expected, but it was something pleasant: not perhaps that day or that month, but at an indefinite future period."

Like most young people, Jane quickly discovers that her new life, uncertain and indefinite though its future course might be, is no less encumbered by authority relations than the old one. Upon meeting the "affable and kind" Mrs. Fairfax, who has hired her as governess at Thornfield, she is surprised by what she takes to be her "condescension": "I felt rather confused," she reports, "at being the object of more attention than I had ever before received, and, that too, shown by my employer and superior; but as she did not herself seem to consider she was doing anything out of her place, I thought it better to take her civilities quietly." This impression of *noblesse oblige* is apparently confirmed by Mrs. Fairfax's casual remark that the household staff "are only servants, and one can't converse with them on terms of equality: one must keep them at due distance, for fear of losing one's authority." The dramatic irony of these opening scenes at Thornfield is revealed the next morning – shortly after the revery described above – when Mrs. Fairfax explains that she is "only the housekeeper – the manager," adding that "I consider myself quite in the light of an ordinary housekeeper: my employer is always civil, and I expect nothing more." The employer, the real "superior" – in the form of Mr. Rochester – has yet to make his memorable entrance. In the meantime, Jane finds with relief that, as the epigraph to this chapter states, her position with respect to Mrs. Fairfax is "all the freer" because of the newly discovered "equality" between them.

This homely episode, with its pithy articulation of the complicated nexus between freedom, equality, authority, and dependence, neatly captures the theme of this chapter, which explores the emergence and development of the liberal tradition out of the conflict between republican freedom – centrally concerned with the "fear of losing one's authority" – and market freedom – centrally concerned with one's hopes and fears about an "indefinite future period." My thesis is that the decline of traditional hierarchies over the course of the nineteenth century – and the resulting expectation that even a young woman of modest means like Jane Eyre might have a story worth telling – made the conflict between these two values apparent and led to the formation of a tradition of political thought and practice – the liberal tradition – that sought to harmonize them. *Jane Eyre* provides a fitting starting point for exploring this development. The novel is set during the Regency period, a time when the contrast between the conspicuous consumption of the ruling class and the squalid living conditions of the working poor in England was especially pronounced, and when the social disruptions of the Industrial Revolution – and of the backlash against it – were beginning to be felt.

It was published in October 1847, on the eve of the revolutions that swept the European continent in the spring of 1848, and just a few months before the publication of the most influential anti-liberal tract of the nineteenth century; Marx and Engels' *Manifesto of the Communist Party*.

Any effort to come to terms with the shape of the liberal tradition has to start by responding to two obvious – albeit contradictory – objections. On the one hand, liberalism has often been seen, especially by its admirers, as a loosely defined collection of political ideas and practices; an ideological label whose referents have changed so fundamentally over time that it has no essential core and yields no coherent set of normative or practical commitments. Alan Ryan points out, for example, that "[i]t is easy to list famous liberals; it is harder to say what they have in common," and suggests that "we should be seeking to understand liberalisms, not liberalism." Helena Rosenblatt begins her sympathetic history of the tradition by observing that "we are muddled about what we mean by liberalism," and Edmund Fawcett begins his by admitting that "[i]f a satisfying, non-circular definition of 'liberalism' is still wanted none is available."[1] On the other hand, liberalism has often been seen, especially by its critics, as an all-too-stable collection of metaphysical, anthropological, and sociological dogmas. Chantal Mouffe, writing from the left, holds that "the dominant tendency in liberal thought ... is characterized by a rationalist and individualist approach"; a "belief in the availability of a universal consensus based on reason" that is "unable to understand the formation of collective identities." Michael Sandel, writing from the "communitarian" center, agrees that liberals "construe all obligation in terms of duties universally owed or obligations voluntarily incurred," and view the self as "free and independent, unencumbered by aims and attachments it does not choose for itself." Patrick Deneen, writing from the right, argues that liberalism is "fundamentally constituted by a pair of deep[] anthropological assumptions," namely "anthropological individualism and the voluntarist conception of choice" and "human separation from and opposition to nature."[2]

---

[1] Alan Ryan, *The Making of Modern Liberalism* (Princeton, NJ: Princeton University Press, 2012), pp. 21–2; Helena Rosenblatt, *The Lost History of Liberalism: From Ancient Rome to the Twenty-First Century* (Princeton, NJ: Princeton University Press, 2018), p. 1; Edmund Fawcett, *Liberalism: The Life of an Idea* (2nd ed., Princeton, NJ: Princeton University Press, 2018 [2014]), p. 22.

[2] Chantal Mouffe, *Agonistics: Thinking the World Politically* (New York: Verso, 2013), pp. 3–4; Michael J. Sandel, *Democracy's Discontent: America in Search of a Public Philosophy*

Needless to say, these characterizations of the liberal tradition cannot both be right[3]; I hope to show that neither of them is. In particular, I will argue that liberalism, like all ideological traditions, is not bound together by a common set of beliefs and practices to which it is committed, but rather by a common problem with which it is concerned[4]: in the case of liberalism, the problem of striking an appropriate balance between republican and market freedom. The diversity that we find within the liberal tradition – and it is not any more or less diverse in this respect than (for example) the democratic and socialist traditions with which it has often been entangled – arises from the fact that liberals not only disagree about how to solve this problem, but also about what would *count* as a solution: this is why it is properly described as a problem and not simply as a goal. In order to explain the emergence of the liberal tradition, then, we have to explain how the problem of balancing republican and market freedom first appeared *as* a problem and show how changing perceptions of the problem – and the changing shape of the problem itself in the face of the various efforts to respond to it – accounts for the development of the tradition over time, lending it a kind of unity while also accounting for its diversity. We also have to show that this way of defining the boundaries of the tradition can account for and exclude illiberal and anti-liberal modes of thought and practice, which do not treat the problem of balancing republican and market freedom as a salient political problem – a task that I take up in Chapter 5.

As I have already suggested, it was the decline of traditional hierarchies over the course of the nineteenth century that brought the problem of

---

(Cambridge, MA: Harvard University Press, 1996), pp. 14, 12; Patrick J. Deneen, *Why Liberalism Failed* (New Haven, CT: Yale University Press, 2018), p. 31.

[3] Nor are these the only contradictory characterizations on offer: Rosenblatt points out, for example, that "[a]ccording to one recent account ... liberalism originates in Christianity," while "according to another, liberalism originates in a battle *against* Christianity," and that "in France and other parts of the world today being liberal means favoring 'small government,' while in America it signifies favoring 'big government'": *Lost History of Liberalism*, pp. 2–3 (original emphasis). The studies alluded to in the first quotation are Larry Siedentop, *Inventing the Individual: The Origins of Western Liberalism* (Cambridge, MA: Harvard University Press, 2014) and Pierre Manent, *An Intellectual History of Liberalism*, trans. Rebecca Balinski (Princeton, NJ: Princeton University Press, 1995 [1987]).

[4] Here I draw on the conception of ideological traditions that is developed in Eric MacGilvray, *The Invention of Market Freedom* (New York: Cambridge University Press, 2011) – see especially pp. 21–3 – although there I associated liberalism (in passing) with a different orienting problem: that of "making it possible for all individuals to pursue their own good in their own way."

balancing republican and market freedom into focus, and not coincidentally it is also during this period that the word "liberal" was first used to refer to a political party or movement. It follows that this is where we should look for the origins of the liberal tradition.[5] The narrative that is offered here therefore displaces John Locke from his familiar role as a (or the) "founding" liberal,[6] and sidelines Immanuel Kant, the philosopher who had the greatest influence on John Rawls, and thus on the development of contemporary academic liberalism. This does not mean that it is necessarily wrong to describe Locke, Kant, and other early modern thinkers as "liberals." All sufficiently robust ideological traditions construct useful histories for themselves – just as their opponents construct useful counter-histories – and so it is not surprising that nineteenth- and twentieth-century liberals drew to varying degrees on (for example) the defense of ordered liberty that we find in Locke and Burke, the skeptical humanism that we find in Montaigne and Bayle, the celebration of commerce that we find in Hume and Smith, the strategies for fighting despotism that we find in Montesquieu and Madison, and the faith in reason and progress that we find in Voltaire and Kant, and that these thinkers came to be seen as "liberals" too. There is nothing wrong with defining a tradition in this retroactive way, although we will of course tend to read earlier thinkers selectively – and thus, in strictly historical terms, to misread them – if and insofar as we read them (Whiggishly) as liberals *avant la lettre*.

It is nevertheless the case that if we want to understand why there is a liberal tradition in the first place, and why it has the (rough and contested) shape that it does, then we should start by focusing on the orienting problem that led to its formation, and on the social and political conditions that gave rise to that problem. I therefore begin by examining two developments that, taken together, made it possible for the problem of balancing republican and market freedom to be clearly

---

[5] Fawcett begins his history of liberalism in the nineteenth century for the same reason, pointing out that previous thinkers "had [not] understood, let alone felt, a new state of affairs in which society was changing people, often at unprecedented speed and in ways nobody understood"; "[t]o look for political liberalism before then," he concludes, "is like searching for the seventeenth-century carburetor or the eighteenth-century microchip": Fawcett, *Liberalism*, p. 2.

[6] Locke's status as a "founding" liberal is of fairly recent vintage; histories of the liberal tradition that predate the Cold War typically start about a century later, as I do here. See, for example, Duncan Bell, "What Is Liberalism?", *Political Theory* 42 (2014), pp. 682–715, and Timothy Stanton, "John Locke and the Fable of Liberalism," *Historical Journal* 61 (2018), pp. 597–620.

recognized as a problem: the "democratization" of public and private life, and the "industrialization" of economic production (Section 4.2). The liberal response to these developments came in two overlapping stages. First, the rise of democracy made it increasingly clear that the power that we exercise over each other in modern societies is reciprocal, insidious, and pervasive, and thus gave new urgency to the problem of carving out a domain of nonresponsible conduct. This explains the liberal concern with promoting a flexible and entrepreneurial economy, a robust and pluralistic civil society, and an open and tolerant public sphere (Section 4.3). Second, the rise of industrial capitalism exposed the fundamental tension between the dependence that we experience in our "private" lives and the independence that we are expected to display as republican citizens, and thus gave new urgency to the problem of creating the material and social conditions under which people become fit to be held responsible for what they do. This explains the liberal concern with promoting economic independence and security, shared or reciprocal power in "private" domains like the workplace and the family, and equal influence over political decision-making (Section 4.4).

Needless to say – and this is the distinctively liberal insight – these two agendas do not always work together smoothly: promoting economic security often means regulating, and thus reducing the flexibility of, the economy; combating "private" power often means regulating, and thus reducing the pluralism of, civil society; and securing equal political influence often means regulating, and thus reducing the openness of, the public sphere. The liberal tradition was born out of and constituted by the tension between these competing sets of commitments, and liberals have responded to this tension in a number of different ways, some of which give more weight to market freedom, and some more weight to republican freedom. In making the case for why the balance should be struck in one way rather than another, liberal thinkers have of course sometimes appealed to pre-nineteenth-century ideas, and I turn at the end of the chapter to the question of how we should think about this liberal "prehistory." As I have already indicated, to say that the liberal tradition was "born" in the nineteenth century is not to deny or downplay the obvious fact that earlier thinkers and ideas have been incorporated into it. Rather, it allows us to see that this incorporation was retroactive, as nineteenth- and twentieth-century liberals drew selectively on influential precedents that could be used to support their cause. In doing so they reconfigured the lines of alliance and opposition – the defining problems – that those thinkers had used to orient themselves, giving rise to apparent paradoxes that intellectual historians are still working to unravel (Section 4.5).

A methodological note before we begin. The liberal narrative that is offered here focuses mainly on "great thinkers," and only indirectly on the historical events to which they were responding – and even then, mostly through the lens that is provided by their writings. Needless to say, an intellectual history of an ideological tradition – and a highly selective one at that – runs the risk of painting a misleadingly abstract and stylized portrait of that tradition. To some extent this is unavoidable: any effort to make sense of the events and ideas that shaped the development of the liberal tradition will necessarily focus on the figures who were trying to make sense of the social and political challenges of their own time and place in the most general terms. The resulting risk of abstraction is mitigated by the fact that the key thinkers whose ideas we will examine here – Constant, Tocqueville, Mill, Green, Hobhouse, Hobson, and Dewey – were all deeply involved in practical politics, as of course were many of their critics and interlocutors. In this respect they are very different from their present-day successors: as I pointed out in the Introduction, one of the most striking features of contemporary academic liberalism is the fact that its key figures are largely detached from, and their central ideas largely ignored in, the public sphere. The narrative that follows can therefore be seen as a framing device for – or a down payment on – a more detailed historical account. In the meantime, I hope that it will help to dispel the still-prevalent view that the liberal tradition is fundamentally contractarian; that it began with Locke's *Second Treatise of Government* and reached its apotheosis in Rawls's *A Theory of Justice*.

4.2 DEMOCRATIZATION AND INDUSTRIALIZATION

Locke begins the *Second Treatise* by drawing a close connection between freedom and equality: because no one has been picked out by God to exercise political authority over anyone else (equality), he reasons, the only political authority to which we can legitimately be subject is that to which we have consented (freedom).[7] However, despite his egalitarian premises Locke, like all early modern thinkers, was writing in and about a society that was deeply inegalitarian; one that was governed by a hereditary monarch, a hereditary nobility, and the clergy, in rather grudging cooperation with the wealthier segment of the "common"

---

[7] John Locke, *Second Treatise of Government* (1690) §4.

people; one that was deeply implicated (as was Locke himself[8]) in the transatlantic slave trade; and one in which women (unless they happened to be monarchs) had no formal political authority whatsoever. Moreover, the political crisis to which the *Two Treatises* were responding was not a popular uprising but rather an intra-parliamentary dispute about dynastic succession, and radical as the argument is in some respects it does not seek to overturn existing power structures but rather to give them a firmer foundation: Locke proposes not to challenge, but to "establish," King William's title.[9] The equality that he assumes, like the consent that he demands, is thus purely hypothetical: he does not provide much guidance on – or show much interest in – the question of how it might be made real, nor does he suggest any means, short of revolution, of keeping political power within the bounds of natural law to which the people have nominally consented.[10]

The social and political hierarchies that Locke took for granted began to collapse in the wake of the American and French Revolutions, and their decline over the course of the nineteenth and twentieth centuries, while not uninterrupted, was in cumulative terms decisive. Monarchies and hereditary aristocracies were overthrown or saw their powers and privileges sharply curtailed; political authority was increasingly, and often entirely, detached from ecclesiastical authority; property qualifications for the suffrage were removed; the doctrine of legal coverture was repealed and women won the right to vote; slavery was abolished; colonies won their independence[11]; and popular or at least constitutional government became widespread in practice, and almost universally endorsed in theory: today even manifestly authoritarian regimes describe themselves as "democratic" or "people's" republics. These momentous developments forced political thinkers and actors to move beyond the abstract and rather sterile claim that people are equal in theory and start wrestling with the fact that they

---

[8] For discussion see, for example, James Farr, "'So Vile and Miserable an Estate': The Problem of Slavery in Locke's Political Thought," *Political Theory* 14 (1986), pp. 263–89 and "Locke, Natural Law, and New World Slavery," *Political Theory* 36 (2008), pp. 495–522.

[9] Locke, *Two Treatises of Government*, preface. On the political aims of the *Two Treatises* see Richard Ashcraft, *Revolutionary Politics and Locke's* Two Treatises of Government (Princeton, NJ: Princeton University Press, 1986).

[10] Locke's brief endorsement of the separation of executive and legislative power (*Second Treatise* §§143–4) falls far short of the detailed institutional proposals that are found in the political writings of republican contemporaries like John Milton and Algernon Sydney and is in any case undercut by his uncomplaining references to a situation (like England's) in which those powers are mixed (§§151–2, 213).

[11] I consider the legacy of liberal support for colonialism and imperialism in Chapter 5.

were becoming equal in practice. Not surprisingly, they arrived at a more complicated and ambivalent portrait of human equality than their contractarian predecessors. More importantly for our purposes, the shift from hypothetical to real egalitarianism had a profound impact on the modern understanding of freedom as a political value, and led to the emergence of a new and specifically "liberal" – liberty-centered – tradition of political thought.

The most obvious sign of this new egalitarianism was of course the broadening of the suffrage and the gradual transfer of political power from the hereditary nobility to the wealthy, and then finally to the people as a whole. Here as elsewhere the pace of change varied considerably from place to place, from the fairly rapid substitution of freeman for freeholder citizenship in the early decades of the American republic, to the pitched battles over successive Reform Bills in Britain, to the periodic cycles of revolution and reform in France – all overlain with the decades-long struggle for women's suffrage. We should not exaggerate the degree to which the extension of full citizenship to all people was driven by a genuine commitment to equality: the pace of democratization was driven by considerations of political expediency at least as much as it was guided by matters of principle, as various parties and factions sought political advantage by strategically enfranchising previously excluded groups. And, of course, many "democracies" remained conspicuously undemocratic in important ways until well into the twentieth century: France did not extend the suffrage to women until the end of the Second World War, the American South maintained a system of racialized citizenship until the 1960s, and the British aristocracy still retains vestiges of its political power. Nevertheless, the nineteenth century saw a sea change in the norms and practices surrounding the boundaries of citizenship; one in which democracy went from being a term of abuse to a basic test of political legitimacy.

The democratization of access to political power was accompanied by a deeper and more far-reaching democratization of social relations. Indeed Alexis de Tocqueville, whose *Democracy in America* provides one of the earliest and most influential analyses of this phenomenon, argued that democracy does not consist in a particular distribution of political power or a particular set of political institutions, but rather in what he calls the "equality of conditions" that obtains in a given society; the habits of mind and norms of behavior that define an egalitarian way of life. This kind of equality, he writes, "extends far beyond political mores and laws, exercising dominion over civil society as much as government; it creates opinions, gives birth to feelings, suggest customs, and modifies whatever it does not create." Its defining feature is a certain uniformity of beliefs, desires, and aspirations, and Tocqueville warns that left to its own devices its natural endpoint is a kind of complacent mediocrity, overseen and enforced by the new and insidious power of public opinion. Nevertheless – and although he was an aristocrat by birth – Tocqueville did not call for a return to the beliefs and practices of the *ancien régime*; instead he insisted, rather presciently, that the social forces that he saw at work in Jacksonian America were irreversible. "[T]he gradual progress of equality," he argues,

is something fated ... it is universal and permanent, it is daily passing beyond human control, and every event and every man helps it along. Is it wise to suppose that a movement which has been so long in train could be halted by one generation? Does anyone imagine that democracy, which has destroyed the feudal system and vanquished kings, will fall back before the middle classes and the rich? Will it stop now, when it has grown so strong and its adversaries so weak?[12]

However prescient Tocqueville's analysis may have been, it might seem odd and even perverse to say that equality is the defining feature of modern social life. After all, the nineteenth century also saw the rise of industrial capitalism, and with it the advent of significant economic *in*equalities which had, and continue to have, an enormous impact on the shape of social relations and the distribution of political power. The Industrial Revolution was of course made possible in part by the loosening of long-standing legal and customary restrictions on production and trade, and the transformation of land and other traditional markers of social status into commodities. At first blush this development seemed to many people – as it still seems to many people today – like a great victory for equality: where economic opportunity once depended almost entirely on the social position into which one was born, it now lay open to anyone who was alert and energetic enough to pursue it. It soon became clear, however, that the economies of scale and extensive division of labor that were (and are) the engines of prosperity in a commercial society were creating a new class of industrialists whose wealth and power were just as threatening to the ideal of self-government as the old landed aristocracy, and a new class of wage laborers whose degradation and vulnerability made them just as unfit for self-government as their rustic forebears. As early as 1830 Tocqueville saw the first signs of what he called

[12] Alexis de Tocqueville, *Democracy in America* (1835/1840), ed. J. P. Mayer, trans. George Lawrence (New York: Harper & Row, 1966), pp. 9, 12 (author's introduction).

a "manufacturing aristocracy" in the United States; "a constant tendency for very rich and well-educated men to devote their wealth and knowledge to manufactures ... by opening large establishments with a strict division of labor" in which "the workman becomes weaker, more limited, and more dependent." Under such conditions, he points out, workers "soon develop habits of body and mind which render them unsuited to any other work," and thus become trapped in a "vicious circle from which they cannot escape."[13]

Tocqueville describes this "state of dependence and poverty" as "an exception, a monstrosity, within the general social condition" of American democracy as he found it, but he warns his readers that "the friends of democracy should keep their eyes anxiously fixed in that direction. For if ever again permanent inequality of conditions and aristocracy make their way again into the world, it will have been by that door that they entered."[14] Here again his warning was a prescient one: by the end of the nineteenth century the majority of workers were in exactly the "monstrous" position that he describes. Where once it had been possible to view dependence on an employer as a temporary stage in a person's career, and thus as an exceptional feature of an economic system, wage labor was now a basic fact of economic life – as of course it still is today. Nineteenth-century political thinkers and actors therefore struggled, as we still struggle, to reconcile the existence of a hierarchical economic system with a commitment to social and political equality. At first blush the choice seemed to lie between two unattractive options: a corrupt form of mass democracy in which many citizens lack the skills, resources, and independence that are necessary for effective political participation, or a plutocratic republic in which both political and economic power are concentrated in the hands of the new industrialist class. If the machine-driven "spoils system" of the American Gilded Age was the paradigmatic example of the former approach, the oligarchical July Monarchy in France was the paradigmatic example of the latter.

The signal achievement of the nineteenth century liberals was to identify, and ultimately to enact, a workable alternative to these two systems;

---

[13] Ibid., pp. 556, 584 (vol. 2, part 2, chapter 20; vol. 2, part 3, chapter 7). Tocqueville's comments about the pernicious effects of the division of labor closely echo Adam Smith's observation that "[t]he man whose whole life is spent in performing a few simple operations ... generally becomes as stupid and ignorant as is possible for a human creature to become": Adam Smith, *An Inquiry into the Nature and Causes of the Wealth of Nations* (Oxford: Clarendon Press, 1979 [1776]), V.i.f.50.

[14] Tocqueville, *Democracy in America*, pp. 557, 558 (vol. 2, part 2, chapter 20).

one that still defines the basic terms of liberal politics today. As they saw it, the challenge that they faced had two distinct dimensions. First, the democratization of social and political relations raised the new and pressing question of how to limit the power of a state that can plausibly claim to act in the name of the people taken as a whole, and that has the administrative capacity to project its authority into the daily lives of ordinary citizens. Closely related, and even more confounding, was the question of how to prevent the overbearing weight of public opinion – which now had the organs of mass communication at its disposal – from stifling individual creativity and initiative. Although they were sometimes reluctant democratizers, liberals did not respond to this challenge by trying to roll back the rise of social and political equality, as did many of their illiberal contemporaries. Indeed, liberal thinkers like Tocqueville and Mill played a key role in making the case for democracy – setting aside, again, the (imponderable) question of what weight principled arguments like theirs actually held in the heat of political debate. However, their misgivings about unchecked social and political power led them to insist on the importance of establishing a domain of nonresponsible conduct within which individuals can do as they please without having to answer to the authority of the state or of their fellow citizens. In other words, they saw market freedom as an essential complement to republican freedom in an egalitarian society.

Liberals were slower to recognize and respond to the second challenge: the fact that industrial capitalism – and thus market freedom itself – also poses a profound *threat* to republican freedom. As Tocqueville's analysis suggests, this is partly because the social effects of industrialization were slower to be felt (especially in intellectual circles) than those of mass democracy. More importantly, the early liberals were – as many liberals still are – enthusiastic capitalists, not least because the transition from a feudal to a commercial economy represented an undeniable advance from the standpoint both of market and of republican freedom. A belief in the importance of economic independence and the possibility of upward mobility has always played a central role in liberal thought, both as an aspirational ideal and as a way of justifying existing inequalities. However, by the second half of the nineteenth century the claim that self-sufficiency and self-advancement could be achieved purely through individual effort began to seem increasingly far-fetched, and liberals were obliged to consider whether it is possible to reconcile the ideal of individual flourishing and democratic self-government with the reality of widespread economic dependence and vulnerability. The program of action that they arrived at – empowering workers and consumers against employers and corporations, expanding access to education and health care, creating a robust social "safety net," and so on – gave the state a much more active role to play in promoting individual freedom. When combined with the ongoing and equally fundamental liberal commitment to the importance of guaranteeing a domain of nonresponsible conduct, it placed the tension between republican and market freedom firmly at the center of liberal politics.

4.3 EQUALITY AND MARKET FREEDOM: THE "CLASSICAL" LIBERALS

Benjamin Constant, who along with his collaborator and companion Germaine de Staël was possibly the first French-speaking writer to use the word "*liberal*" (as an adjective) to describe his own political position,[15] was also among the first to argue that the French Revolution and its aftermath revealed the need for a fundamental rethinking of the meaning of freedom.[16] Constant's position on this question – and the nature of his innovation – is often misunderstood. In particular, his famous distinction between "ancient" and "modern" liberty cannot be reduced, as it sometimes has been, to the distinction that was later drawn between "positive" and "negative" liberty,[17] nor does it correspond to the distinction between republican and market freedom that I have developed here. Rather, "modern" liberty as Constant defines it has three distinct elements, and the first and third of these – "the right to be subjected only

---

[15] See K. Steven Vincent, *Benjamin Constant and the Birth of French Liberalism* (New York: Palgrave Macmillan, 2011), p. 76 and note; Vincent dates their first use of the term to 1795.

[16] Edmund Burke's *Reflections on the Revolution in France* (1790) – which, it is often forgotten, predated the regicide and the Terror – is more concerned with preserving liberty in its traditional republican sense than with rethinking its meaning. The same can be said, *mutatis mutandis*, of Thomas Paine's *The Rights of Man* (1791) – or, for that matter (as Burke emphasized) of the American Revolutionaries.

[17] Philip Pettit, for example, has argued that "Constant's modern liberty is [Isaiah] Berlin's negative liberty, and his ancient liberty ... is the most prominent variety of Berlin's positive conception": Philip Pettit, *Republicanism: A Theory of Freedom and Government* (2nd ed., New York: Oxford University Press, 1999 [1997]), p. 18; he later refers to this as the "Berlin-Constant framework," p. 27. Rawls also associates Constant's position with Berlin's; see John Rawls, *A Theory of Justice* (2nd ed., Cambridge, MA: Harvard University Press, 1999 [1971]), pp. 176–7 (§32). Cf. Isaiah Berlin, "Two Concepts of Liberty" (1958/1969), in *Liberty*, ed. Henry Hardy (New York: Oxford University Press, 2002), esp. pp. 209–11.

Equality and Market Freedom: The "Classical" Liberals 135

to the laws, and to be neither arrested, detained, put to death or maltreated in any way by the arbitrary will of one or more individuals," and the "right to exercise some influence over the administration of government" – have a distinctly republican flavor. Constant's pioneering defense of liberalism is best understood as an effort to come to terms with the tension between these republican aspects of "modern" liberty and its second and more distinctive aspect; what I have called market freedom, and what he calls "individual" or "civil" liberty:

the right of everyone to express their opinion, choose a profession and practice it, to dispose of property and even to abuse it; to come and go without permission, and without having to account for their motives or undertakings ... to associate with other individuals, or to profess the religion which they and their associates prefer, or even simply to occupy their days or hours in a way which is most compatible with their inclinations or whims.[18]

Constant responds to the tension between political and individual liberty by distinguishing the question of how political power is *constituted* from the question of how it is *limited*; a distinction which, he argues, is "of the greatest importance" and yet "has been overlooked by writers of all parties."[19] Although his concern to limit political power leads him to condemn Rousseau's defense of absolute popular sovereignty in the strongest terms,[20] his concern for the proper constitution of political power leads him to endorse Rousseau's famous claim that all legitimate political authority is derived from the "general will"; that is, from the people taken as a whole. "All authority which does not issue from the general will is undoubtedly illegitimate," he argues, but "authority which issues from the general will is not legitimate merely by virtue of this, whatever its extent may be and whatever objects it is exercised over. The first of these principles is the most salutary truth, the second the most

---

[18] Benjamin Constant, "The Liberty of the Ancients Compared with That of the Moderns" (1819), in *Political Writings*, ed. and trans. Biancamaria Fontana (New York: Cambridge University Press, 1988), pp. 310–11.

[19] Benjamin Constant, *Principles of Politics Applicable to All Governments* (1810), ed. Etienne Hofmann, trans. Dennis O'Keeffe (Indianapolis: Liberty Fund, 2003), p. 5 (book 1, chapter 1).

[20] "Rousseau's theory that political power is unlimited ... is the theory we must hold responsible for most of the difficulties the establishment of freedom has encountered among various nations, for most of the abuses which worm their way into all governments of whatever type, and indeed for most of the crimes which civil strife and political upheaval drag in their wake. It was just this theory which inspired our Revolution and those horrors for which liberty for all was at once the pretext and the victim": ibid., p. 13 (book 1, chapter 3).

dangerous of errors. The former is the basis of all freedom, the latter the justification of all despotism." This tension between popular sovereignty and individual liberty gives rise to the motivating problem of Constant's political thought: the fact (as he sees it) that the enjoyment of individual liberty is even more precarious under a popular regime than under a traditional despotism. "What no tyrant would dare to do in his own name," he argues, popular governments "legitimate by the unlimited extension of boundless social authority. They seek the enlargement of the powers they need, from the very owner of social authority, that is, the people, whose omnipotence is there only to justify their encroachments."[21]

Constant devoted a great deal of energy to the traditional republican project of limiting political power through properly designed institutions, most notably by writing the Napoleonic Charter of 1815 – the so-called Benjamine – a proposal for a constitutional monarchy with a popularly elected Chamber of Representatives that was ratified by plebiscite and then quickly rendered moot by Napoleon's final defeat at Waterloo.[22] However, he was acutely aware that political accountability depends on public engagement, and that this engagement is hard to secure under modern conditions: "the people who, in order to enjoy the liberty which suits them, resort to the representative system, must exercise an active and constant surveillance over their representatives," he points out, but in modern societies "each individual, occupied with his speculations, his enterprises, the pleasures he obtains or hopes for, does not wish to be distracted from them other than momentarily, and as little as possible."[23] The practical aim of the famous lecture on ancient and modern liberty (much of which was drawn from earlier writings[24]) is thus not to demonstrate the infeasibility of reviving "ancient" liberty – Constant takes his audience to be agreed on that point – but rather to call attention to the instability of its "modern" counterpart. "The danger of modern liberty,"

---

[21] Ibid., pp. 31, 19 (book 2, chapter 1; book 1, chapter 6), corrected to translate *autorité social* as "social" instead of "political" authority.
[22] Constant included a detailed defense of the Charter – a kind of Napoleonic *Federalist Papers* – in the 1815 edition of the *Principles of Politics*; see Constant, *Political Writings*, pp. 183–257.
[23] Constant, "Ancient and Modern Liberty," pp. 326, 315.
[24] See, for example, Constant, *Principles of Politics*, book 16 *passim* and *The Spirit of Conquest and Usurpation and Their Relation to European Civilization* (1814), part 1, chapter 2 and part 2, chapters 6–7, 18 (*Political Writings*, pp. 53–5, 102–4, 105–8, 140–1), each of which contains extended passages that are included verbatim or nearly so in the 1819 lecture.

he argues, "is that, absorbed in the enjoyment of our private independence, and in the pursuit of our particular interests, we should surrender our right to share in political power too easily." The result, he warns, would be the loss not only of republican freedom, but of individual liberty itself: "Could we be made happy by diversions," he asks rhetorically, "if these diversions were without guarantees? And where should we find guarantees, without political liberty?"[25]

It is here that the distinctively liberal aspects of Constant's political thought come to the fore: he insists that "we [moderns] have means to defend [individual liberty] which the ancients did not"; means that do not depend on a traditional republican appeal to virtuous citizenship or accountable institutions, but rather on the uncoordinated actions of private individuals – that is, on the exercise of individual liberty itself. The most notable such means is the operation of commerce, which he describes as the "universal tendency" of modern societies – "the true life of nations" – having replaced war as the primary means of "getting what one wants." Commerce, Constant points out, "confers a new quality on property, circulation," which "makes the action of arbitrary power easier to elude" and "places authority itself in a position of dependence," since "to obtain the favours of wealth one must serve it." According to this line of argument modern governments are deterred from acting arbitrarily by the threat of spontaneous resistance by "private" citizens; resistance that is motivated not by any concern for the common good but simply by a jealousy for their own property, and that consists not in open rebellion but rather in a silent – albeit politically potent – withdrawal of resources. Constant concludes that whereas "governments in antiquity were necessarily stronger than individuals," "[i]ndividuals are today stronger than their governments": "thanks to trade, individuals shape their own futures, despite events. They move their assets far away; governments cannot penetrate their transactions; they take along with them all the comforts of private life."[26]

Although it is only mentioned in passing in the lecture on ancient and modern liberty,[27] Constant identifies a second and even more potent "modern" means of preventing the abuse of political power; one that also depends on the uncoordinated actions of private individuals.

---

[25] Constant, "Ancient and Modern Liberty," p. 326.
[26] Ibid., pp. 313–14, 324–5; Constant, *Principles of Politics*, p. 357 (book 16, chapter 4). We may detect an allusion in the last passage to Constant's own peripatetic life.
[27] See in particular Constant, "Ancient and Modern Liberty," p. 322.

Modern liberty, he argues, is "guaranteed first of all by the same force which upholds all recognized truths, that is, by public opinion. Afterward we can get busy with guaranteeing [it] in a more fixed way, via the specific organization of political powers. But having obtained and consolidated the first guarantee will always be a great good."[28] As in the case of commerce, this means of preserving liberty depends on the existence of a robust public sphere in which information circulates freely: "if you allow public opinion free expression," he argues, "you will have no difficulty in knowing its feelings ... if authority will only remain silent, the individuals will speak up, the clash of ideas will generate enlightenment, and it will soon be impossible to mistake the general feeling." Above all, he insists, the liberty of the press – an "infallible" means of spreading information and ideas – must be respected: it is a "freedom which is as necessary to governments as it is to the people ... the violation of which, in this respect, is a crime against the state." Despite this note of warning, Constant comes to the rather optimistic conclusion that public opinion, like commerce, is ultimately beyond the power of the would-be modern despot: it "cannot be stifled," he insists; "blood flows but public opinion remains afloat, charges once more and triumphs. The more it is repressed, the more terrible it becomes; it penetrates minds with the air they breathe; it becomes everyone's habitual sentiment, everyone's obsessive conviction."[29]

Tocqueville offers a much more pessimistic analysis of the relationship between freedom, equality, and public opinion. As we have already seen, he associates democracy with the "equality of conditions" that obtains in a society, not with a particular set of political institutions. This emphasis on social conditions makes it possible for him to speak without contradiction of "democratic despotism"; that is, of a kind of domination that is exercised over a democratic society but not (necessarily) by a democratic government. The fear of democratic despotism defines the central aim of *Democracy in America*: to "educate" democracy in such a way that it is compatible with the enjoyment of freedom. Tocqueville emphasizes that these two values are not necessarily incompatible; indeed, he argues that "[t]he completest possible form for equality on this earth" would be one in which "all the citizens take a part in the government and ... each of them has an equal right to do so. Then no man is different from his fellows [equality], and nobody can wield tyrannical power [freedom]." However,

---

[28] Constant, *Principles of Politics*, p. 38 (book 2, chapter 4).
[29] Constant, *Spirit of Conquest and Usurpation*, pp. 150, 139.

he also emphasizes that democracy and freedom are not easily combined: "[O]f all forms of society," he argues "the one where aristocracy does not and cannot exist is just the one which will have the most difficulty escaping absolute government for long." Democratic people "want equality in freedom," he concludes, but "if they cannot have that, they still want equality in slavery."[30]

Tocqueville identifies two threats in particular that democracy poses to freedom. On the one hand, the rise of social equality gives the majority a kind of "omnipotence": "When once its mind is made up on any question," he argues, "there are, so to say, no obstacles which can retard, much less halt, its progress and give it time to hear the wails of those it crushes as it passes." The fear of unchecked power is of course a traditional republican concern; as Tocqueville puts it, when "the right and capacity to do all [is] given to any authority whatsoever, whether it be called people or king, democracy or aristocracy ... the germ of tyranny is there." However, this fear takes on a new and more sinister form in a modern democracy because the power of the majority is not just the power to imprison or kill, but also and more importantly to socialize and to ostracize. It therefore "acts as much upon the will as upon behavior and at the same moment prevents both the act and the desire to do it." "Under the absolute government of a single man," Tocqueville writes, "despotism, to reach the soul, clumsily struck at the body, and the soul, escaping from such blows, rose gloriously above it; but in democratic republics that is not at all how tyranny behaves; it leaves the body alone and goes straight for the soul." He draws the striking conclusion that there is "no country in which, generally speaking, there is less independence of mind and true freedom of discussion than in America."[31]

On the other hand, the corollary of the omnipotence of the majority is the relative impotence of the individual. Like Constant, Tocqueville finds that "in times of democracy private life is so active and agitated, so full of desires and labor, that each individual has scarcely any leisure or time left for political life." Moreover, where in aristocratic societies there is "a small number of very rich and powerful men, each of whom can carry out great undertakings on his own," Tocqueville points out that "among democratic peoples all the citizens are independent and weak," and "can do hardly anything for themselves." The result is what he calls "individualism": "a calm and considered feeling which disposes each citizen to

---

[30] Tocqueville, *Democracy in America*, pp. 503, 506 (vol. 2, part 2, chapter 1).
[31] Ibid., pp. 248, 252, 254–5 (vol. 1, part 2, chapter 7).

isolate himself from the mass of his fellows and withdraw into the circle of family and friends ... leav[ing] the greater society to look after itself."[32] Needless to say – and here again Constant is in agreement – this kind of individualism poses a threat to freedom; as Tocqueville puts it, "[d]espotism, by its very nature suspicious, sees the isolation of men as the best guarantee of its own permanence" and so "is particularly to be feared in ages of democracy." Taken together, these concerns lead him to warn his readers about the "novel" kind of despotism to which democratic societies are vulnerable, characterized on the one hand by "an innumerable multitude of men, alike and equal, constantly circling around in pursuit of the petty and banal pleasures with which they glut their souls," and on the other hand by "an immense protective power which alone is responsible for securing their enjoyment and watching over their fate ... absolute, thoughtful of detail, orderly, provident, and gentle."[33]

Tocqueville calls attention throughout *Democracy in America* to a variety of strategies that the Americans of his day had hit upon to forestall the rise of democratic despotism. Some of these fit neatly within the traditional republican project of designing accountable and responsive political institutions: for example, he praises the federal system for preventing the centralization of power and giving citizens more opportunities to get involved in public life, and highlights the crucial role that an independent judiciary plays in guaranteeing the rule of law.[34] Like Constant, however, Tocqueville gives special attention to the freedom-promoting effects of conduct that takes place outside the bounds of politics as traditionally conceived. His most influential argument along these lines[35] is his analysis of the vital role of voluntary associations, which "take the place of the powerful private persons whom equality of conditions has eliminated," and thereby counteract each of the three

---

[32] Ibid., pp. 671 (vol. 2, part 4, chapter 3), 514 (vol. 2, part 2, chapter 5), 506 (vol. 2, part 2, chapter 2). Other factors that contribute to democratic "individualism" include the absence of fixed authority relations and the instability of individual fortunes: ibid., pp. 507–8 (vol. 2, part 2, chapter 2).

[33] Ibid., pp. 509–10 (vol. 2, part 2, chapter 4), 691–2 (vol. 2, part 4, chapter 6).

[34] On federalism see ibid., vol. 1, part 1, chapter 5, vol. 1, part 2, chapter 8, and vol. 2, part 2, chapter 4; on judicial independence see ibid., vol. 1, part 2, chapter 8, and see also the summary discussion at pp. 696–9 (vol. 2, part 4, chapter 7).

[35] Other important lines of argument include his discussion of the freedom-promoting effects of religious belief and practice – which depend, in his view, on religious disestablishment – and his emphasis (echoed, as we have seen, by Constant) on the importance of protecting the freedom of the press. On the former point see ibid., vol. 1, part 2, chapter 9; vol. 2, part 1, chapter 5; on the latter see ibid., vol. 1, part 2, chapter 3; vol. 2, part 2, chapter 6; and the summary discussion at pp. 697–8 (vol. 2, part 4, chapter 7).

Equality and Market Freedom: The "Classical" Liberals 141

democratic pathologies that he identifies. First and most obviously, associations counteract individualism by cultivating a sense of efficacy in their members and by demonstrating the value of cooperation to others.[36] Second, they counteract conformism by creating communities of belief and practice that are distinct from the "omnipotent" majority, and whose size and influence help to give contrarians the courage of their convictions.[37] And third, they counteract democratic despotism by dispersing power away from the state and creating potential sites of resistance.[38] Needless to say, these benefits can only be enjoyed if people are allowed to organize as they see fit, even (within limits) when allowing them to do so poses a threat to public order.[39] "If men are to remain civilized or become civilized," Tocqueville concludes, "the art of association must develop and improve among them at the same speed as equality of conditions spreads."[40]

The most influential modern discussion of the tension between freedom and equality is found in the political writings of John Stuart Mill, who was of course the pivotal liberal thinker of the nineteenth century. Mill was a great admirer of Constant; he called his death in 1830 "a misfortune to the world" and declared that "France, since the first revolution, has not produced his equal."[41] Like Constant, Mill believed that legitimate political authority ultimately rests with the people, but should be exercised by their representatives,[42] and like Constant he insisted that popular sovereignty is a necessary, but not a sufficient, condition for the enjoyment of individual

---

[36] "It is clear that unless each citizen learned to combine with his fellows to preserve his freedom at a time when he individually is becoming weaker and so less able in isolation to defend it, tyranny would be bound to increase with equality": ibid., p. 513 (vol. 2, part 2, chapter 5).

[37] "[T]hey are no longer isolated individuals, but a power conspicuous from the distance [sic] whose actions serve as an example; when [an association] speaks, men listen": ibid., p. 516 (vol. 2, part 2, chapter 5).

[38] "An association ... is an educated and powerful body of citizens which cannot be twisted to any man's will or quietly trodden down, and by defending its private interests against the encroachments of power, it saves the common liberties": ibid., p. 679 (vol. 2, part 4, chapter 7).

[39] "By the use of a dangerous liberty, the Americans learn the art of rendering the dangers of freedom less formidable": ibid., p. 524 (vol. 2, part 2, chapter 7).

[40] Ibid., p. 517 (vol. 2, part 2, chapter 5).

[41] John Stuart Mill, "French News [7]" (1830), in *Collected Works*, ed. J. M. Robson (Toronto: University of Toronto Press, 1963–91), vol. 22, p. 214.

[42] "[N]othing less can be ultimately desirable, than the admission of all to a share in the sovereign power of the state. But since all cannot, in a community exceeding a single small town, participate personally in any but some very minor portions of the public business, it follows that the ideal type of a perfect government must be representative": Mill,

liberty.[43] Mill's admiration for Tocqueville was even greater; he hailed *Democracy in America* on its appearance as "the beginning of a new era in the scientific study of politics," and later wrote that "[the] shifting of my political ideal from pure democracy, as commonly understood by its partisans, to the modified form of it, which is set forth in my *Considerations on Representative Government* ... dates its commencement from my reading, or rather study," of that book.[44] It is not surprising to find, then, that *On Liberty*, like *Democracy in America*, centers on the problem of resisting what Mill calls "the tyranny of the prevailing opinion and feeling" in a democratic society; "a social tyranny more formidable than many kinds of political oppression, since, though not usually upheld by such extreme penalties, it leaves fewer means of escape, penetrating much more deeply into the details of life, and enslaving the soul itself." Left to its own devices, Mill warns, a democratic society will "fetter the development, and, if possible, prevent the formation, of any individuality not in harmony with its ways, and compel all characters to fashion themselves upon the model of its own."[45]

What makes Mill's response to this challenge distinctive is the appeal that it makes to social progress: where Constant treats individual liberty as the prized possession of modern peoples, and Tocqueville sees it as something that can forestall (at least for a time) the rise of democratic despotism, Mill holds that a proper regard for individual liberty, if only a "strong barrier of moral conviction" can be raised on its behalf, will set into motion a virtuous cycle in which human capacities are indefinitely expanded over time.[46] Thus – to use the typology that we developed in Chapter 3 – where

---

Considerations on Representative Government (1861), *Collected Works*, vol. 19, p. 412 (chapter 3).

[43] "[T]he people ... *may* desire to oppress a part of their number: and precautions are as much needed against this as against any other abuse of power. The limitation, therefore, of the power of government over individuals loses none of its importance when the holders of power are regularly accountable to the community": Mill, *On Liberty* (1859), *Collected Works*, vol. 18, p. 219 (chapter 1, original emphasis).

[44] Mill, "De Tocqueville on Democracy in America (II)" (1840), *Collected Works*, vol. 18, p. 156; Mill, *Autobiography* (1873), *Collected Works*, vol. 1, p. 199 (chapter 6).

[45] Mill, *On Liberty*, pp. 219–20 (chapter 1).

[46] Ibid., p. 227 (chapter 1). Mill emphasizes that the expansion of human capacities does not necessarily entail an expansion of material wealth or consumption: "a stationary condition of capital and population," he argues, "implies no stationary state of human improvement. There would be as much scope as ever for all kinds of mental culture, and moral and social progress; as much room for improving the Art of Living, and much more likelihood of its being improved, when minds ceased to be engrossed by the art of getting on": Mill, *Principles of Political Economy, with Some of Their Applications to Social Philosophy* (1848), *Collected Works*, vols. 2–3, p. 756 (book 4, chapter 6).

Constant is a paragon of individualist liberalism, and Tocqueville of tragic liberalism, Mill is the paradigmatic progressive liberal: "the one indispensable merit of a government," he argues, "is that its operation on the people is favorable, or not unfavorable, to the next step which it is necessary for them to take in order to raise themselves to a higher level."[47] Despite the rather ominous-sounding reference to "operation on the people," Mill contends that modern governments often best serve the cause of progress through inaction; that is, by granting citizens an extensive domain of individual liberty: "The perfection both of social arrangements and of practical morality," he argues in the *Principles of Political Economy*, "would be, to secure to all persons complete independence and freedom of action, subject to no restriction but that of not doing injury to others" – or, as he more famously puts it in *On Liberty*, "the only purpose for which power can be rightfully exercised over any member of a civilized community, against his will, is to prevent harm to others."[48]

The central aim of *On Liberty*, then, is to persuade the reader that "[m]ankind are greater gainers by suffering each other to live as seems good to themselves, than by compelling each to live as seems good to the rest."[49] Like Tocqueville, and in sharp contrast to Constant, Mill takes himself to be working against the grain of public opinion in pursuing this line of argument. In a modern democracy, he argues, "[t]he only power deserving the name is that of masses … that is to say, [of] collective mediocrity," and "masses" are no great lovers of liberty, at least insofar as its exercise challenges the status quo: "The majority, being satisfied with the ways of mankind as they now are (for it is they who make them what they are) cannot comprehend why those ways should not be good enough for everybody." Life in a genuinely free society, by contrast, is fundamentally open-ended and unpredictable, and so its members will often be, if not offended, then at least bewildered by one another: "Originality is the one thing," he points out, "which unoriginal minds cannot feel the use of." Indeed, Mill suggests that the diversity of beliefs and ways of life that European *societies* exhibit, and the progress that they have achieved as a result, has come about despite the best efforts of European *people*:

although at every period those who travelled in different paths have been intolerant of one another, and each would have thought it an excellent thing if all the rest

---

[47] Mill, *Considerations on Representative Government*, p. 394 (chapter 2).
[48] Mill, *Principles of Political Economy*, pp. 208–9 (book 2, chapter 1); Mill, *On Liberty*, p. 223 (chapter 1).
[49] Mill, *On Liberty*, p. 226 (chapter 1).

could have been compelled to travel his road, their attempts to thwart each other's development have rarely had any permanent success, and each has in time endured to receive the good which the others have offered.[50]

Thus while Mill rests his defense of liberty on an appeal to utility, he admits that the state of continual social ferment that the exercise of liberty brings about is likely to make many people unhappy, at least in the short run. This is presumably why he does not appeal to utility understood as the satisfaction of actually existing desires, but rather "in the largest sense, grounded on the permanent interests of man as a progressive being."[51] Mill's liberalism therefore depends, more explicitly than either Constant's or Tocqueville's, on the willingness of public officials and ordinary citizens to tolerate behavior that they believe to be misguided or wrong; "to see that it is good there should be differences, even though not for the better, even though, as it may appear to them, some should be for the worse." However, the mere toleration of differences is not enough for Mill; like Tocqueville he recognizes that "the very idea of resisting the will of the public" is hard to awaken in a democratic society, and that the existence of free-thinking and free-acting individuals therefore cannot be taken for granted. Where Tocqueville focuses on collective solutions to this problem – on the experience and self-confidence that we can gain by participating in voluntary associations – Mill looks instead to the influence of "exceptional" individuals. He and Tocqueville nevertheless agree in thinking that it is less important *how* people go about resisting the "despotism of custom" than that they do: "In other times," Mill argues, "there was no advantage in their doing so, unless they acted not only differently, but better. In this age, the mere example of nonconformity, the mere refusal to bend the knee to custom, is itself a service."[52]

---

[50] Ibid., pp. 268, 261, 268, 274 (chapter 3). Mill borrows this analysis of European history from the second lecture of François Guizot's *Histoire générale de la civilisation en Europe* (1828); see in particular the discussion in Mill, "De Tocqueville on Democracy in America (II)," p. 197, where Guizot is explicitly cited.

[51] Mill, *On Liberty*, p. 224 (chapter 1). This appreciation of the destabilizing effects of free choice is what distinguishes Mill's treatment of liberty most sharply from that of his teacher Jeremy Bentham. As Douglas Long remarks, "[t]he indeterminate, open-ended quality of the libertarian view of man was alien to Bentham. He sought rather the perfection of a neo-Newtonian social physics" in which "[t]he realm of liberty is ... not a subjective, boundless world of potentiality, but a circumscribed space reserved for the use of some particular agent as a means to the omnipresent end of happiness": Douglas G. Long, *Bentham on Liberty: Jeremy Bentham's Idea of Liberty in Relation to His Utilitarianism* (Toronto: University of Toronto Press, 1977), pp. 164, 101.

[52] Mill, *On Liberty*, pp. 275, 269 (chapter 3).

In addition to this open-ended appeal to nonconformity, Mill offers a second, independent line of argument in favor of individual liberty; one that "rests on grounds different from, though equally solid with," the position that he defends in the main body of *On Liberty*. This is of course his defense of the "*laisser-faire* principle" in economics. Here the connection to utility is more straightforward: Mill holds that "the cheapness and the good quality of commodities are most effectually provided for by leaving the producers and sellers perfectly free, under the sole check of equal freedom to the buyers for supplying themselves elsewhere." While some people are indeed harmed by economic competition, and while economic regulations therefore "affect only that part of conduct which society is competent to restrain," such regulations, he insists, "do not really produce the results which it is desired to produce by them": rather "the general prosperity attains a greater height, and is more widely diffused, in proportion to the amount and variety of the personal energies enlisted in promoting it."[53] Mill seems to expect this line of argument to find better favor with his readers than his defense of eccentricity – he remarks that "[t]he spontaneity and unfettered action of the individual, and of voluntary association, are, *as all know*, the life of modern political economy"[54] – but like Adam Smith, who he follows closely on this point, he does not treat prosperity as an end in itself. On the contrary, the claim in the final chapter of the *Principles of Political Economy* that "*[l]aisser-faire* ... should be the general practice," and that "every departure from it, unless required by some great good, is a certain evil," comes at the end of a discussion that ranges well beyond economic matters to anticipate the broader appeal to personal development and social progress that is laid out in *On Liberty*.[55]

Despite their differences in emphasis and approach, Constant, Tocqueville, and Mill share three beliefs which, taken together, define their political position as a liberal one. First, they agree in thinking that the distinguishing feature of their time and place is the advent of social and political equality. As we have seen, for Constant this is a normative claim (borrowed from Rousseau) about the proper grounds of political authority in the wake of the French Revolution, for Tocqueville it is an empirical claim about the inevitable trajectory of European history, and for Mill it is

---

[53] Ibid., p. 293 (chapter 5); Mill, *Considerations on Representative Government*, p. 404 (chapter 3).
[54] Mill, "Centralisation" (1862), *Collected Works*, vol. 19, p. 583 (emphasis added).
[55] Mill, *Principles of Political Economy*, p. 945 (book 5, chapter 11).

a developmental claim about the stage of progress that European societies have reached. Whatever the underlying reason, the practical implication is that government is no longer the special province of an hereditary class or virtuous elite: for better or worse – and liberals have sometimes been, like Tocqueville, ambivalent democrats – the rights and responsibilities of citizenship now belong, at least in principle, to all (male) citizens.[56] Second, these thinkers agree in thinking that the new egalitarianism makes social and political power both harder to control and harder to avoid. On the one hand, the admission to citizenship of people who have many other demands on their time and attention, and whose voice is, as a result of democratization, greatly diluted, gives rise to a pervasive sense of political disengagement and impotence. On the other hand, the identification of political power with the popular will, and the replacement of traditional authority relations with the more amorphous authority of public opinion, makes it tempting to treat the power of the state as unlimited, and to use that power to secure conformity with the implicit or explicit wishes of the majority or those who claim to speak for it.

Third, and most importantly for our purposes, these thinkers agree in thinking that the proper response to these developments is neither to turn away from democracy nor to embrace unlimited popular sovereignty, but rather to carve out a domain of conduct within which people are not responsible to the state or to each other for what they do; in which they enjoy market freedom in the broad sense in which I have defined that term. The key move here is not the assertion of individual liberty against public power, which is of course a perennial concern, but rather the claim that the existence of a domain of unregulated conduct in which people make choices that have unpredictable and potentially harmful consequences is an essential complement to democratic self-government. As we have seen, this line of argument takes a number of different forms both within and between the political writings of Constant, Tocqueville, and Mill, just as it takes a number of different forms among their contemporaries and among later liberal thinkers. As we saw in Chapter 3, the liberal case for market freedom consists of an overlapping set of claims about the importance of respecting individual sovereignty, preventing the concentration of political power, advancing material prosperity, promoting social progress, creating the conditions for personal development, and so on. What

---

[56] Mill was of course a pioneering defender of the view that full citizenship should also be extended to women, an ideal that was not widely realized until nearly half a century after his death.

binds these claims together – what makes them both distinctive and groundbreaking – is their willingness to treat a certain renunciation of collective control and a certain experience of mutual incomprehension as central and desirable features of life in a free society.

4.4 EQUALITY AND REPUBLICAN FREEDOM: THE "NEW" LIBERALS

Liberal enthusiasm for market freedom in the narrow economic sense reached its peak in the middle decades of the nineteenth century and was strong enough during that period that liberalism is still identified in some quarters – especially on the European continent – with the doctrine of *laissez-faire*. It is important to keep in mind, however, that even the "classical" liberals were not united on this point; as Helena Rosenblatt points out, "it would be wrong to conclude that all mid-nineteenth century liberal thinkers believed in laissez-faire or that liberal governments pursued strictly laissez-faire policies" because "[t]here simply was no unified liberal position on economics."[57] Even liberals who did embrace *laissez-faire* treated it more as a rule of thumb than as a piece of economic or moral dogma: François Guizot describes it as "one of those vague axioms, true or false depending how one uses it,"[58] and Mill begins the final chapter of his *Principles of Political Economy* by admitting that the problem of defining the limits of government interference in the market "does not, as I conceive, admit of any universal solution."[59] Indeed, Mill's open-mindedness on the question of the proper extent of economic regulation – and his flexibility on the question of property rights[60] – proved to be so influential that Ludwig von Mises, one of the leading twentieth-century defenders of *laissez-faire*, named him as "the originator of the thoughtless confounding of liberal and socialist ideas that led to the decline of English liberalism": "In comparison with Mill," he concluded, "all other socialist writers – even Marx, Engels, and Lassalle – are scarcely of any importance."[61]

---

[57] Rosenblatt, *Lost History of Liberalism*, p. 105.
[58] François Guizot, *Des moyens de gouvernement et d'opposition dans l'état actuel de la France* (Paris: Librairie Française de L'Advocat, 1821), pp. 172–3, my translation.
[59] Mill, *Principles of Political Economy*, pp. 945, 937 (book 5, chapter 11).
[60] See especially the discussion in ibid., book 2, chapters 1–2.
[61] Ludwig von Mises, *Liberalism: The Classic Tradition*, trans. Ralph Raico (Indianapolis: Liberty Fund, 2005 [1927]), pp. 153–4. For a detailed examination of Mill's credentials as a socialist thinker, and of the relationship between his socialism and his liberalism, see

We have seen that the classical liberals were committed to the enjoyment not only of market but also of republican freedom, and indeed that they were driven to embrace market freedom in part by their concerns about the compatibility of republican government with social and political equality. These concerns provided the entering wedge for the qualified embrace of socialism that became an increasingly prominent feature of liberal thought and practice in the latter part of the nineteenth century, and that neoliberals like Mises held in such contempt. This is largely a story of self-correction, as liberals began to appreciate the extent of the threat that market freedom – understood, again, in the narrow economic sense – poses to the equal enjoyment of republican freedom. The key development, as I have already indicated, was the rise of industrial capitalism: the defense of *laissez-faire* had a very different character, politically speaking, when its most visible victims were the great landlords and monopoly guilds than when its most visible victims were ordinary workers and consumers. The pursuit of market freedom was originally a cause of the left, and the early liberals were called "radicals" for good reason: they were aligned against the economic powers of the age,[62] and their support for market freedom in the broader sense that includes freedom of thought, expression, and assembly also aligned them against the political and religious powers of the age. This helps to explain why John Maynard Keynes, one of the leading twentieth-century critics of *laissez-faire*, nevertheless remarked in 1925 that "I hope that I should have belonged to [that] party if I had been born a hundred years earlier."[63]

Republicans have always insisted that people need to be equipped with certain skills and resources in order to participate effectively in the project of self-government. As we saw in Chapter 2, this idea served for most of the history of republican thought as a principle of exclusion: those who

---

Helen McCabe, *John Stuart Mill, Socialist* (Montreal: McGill-Queen's University Press, 2021).

[62] Beatrice Webb (of all people) remarked in an 1886 diary entry that "[t]he Political Economy of Adam Smith was the scientific expression of the impassioned crusade of the 18th century against class tyranny and the oppression of the Many by the Few": "By what silent revolution of events," she asks, "did it change itself into the 'Employers' Gospel' of the 19th century?": quoted in Emma Rothschild, *Economic Sentiments: Adam Smith, Condorcet, and the Enlightenment* (Cambridge, MA: Harvard University Press, 2001), p. 65. For an excellent discussion of the radical origins of free-market ideology see Elizabeth Anderson, *Private Government: How Employers Rule Our Lives (and Why We Don't Like to Talk about It)* (Princeton, NJ: Princeton University Press, 2017), chapter 1.

[63] John Maynard Keynes, "Am I a Liberal?" (1925), in *Essays in Persuasion* (New York: Harcourt, Brace and Company, 1932), pp. 329–30.

were deemed too poor, too ignorant, or too dependent on another person (such as a landlord, a patron, an employer, or a husband) to offer informed and independent judgments about matters of public concern were *ipso facto* excluded from the enjoyment of republican freedom. Despite their professed egalitarianism, the classical liberals largely agreed in thinking that the rights and responsibilities of citizenship should be restricted to those who were suitably qualified. Constant held, for example, that "[o]nly property can render men capable of exercising political rights," because it confers "the leisure needed for developing an informed outlook and soundness of judgment"; "[t]o counter this with natural equality," he argued, "is to be reasoning within a hypothesis inapplicable to the present state of societies."[64] Mill agreed that knowledge and judgment are essential qualities in a citizen, although he saw education rather than property as the key criterion: he infamously argued that multiple votes should be given to the "better and wiser" citizens, and held that it is "wholly inadmissible that any person should participate in the suffrage, without being able to read, write, and ... perform the common operations of arithmetic." Mill also held that the recipients of public charity ("parish relief") should be disenfranchised, not because they lacked leisure, but rather out of a traditional fear that they would expropriate the wealthy: "He who cannot by his labour suffice for his own support," he argued, "has no claim to the privilege of helping himself to the money of others."[65]

The classical liberals tried to reconcile their defense of political exclusion with their underlying egalitarianism by emphasizing that access to the rights of citizenship was no longer determined at birth or left to the discretion of the already-enfranchised, but was available to anyone who could acquire the necessary qualifications: to use T. H. Marshall's terminology, the suffrage was now (for men) an "open group" and not a "closed group" monopoly.[66] Thus Constant defended his support for a (fairly modest) property qualification for the suffrage by appealing to the ideal of

---

[64] Constant, *Principles of Politics*, p. 166 (book 10, chapter 2).
[65] Mill, *Considerations on Representative Government*, pp. 478, 470, 472 (chapter 8). Mill is nevertheless careful to distinguish the claims of education from those of wealth: he argues that to base plural voting on property "is always, and will continue to be, supremely odious," and insists "that it be open to the poorest individual in the community to claim its privileges, if he can prove that, in spite of all difficulties and obstacles, he is, in point of intelligence, entitled to them:" ibid., pp. 474, 476 (chapter 8).
[66] T. H. Marshall, "Citizenship and Social Class," in *Citizenship and Social Class and Other Essays* (New York: Cambridge University Press, 1950), pp. 19–20.

upward mobility: "If property were immobile and always stayed in the same hands," he concedes, "[i]t would split the human race in two," but in a commercial society property "tends to a continual changing of hands," and so "[t]he necessary purpose of the propertyless is to manage to become propertied." The same thought lay behind Guizot's notoriously blithe response to those who complained about the (much higher) property qualification for the suffrage under the July Monarchy: "*enrichissez-vous.*"[67] Mill similarly points to the positive incentives that an educational requirement for the suffrage would create: "To make a participation in political rights the reward of mental improvement," he argues, would "make an honourable distinction in favour of the educated, and create an additional motive for seeking education." Indeed, he suggests that "[t]he very novelty of the requirement – the excitement and discussion which it would produce in the class chiefly affected by it – would be the best sort of education; would make an opening in their minds that would let in light – would set them thinking in a perfectly new manner respecting political rights and responsibilities."[68]

Despite their sometimes patronizing tone, Mill's political writings mark a sea change in the liberal understanding of the proper boundaries of citizenship: unlike Constant and Guizot,[69] he saw universal (albeit graduated) suffrage – including women's suffrage – as desirable in itself, and indeed as a defining feature of a truly free society. His defense of this position rests on three interlocking claims. The first is the familiar republican claim that "the rights and interests of every or any person are only secure from being disregarded, when the person interested is himself able, and habitually disposed, to stand up for them." Mill gives this claim an egalitarian twist: "it is a personal injustice," he argues, "to withhold from any one, unless for the prevention of greater evils, the ordinary privilege of having his voice reckoned in the disposal of affairs in which he has the same interest as other people." The second and more distinctively liberal claim, which we have already encountered, is that "the general prosperity

---

[67] Constant, *Principles of Politics*, pp. 183, 170 (book 10, chapters 10 and 4). Constant held that the suffrage should be extended to "anyone whose income from land is ... sufficient to see him through the year, without having to work for other people" (ibid., p. 182; book 10, chapter 9); under the July Monarchy the property qualification restricted the suffrage to less than 1 percent of the population.

[68] Mill, "Thoughts on Parliamentary Reform" (1859), *Collected Works*, vol. 19, pp. 327–8.

[69] As we have seen, Tocqueville saw universal male suffrage as a *fait accompli* – something that had already been realized in the United States, and that was destined to be realized in France – and therefore treated it as a fact to be taken into account rather than as a principle to be argued for.

Equality and Republican Freedom: The "New" Liberals 151

attains a greater height, and is more widely diffused, in proportion to the amount and variety of the personal energies enlisted in promoting it" (recall that Mill's conception of "prosperity" refers to human flourishing in the widest sense and not simply to *material* prosperity). Combining these two claims – which, he argues, are "of as universal truth and applicability as any general propositions which can be laid down respecting human affairs" – Mill concludes that

> human beings are only secure from evil at the hands of others, in proportion as they have the power of being, and are, self-*protecting*; and they only achieve a high degree of success in their struggle with Nature, in proportion as they are self-*dependent*, relying on what they themselves can do, either separately or in concert, rather than on what others do for them.[70]

The third and crucial claim in Mill's defense of universal suffrage – which he borrows from Tocqueville's analysis of American democracy – is that republican freedom has an edifying effect on those who enjoy it and is therefore a necessary condition of personal development and social progress. "The maximum of the invigorating effect of freedom upon the character," he argues, "is only obtained when the person acted on either is, or is looking forward to becoming, a citizen as fully privileged as any other," because

> [h]e is called upon, while so engaged, to weigh interests not his own; to be guided, in case of conflicting claims, by another rule than his private partialities; to apply, at every turn, principles and maxims which have for their reason of existence the general good; and he usually finds associated with him in the same work minds more familiarized than his own with these ideas and operations, whose study it will be to supply reasons to his understanding, and stimulation to his feeling for the general interest.

Unlike Tocqueville, Mill draws a direct connection between the positive effects of political participation and the dilemma of maintaining free government under conditions of industrial production – a dilemma which was of course even more pressing in the 1860s than it had been in the 1830s. "It is by political discussion," he argues,

> that the manual labourer, whose employment is a routine, and whose way of life brings him in contact with no variety of impressions, circumstances, or ideas, is taught that remote causes, and events which take place far off, have a most sensible effect even on his personal interests; and it is from political discussion, and

---

[70] Mill, *Considerations on Representative Government*, pp. 404, 469 (chapters 3 and 8; original emphasis).

collective political action, that one whose daily occupations concentrate his interests in a small circle round himself, learns to feel for and with his fellow-citizens, and becomes consciously a member of a great community.[71]

Mill's faith in the edifying effects of political participation will seem rather quaint to many readers today, but it highlights the expansive nature of his conception of the boundaries of citizenship – a conception that soon came to define the mainstream of liberal thought and practice.[72] Instead of centering on the question of who is *already* worthy of citizenship, the pursuit of republican freedom was now understood to require that each person be provided with the resources and opportunities that would *make* them worthy. Thus, with regard to the literacy test, Mill argues that "the means of attaining these elementary acquirements should be within the reach of every person, either gratuitously, or at an expense not exceeding what the poorest, who earn their own living, can afford." With regard to the exclusion of the economically dependent, he holds that "[t]hese exclusions are not in their nature permanent," and "exact such conditions only as all are able, or ought to be able, to fulfil if they choose." With regard to plural voting, he suggests that giving more votes to the "better and wiser" is a necessary step toward giving regard for personal merit its proper place in public morality: "as it is for [the citizen's] good that he should think that every one is entitled to some influence, but the better and wiser to more than others, it is important that this conviction should be professed by the State, and embodied in the national institutions."[73] Taken together, these three claims – that a basic education should be available to all regardless of ability to pay, that poverty should be a rare and temporary condition, and that public institutions should embody and promote an ideal of self-improvement – go a long way toward defining the agenda of the "new" liberalism of the ensuing decades, and indeed of liberal politics through to the present day.

Like Mill, the "new" liberals held that the extension of the rights of citizenship to all people would benefit not only the currently excluded groups, but society as a whole. Indeed, T. H. Green, whose "positive"

---

[71] Ibid., pp. 411–12, 469 (chapters 3 and 8).

[72] In England the association of liberalism with political inclusion was close enough by 1862 – a year after the publication of Mill's *Considerations on Representative Government* – that James Fitzjames Stephen described the Liberals (rather grumpily) as "the party which wishes to alter existing institutions with the view of increasing popular power," adding that the words "liberalism" and "liberal" "are not greatly remote in meaning from the words 'democracy' and 'democratic'": quoted in Bell, "What Is Liberalism?", p. 694.

[73] Mill, *Considerations on Representative Government*, pp. 470, 472, 478 (chapter 8).

theory of freedom had a profound influence on early twentieth-century liberal thinkers such as J. A. Hobson, L. T. Hobhouse, and John Dewey, *defined* freedom as "the increasing development and exercise on the whole of those powers of contributing to social good with which we believe the members of society to be endowed."[74] Green was among the first generation of English thinkers to have been deeply influenced by German idealism, and his theory of freedom emerged out of a systematic philosophical treatment of the relationship between mind, will, and society. It is therefore tempting to see the shift in emphasis in liberal thought and practice that he helped to bring about as the byproduct of a broader philosophical shift from a utilitarian individualism to an idealistic holism. However, this would understate the extent to which the aims of the "new" liberals were continuous with those of their "classical" predecessors, and overstate the extent to which those aims were grounded in a particular philosophical position: as the political theorist Michael Freeden puts it, "[r]ather than Idealism giving birth to a new version of liberalism, it was liberalism that was able to assimilate certain aspects of Idealism into its mainstream and thus bestow new meaning upon Idealist tenets."[75] Many of Green's liberal contemporaries and successors did not endorse, and were no doubt often unaware of, the idealist underpinnings of his theory of freedom; indeed, Hobhouse devoted an entire book to refuting them.[76] As we will now see, the program of action that they defended and ultimately enacted is better understood as an effort to reconcile the demands of self-government with the realities of life in an advanced industrial economy.

The new liberals gave particular attention to the question of whether the vulnerable parties in a market economy – especially wage laborers and their dependents – are fit to be held responsible for the choices that they make within it. They were struck not only by the inequality of power between the employing and laboring classes – by the fact that, as Louis

---

[74] T. H. Green, "Liberal Legislation and Freedom of Contract" (1881), in *Lectures on the Principles of Political Obligation and Other Writings*, ed. Paul Harris and John Morrow (New York: Cambridge University Press, 1986), p. 199.
[75] Michael Freeden, *The New Liberalism: An Ideology of Social Reform* (New York: Oxford University Press, 1978), p. 18.
[76] L. T. Hobhouse, *The Metaphysical Theory of the State: A Criticism* (London: George Allen and Unwin, 1918). Hobhouse remarks that "the Hegelian influence has ... permeated the British world, discrediting the principles upon which liberal progress has been founded and in particular depreciating all that British and French thinkers have contributed. Perhaps it has been none the less dangerous because it has captivated men of real humanity, genuinely interested in liberal progress": ibid., p. 24.

Brandeis put it, "[m]en are not free if dependent industrially upon the arbitrary will of another"[77] – but also and more profoundly by the capriciousness of market outcomes, and by the standing threat that they pose even to the prudent and industrious. "The opportunities of work and the remuneration for work," Hobhouse pointed out, "are determined by a complex mass of social forces which no individual, certainly no individual workman, can shape":

> [i]t is not his fault if there is over-production in his industry, or if a new and cheaper process has been introduced which makes his particular skill, perhaps the product of years of application, a drug in the market. He does not direct or regulate industry. He is not responsible for its ups and downs, but he has to pay for them.[78]

Hobson strikes a similar note: "the great majority of the population in our rich and civilized country," he writes,

> are conscious always of standing in a precarious condition. They and their families may be plunged into poverty and its attendant degradation and disease at any time by the ill-health or other disablement of the bread-winner, by the failure of an employer, by some change of public taste, some shift of market, some introduction of improved machinery, or some trade depression. Few of these emergencies can be foreseen; against the graver ones no adequate provision can be made.

"No man," he concludes, "whose standard of life lies at the mercy of a personal accident or a trade crisis, has the true freedom which it is the first duty of the civilised State to furnish."[79]

The new liberals therefore agreed in thinking that, as Green put it, "[i]t is the business of the state, not indeed directly to promote moral goodness, but to maintain the conditions without which a free exercise of the human faculties is impossible": "Left to itself, or to the operation of casual benevolence," he argued, "a degraded population perpetuates and increases itself," and "there [is] nothing on their part, in the way either of self-respect or established demand for comforts, to prevent them from working and living, or from putting their children to work and live, in a way in which no one who is to be a healthy and free citizen can work and live."[80] What made this

---

[77] Louis Brandeis, "True Americanism" (1915), in Philippa Strum, ed., *Brandeis on Democracy* (Lawrence: University Press of Kansas, 1995), p. 28.
[78] L. T. Hobhouse, *Liberalism* (1911), in *Liberalism and Other Writings* (New York: Cambridge University Press, 1994), pp. 79, 77 (chapter 7).
[79] J. A. Hobson, "Equality of Opportunity," in *The Crisis of Liberalism: New Issues of Democracy* (London: P. S. King & Son, 1909), pp. 106–7.
[80] Green, "Liberal Legislation and Freedom of Contract," pp. 202, 203–4.

Equality and Republican Freedom: The "New" Liberals

line of argument "new" is not of course the appeal to freedom, but the claim that it is the "business of the state" to secure it: "this is the point," Hobhouse conceded, "at which we stand furthest from the older Liberalism."[81] The reforms that the new liberals enacted in the name of this ideal were incredibly wide-ranging and, from a contemporary standpoint, utterly familiar: they included the socialization of "natural" monopolies such as communication, transportation, and utility systems; the creation of social insurance programs for the disabled, the elderly, and the unemployed; the passage of workplace and consumer safety regulations and of minimum wage and maximum hours laws; the provision of free and compulsory public schooling for children; anti-trust and pro-union legislation; and (to pay for it all) the levying of a progressive income tax.[82] What bound these efforts together was a belief that a free society is one whose citizens are able to exercise some degree of control over their lives, and therefore enjoy freedom in the republican sense; that, as Hobhouse put it, "the self-governing State is at once the product and the condition of the self-governing individual."[83]

Despite the obvious practical differences between themselves and their classical predecessors, the new liberals often emphasized that their underlying goals were the same. Green, for example, acknowledged that there was "a noticeable difference between the present position of political reformers and that in which they stood a generation ago," but insisted that "those who think a little longer about it can discern the same old cause of social good against class interests, for which, under altered names, liberals are fighting now as they were fifty years ago."[84] Hobhouse likewise contrasted the "earlier and more negative aspect" of the liberal movement with the "constructive theory ... of our own day," but saw "Liberalism in every department as a movement fairly denoted by the name – a movement of liberation, a clearance of obstructions, an opening of channels for the flow of free spontaneous vital activity."[85] Hobson went so far as to suggest that "Liberals ... as a party *never* committed themselves either to the theory or the policy of ... narrow *laissez-faire* individualism," although he conceded that earlier liberals "tended to lay an excessive emphasis upon the aspect of liberty which

---

[81] Hobhouse, *Liberalism*, p. 64 (chapter 6).
[82] For a useful overview see Fawcett, *Liberalism*, pp. 160–7, and Rosenblatt, *Lost History of Liberalism*, pp. 220–33.
[83] Hobhouse, *Liberalism*, p. 74 (chapter 7).
[84] Green, "Liberal Legislation and Freedom of Contract," pp. 195–6.
[85] Hobhouse, *Liberalism*, pp. 22–3 (chapter 2).

consists in absence of restraint, as compared with the other aspect which consists in presence of opportunity."[86] John Dewey later argued that "[i]f we strip its creed from adventitious elements, there are ... enduring values for which earlier liberalism stood," namely "liberty, the development of the inherent capacities of individuals made possible through liberty, and the central role of free intelligence in inquiry, discussion, and expression": "It is the business of liberalism," he concluded, "to state these values in ways, intellectual and practical, that are relevant to present needs and forces."[87]

Despite (or maybe because of) these assurances, critics of the new liberalism – Mises prominent among them – argued that its agenda was not "liberal" at all, but rather a thinly disguised brand of socialism. Many new liberals embraced the label; Hobhouse held that "true Socialism ... serves to complete rather than to destroy the leading Liberal ideas,"[88] and in an 1887 House of Commons speech the prominent Liberal MP William Harcourt made the striking and widely repeated declaration that "we are all socialists now." However, the liberal embrace of socialism came with significant caveats. As Hobhouse put it,

> a Liberal Socialism ... must clearly fulfill two conditions. In the first place it must be democratic. It must come from below, not above ... It must engage the efforts and respond to the genuine desires not of a handful of superior beings, but of great masses of men. And secondly, and for that very reason, it must make its account with the human individual. It must give the average man free play in the personal life for which he really cares. It must be founded on liberty, and must make not for the suppression but for the development of personality.[89]

Hobhouse's appeal to democracy identifies liberalism as the party of persuasion and reform rather than of violence and revolution; it rules out a "vanguardist" socialism of the kind that was soon to be imposed by

---

[86] Hobson, "The Vision of Liberalism," *Crisis of Liberalism*, p. 92 (emphasis added).

[87] John Dewey, *Liberalism and Social Action* (1935), in Jo Ann Boydston, ed., *The Later Works of John Dewey, 1925–1953* (Carbondale: Southern Illinois University Press, 1981–1991), vol. 11, pp. 25, 35 (chapter 2).

[88] L. T. Hobhouse, "Liberalism and Socialism," in *Democracy and Reaction* (London: T. Fisher Unwin, 1904), p. 229.

[89] Hobhouse, *Liberalism*, pp. 83–4 (chapter 8). Dewey struck a similar note some 25 years later: "Freedom," he argued, "is not something that can be handed to men as a gift from outside, whether by old-fashioned dynastic benevolent despotisms or by new-fashioned dictatorships, whether of the proletarian or of the Fascist order. It is something which can be had only as individuals participate in winning it, and this fact, rather than some particular political mechanism, is the essence of democratic liberalism": Dewey, "A Liberal Speaks Out for Liberalism" (1936), *Later Works*, vol. 11, p. 288.

Equality and Republican Freedom: The "New" Liberals 157

the Bolsheviks in Russia.[90] His appeal to "free play in ... personal life" establishes that a liberal polity, whatever "socialist" measures it might enact, also has to make room for a flexible and entrepreneurial economy, a robust and pluralistic civil society, and an open and tolerant public sphere. The characteristic note of the new liberalism, as of liberalism more generally, is thus one of balance and compromise: its fundamental commitment to republican freedom – to realizing what Hobhouse called a "self-governing State" – is matched by an equally fundamental commitment to market freedom – to promoting what Green called "the free exercise of the human faculties."

In short, the new liberals saw socialism as a complement, and not as an alternative, to capitalism: "economic Liberalism," Hobhouse wrote, "seeks to do justice to the social and individual factors in industry alike, as opposed to an abstract Socialism which emphasizes the one side and an abstract Individualism which leans its whole weight on the other."[91] Hobson similarly appealed to a "practicable Socialism" which "aims primarily not to abolish the competitive system, to socialise all instruments of production, distribution, and exchange, and to convert all workers into public employees – but rather to supply all workers at cost price with all the economic conditions requisite to the education and employment of their personal powers for their personal advantage and enjoyment": "wherever ... obstructions to economic liberty are found," he insisted, "the State must exert its powers, either to restore free competition, or, where that is impracticable or unwise, to substitute a public monopoly in which all share for a private monopoly the profits of which pass to a favoured few."[92] Nor was this belief in the complementarity of socialism and capitalism confined to the realm of what we would now call liberal theory: in 1909 a young Liberal MP named Winston Churchill argued, in an essay called "Liberalism and Socialism," that "[n]o man can be a collectivist alone or an individualist alone. He must be both an individualist and a collectivist. The nature of man is a dual nature. The character of the organisation of human society is dual." "We want to draw a line," he concluded, "below which we will not allow persons to

---

[90] Hobhouse contrasts "liberal" socialism so understood with two "illiberal" varieties: "mechanical" socialism, which appeals to the doctrine of economic determinism, and "official" socialism, which calls for the despotic exercise of political power in the name of the working class: Hobhouse, *Liberalism*, pp. 81–3 (chapter 8).
[91] Ibid., p. 101 (chapter 8).
[92] Hobson, "Poverty: Its Causes and Cures," *Crisis of Liberalism*, pp. 172–3; Hobson, "Crisis of Liberalism," p. 4.

live and labour, yet above which they may compete with all the strength of their manhood."[93]

Not surprisingly, this emphasis on the importance (and difficulty) of striking a balance between republican and market freedom – and thus, among other things, between socialism and capitalism – led some critics to conclude that liberalism is a wavering ideology; as Dewey observed, "in the minds of many persons, liberalism has fallen between two stools, so that it is conceived as the refuge of those who are unwilling to take a decided stand in the social conflicts going on."[94] There is of course an irony here: where contemporary critics take liberalism to task for its allegedly dogmatic commitment to individualism, rationalism, and universalism, prewar critics focused on its lack of a clear normative vision. As we might expect, liberals see this kind of flexibility as a strength rather than a weakness, and argue that it is not only compatible with but essential to the pursuit of social and political progress. Adam Gopnik, for example, has recently offered an eloquent defense of what he calls the "moral adventure" of a political ideology that depends on "shadings and qualifications"; one whose foundations are "cracked in advance," but that has nevertheless realized "vistas of general legal and social equality far outstripping anything previously known to mankind, and largely achieved by peaceful and parliamentary means."[95] Hobson, writing more than a century earlier, found poetry in this appeal to an uncertain but hopeful future: "It is the peril, as it is the glory, of Liberalism," he writes, "that it is required to drive several teams of personal liberty abreast along the road of progress"; "this illimitable character of Liberalism, based on the infinitude of the possibilities of human life, in its individual and social aspects, affords that vision without which not only a people but a party perishes, the vision of 'That untravelled world whose margin fades/For ever and for ever when I move.'"[96]

4.5 LIBERALS BEFORE LIBERALISM?

We can draw four general conclusions from this overview of the formative period for the liberal tradition; the period that runs roughly from the

---

[93] Quoted in Freeden, *New Liberalism*, p. 161.
[94] Dewey, *Liberalism and Social Action*, p. 5 (chapter 1).
[95] Adam Gopnik, *A Thousand Small Sanities: The Moral Adventure of Liberalism* (New York: Basic Books, 2019), pp. 24, 26.
[96] Hobson, "Vision of Liberalism," p. 95; the quotation (slightly misprinted in Hobson's text) is from Tennyson's "Ulysses."

French Revolution to the beginning of the First World War. First and most straightforwardly, the liberals of this period put liberty squarely at the center of their political agenda, as their party label would lead us to expect. For all of their differences, Constant, Tocqueville, Mill, Green, Hobhouse, Hobson, Dewey, and their fellow-travelers agree in treating freedom, and not justice, as the "first virtue" of social institutions. Second, these liberals also agree in thinking that the rise of social and political equality requires a fundamental rethinking of the practical implications of the pursuit of freedom under modern conditions, and pay particular attention to the complementary relationship between republican and market freedom. Third, these liberals spend little if any time speculating about abstract questions like the origins of political authority, the nature of political obligation, or the features of an ideal political order. They focus instead on the practical question of how the pursuit of freedom in their own time and place was affected by the design of political institutions, the workings of the economy, and what we would now call the sociological underpinnings of public life. Finally, and relatedly, these liberals, like most nineteenth-century thinkers, constantly emphasize the importance of historical context: recall Constant's analysis of the differences between ancient and modern liberty, Tocqueville's appeal to equality as the engine of historical change, Mill's concern with the "stage of progress" that a given society has reached, and the new liberals' focus on, well, "newness"; that is, on the pressing need to adapt liberal practices to changing social conditions.

In each of these ways, the liberals of this formative period defy the caricature of liberalism that is painted by its contemporary critics: none of them believed that there is such a thing as "the individual" that stands apart from the social, economic, and political relationships through which personal identity is formed, none of them believed that there are such things as universal or pre-political rights, obligations, or principles – or at least none that can be given practical meaning without reference to the circumstances of a specific time and place – and none of them believed in the perfectibility of human nature, the inevitability of social progress, or the value of utopian thinking. This raises the obvious question of how this caricature came to be so widespread, and how liberalism came to be associated, especially in the academy, with the identification of abstract principles of justice that can be endorsed by all reasonable people. We can break this question down into two distinct parts. First, we have to consider how the early modern thinkers who fit the contemporary caricature of liberalism more closely – most notably John Locke and Immanuel Kant – came to be seen as liberals, even though they did not – and, given the terminology that was available to them, *could* not – identify as liberals themselves. We have to consider, in short, how nineteenth- and twentieth-century liberals went about constructing a useful history for themselves. Second, and more perplexingly, we have to consider how these proto-liberals (as we might call them) were not only *incorporated* into the liberal tradition, but came to be seen as the *paradigmatic* liberals, largely to the exclusion of the genuinely liberal thinkers whose ideas we have just surveyed.

We will look more closely at how this piece of ideological alchemy was performed in Chapter 5; here I will simply point out that the incorporation of the early modern contractarians into the liberal tradition was almost entirely a twentieth-century – and largely a postwar – phenomenon. In the nineteenth century, as the historian Duncan Bell observes, "[m]ost accounts of the historical development of modern political thought contended that there had been a radical break – both intellectual and political – at the end of the eighteenth century. A new world had dawned, and there was little space in it for Lockean political theory."[97] This assessment is borne out in the thinkers that we have focused on here. Mill was a great – though not uncritical – admirer of Locke's *Essay on Human Understanding*, but I find only a single reference to the *Two Treatises of Government* in his (vast) published corpus.[98] Constant's *Principles of Politics* contains an allusion to the *Essay*, but no mention of the *Treatises*.[99] Locke's name does not appear in either of Tocqueville's major works, *Democracy in America* and *The Old Regime and the*

---

[97] Bell, "What Is Liberalism?", p. 695; he adds that "[l]iberalism was figured as the progeny of this gestalt switch": ibid. Pierre Manent, who identifies liberalism with the Lockean idea of the individual "who, because he is human, is naturally entitled to ... rights that are attributed to him independently of his function or place in society," nevertheless admits that there is a "second liberalism, which emerged in the first half of the nineteenth century," and which "bore little resemblance to the first." He does not explain why we should treat the "first" liberalism, which unlike the "second" never used that term to describe itself, as paradigmatic. Manent, *Intellectual History of Liberalism*, pp. xvi, 80.

[98] In an unsigned review of George Cornewall Lewis's "Remarks on the Use and Abuse of Political Terms," published in *Tait's Edinburgh Magazine* in 1832: Mill, *Collected Works*, vol. 18, pp. 10–11. Mill takes Lewis to task for treating Locke's social contract theory with "unqualified contempt," but offers some qualified contempt of his own, singling out in particular "a certain wavering and obscurity in [Locke's] notion of the grounds of morality" and his "rude and unskillful" treatment of the limits of governmental authority.

[99] Constant remarks that "[i]t was far from his country, whence tyranny had banished him, that Locke analyzed man's faculties": Constant, *Principles of Politics*, p. 307 (book 14, chapter 4). The Cambridge edition of Constant's *Political Writings* contains no mention of Locke.

Revolution. Green's *Lectures on the Principles of Political Obligation* contain, as we might expect, a discussion of social contract theory, but he takes a negative stance toward the tradition and lumps Locke in with nonliberals like Hobbes and Rousseau – though he concedes that "for practical purposes, Locke's doctrine is much the better."[100] Not until Hobhouse's *Liberalism* (1911) is Locke named as an important early liberal, but even there he receives only two passing mentions: once as a prominent critic of absolute monarchy at the time of the Glorious Revolution, and once (along with Thomas Paine, who unlike Locke is actually quoted) as a proponent of natural rights – a doctrine, Hobhouse remarks, that "long outlived the theory on which it rested."[101]

As we might expect given the discussion so far, the key early modern sources for the nineteenth-century liberals were not the contractarians, but rather the eighteenth-century defenders of market freedom, and the overlapping group of thinkers who sought to adapt the principles of republican government for modern commercial societies. Adam Smith is of course the most important figure in the first category: *The Wealth of Nations* served for the early liberals – as it still serves for many liberals today – as a kind of primer on the promises and pitfalls of unregulated production and trade. Constant's *Principles of Politics* and Mill's *Principles of Political Economy* each contain dozens of references to *The Wealth of Nations*; Tocqueville is less scrupulous about citing his sources, but Smith's influence is clearly felt in *Democracy in America*'s scattered chapters on economic issues. None of the nineteenth-century liberals engages Smith's great work in moral philosophy, *The Theory of Moral Sentiments* (1759), on which his fame during his own lifetime largely rested. An avalanche of scholarship over the past several decades has shown that a one-sided focus on *The Wealth of Nations* yields a partial and misleading picture of Smith's thought, and has sought to dissolve the so-called Adam Smith problem of how the same thinker could have promoted a political economy based on self-interest and a moral psychology based on mutual sympathy.[102] As valuable as this scholarship is, it is important to keep in mind that Smith's liberal readers were not trying to understand him on his own terms; they were drawing selectively on his ideas to address the political challenges of their own time and place.

---

[100] Green, *Lectures on the Principles of Political Obligation*, pp. 45–55, quoted at p. 52.
[101] Hobhouse, *Liberalism*, pp. 11, 26–7 (chapters 2 and 3).
[102] A pioneering English-language contribution to this now vast literature is the volume *Essays on Adam Smith*, ed. A. S. Skinner and T. Wilson (New York: Oxford University Press, 1975), which was issued in conjunction with the publication of the first volumes of the Glasgow Edition of Smith's works.

As we saw in Chapter 2, there was a broader shift over the course of the eighteenth century from a virtue- to an interest-centered conception of politics, and a corresponding reconsideration of the value of commerce, which came to be seen as the defining feature of modern social and political life.[103] As obvious as the parallels are between these developments and the concerns of the nineteenth-century liberals, it is surprisingly difficult to identify direct lines of influence. Constant's appeal to the politically beneficial effects of commerce in checking arbitrary rule, which draws on a line of argument that can be traced back through Smith to Charles de Montesquieu's seminal book *The Spirit of the Laws* (1748) and the writings of the Scottish mercantilist James Steuart, is probably the most straightforward example.[104] Another important source of inspiration was the American republic, the only example of a large, stable, and commercially oriented democracy for most of the nineteenth century. Tocqueville's comparison of the American and French cases was of course enormously influential, and Mill praised the *Federalist* as "the most instructive treatise we possess on federal government,"[105] although both thinkers found that the American statesmen of their own day had fallen far from the high standard that was set at the Founding. Tocqueville's emphasis on the importance of social mores and "intermediate powers" owes a clear debt to Montesquieu's *Spirit of the Laws*, but the content of the latter book highlights even more clearly the vast gulf that lies between eighteenth- and nineteenth-century political thought: as Mill put it, *Democracy in America* "is such [a book] as Montesquieu might have written, if to his genius he had superadded good sense, and the lights which mankind have since gained from the experiences of a period in which they may be said to have lived centuries in fifty years."[106]

As I have already emphasized, it does not follow that it is wrong to describe early modern thinkers as "liberals," if by this we mean that some of their ideas had an important influence on (or provided useful precedents for) later thinkers who used that label to describe themselves. It does follow, however, that we should be cautious about doing so. Where nineteenth- and

---

[103] Here again the literature is vast; my version of the story is told in *The Invention of Market Freedom*, chapters 3 and 4.

[104] See Montesquieu, *The Spirit of the Laws* (1748), book 21, chapter 20; Steuart, *An Inquiry in the Principles of Political Economy* (1767), book 2, chapters 13 and 22; and, for an influential discussion, Albert O. Hirschman, *The Passions and the Interests: Political Arguments for Capitalism Before Its Triumph* (Princeton, NJ: Princeton University Press, 1977).

[105] Mill, *Considerations on Representative Government*, p. 555 (chapter 17).

[106] Mill, "Tocqueville on Democracy in America (I)" (1835), *Collected Works*, vol. 18, pp. 57–8.

Liberals Before Liberalism? 163

twentieth-century figures like Constant, Tocqueville, Mill, Green, Hobson, Hobhouse, and Dewey, for all of their differences, saw themselves as part of a continuous ideological tradition, their appropriation of earlier thinkers was just that – an *appropriation* – and like all such appropriations it was partial and selective. As a result of their efforts the philosophical and political lines that divided seventeenth- and eighteenth-century thinkers were redrawn, and figures who had been on the same side of certain issues (for example, Hobbes and Locke on the origins of government, or Smith and Rousseau on the question of natural sociability) were placed on opposite sides of the liberal-illiberal divide, and figures who were on opposite sides of certain issues (for example, Locke and Hume on the origins of government, or Montesquieu and Hume on the question of parliamentary independence) were placed on the same side. Historians of political thought have spent decades trying to correct the anachronisms that this way of carving up the terrain introduces, and to dissolve the apparent paradoxes to which it gives rise. This scholarship is, again, valuable in its own right, but its chief value for our understanding of the liberal tradition is to remind us how misleading it can be to apply the label "liberal" to thinkers who would not (and could not) have applied it to themselves.[107]

I began this chapter by pointing out that the freedom, born of equality, that obtained between the lowly Jane Eyre and the only somewhat less lowly Mrs. Fairfax was enjoyed under the auspices of a real authority, their employer Mr. Rochester, who had yet to make his memorable entrance. That entrance is described in the next chapter of the novel – chapter 12 – which is a kind of mirror image of its predecessor. Where the earlier chapter has Jane arriving at Thornfield and enjoying a reverie on a sunlit lawn, here she travels anxiously away from Thornfield along a dark and icy road. Where before she mistakes the "affable and kind" Mrs. Fairfax for her "superior," here she fails to recognize the "dark, strong, and stern" master of the house for who he really is. Rochester nevertheless appears on the scene clothed in an unmistakable and rather ominous aura of mastery; mounted on a "tall steed" and accompanied by a "Gytrash" of a hound. The illusion is quickly shattered, as with

---

[107] As J. G. A. Pocock reminds us, "[t]he term [liberalism] was not used in the eighteenth century, where the adjective 'liberal' did not bear its modern meaning, and though elements were present which would in due course be assembled by means of this formula, there was no system of doctrine corresponding to its later use": J. G. A. Pocock, "Afterword" (2003) to *The Machiavellian Moment: Florentine Political Thought and the Atlantic Republican Tradition* (2nd ed., Princeton, NJ: Princeton University Press, 2003 [1975]), p. 579.

a "clattering tumble . . . [m]an and horse were down," having "slipped on the sheet of ice which glazed the causeway." The scene that follows – like the pratfall itself – is comically awkward, as Rochester, despite his pride, gradually admits that he is injured and in need of help, and Jane, despite her diffidence and her fear of dog, horse, and (she all but admits) men, gradually realizes that she is in a position to provide it. The rest of the novel is devoted to correcting the disequilibrium that is introduced here between its two central characters, and it ends (spoiler alert!) with Thornfield in ashes, Rochester blind and maimed, and Jane financially independent and emotionally mature at last. "Am I hideous, Jane?" he asks upon their reunion. "Very, sir," she replies (rather freely): "you always were, you know."

It would be misleading to exaggerate the parallels between Jane Eyre's rise in the world and the rise of the common person over the course of the nineteenth century, or between Mr. Rochester's fall and the fall of the landed aristocracy. Jane's wealth is not won through her own efforts or as the result of any liberalization of economic opportunity but is bestowed – as is so often the case in Victorian fiction – by a long-lost uncle. Mr. Rochester's downfall is not brought about by any movement of social or political reform, but rather (spoiler alert!) by an act of self-destructive revenge on the part of his insane first wife. Jane ends her remarkable story by resolving, rather unremarkably, to devote herself to the traditional feminine roles of wife, mother, and caretaker. It is not fanciful, however, to suppose that much of the novel's popularity, then as now, arises from its portrait of a social world in which traditional lines of authority are being redrawn, and in which, as I said at the beginning of this chapter, even a young woman of modest means could have a story worth telling. Nor was this fact lost on the novel's early readers. Elizabeth Rigby, writing (anonymously) for the influential *Quarterly Review*, declared it to be "pre-eminently an anti-Christian composition," marked by "a murmuring against the comforts of the rich and against the privations of the poor" and "a proud and perpetual assertion of the rights of man": "the tone of mind and thought," she concluded, "which has overthrown authority and violated every code human and divine abroad, and fostered Chartism and rebellion at home, is the same which has also written *Jane Eyre*."[108] We turn now to the contemporary legacy of this "rebellious" brand of egalitarianism, and the twofold conception of freedom to which it gave rise.

---

[108] Elizabeth Rigby, "*Vanity Fair, Jane Eyre,* and *Governesses' Benevolent Institution Report for 1847*," *Quarterly Review* 84 (1848), p. 174.

5

Liberalism and the Problem of Polarization

> Justice is the end of government. It is the end of civil society. It ever has been, and ever will be pursued, until it be obtained, or until liberty be lost in the pursuit.
> James Madison, *Federalist* 51

5.1 LIBERALISM AND POLARIZATION

I began this book by arguing that the problem of polarization – our growing inability to talk to each other constructively across lines of political disagreement – is the most fundamental challenge facing modern societies, and by suggesting that a freedom-centered liberalism offers a promising set of resources for responding to that challenge. In the intervening chapters I have developed an account of what liberal freedom consists in, conceptually speaking, and I have argued that the liberal tradition has been committed, historically speaking, to the pursuit of freedom so understood. In this concluding chapter I return to the problem of polarization and show how a freedom-centered liberalism can help us both to account for and to combat it. Of course, it is not enough to show that liberalism offers a response to this problem – presumably every political ideology offers *some* kind of response, at least implicitly – we also have to show that its response is preferable to the going alternatives, and in order to do *that* we have to give an account of what those alternatives are. This chapter therefore weaves together an application of liberal principles to contemporary political debates with a defense of those principles against some of their most influential contemporary critics. As we will see, this criticism has been strongly shaped by the rise of a justice-centered, contractarian brand of liberalism in the latter part of the twentieth century, and so part of our task here will be to distinguish that way of thinking (again) from its freedom-centered counterpart. I conclude by offering a proposal for how contractarian intuitions about legitimacy and consent might be accommodated within a more traditional liberal framework.

As we have seen, the liberal conception of freedom is internally complex: liberals are committed to the pursuit and enjoyment of both republican and market freedom. From the standpoint of republican freedom, we are free if and to the extent that we are self-governing, in the sense that we have collectively authorized the social conditions under which we act or are able to supervise and control those who did. From the standpoint of market freedom we are free if and to the extent that we are able to make decisions about certain aspects of our lives – who to associate with, how to express ourselves, what career to pursue, what religion to practice (if any), how to dispose of our property, and so on – without being accountable to other people (unless we choose to be) for the decisions that we make or the consequences that they have. A liberal polity is thus one in which certain domains of conduct that might in principle be matters of public concern, and that could in principle be placed under public control, are nevertheless left in the hands of "private" actors, and in which the state's performance of tasks that could in principle be handled by "private" actors comes with significant procedural strings attached. Each of these dimensions of liberal freedom directs our attention to a daunting political problem: republican freedom to the problem of securing the conditions of self-government, and market freedom to the problem of protecting a domain of individual liberty against public and private interference. Because republican and market freedom are often in tension – because the effort to solve one of these problems often exacerbates the other – a liberal politics is concerned above all with the problem of striking an appropriate balance between them.

It follows that those of us who are unhappy with the political status quo – as we all no doubt are, albeit in very different ways and to very different extents – have four possible (and not always mutually exclusive) courses of action open to us within the bounds of a liberal politics. First, we can work to expand the domain of market freedom for some people, with the understanding that this will generally result in a loss of republican freedom for others[1]: we might argue, for example, that economic regulations are stifling innovation and

---

[1] I say "generally" here and in the following case because, as we saw in Chapter 2, expanding the domain of market freedom can be an important means of limiting the arbitrary power of the state, and thus (to that extent) of promoting republican freedom as well.

opportunity, or that efforts to regulate individual conduct are restricting people's ability to live as they see fit and pursue the goods that they want to pursue, or that efforts to reduce inequality are infringing on associational or expressive freedoms. Conversely, we can work to expand the enjoyment of republican freedom for some people, with the understanding that this will generally result in a loss of market freedom for others: we might argue, for example, that inadequate economic regulation is leading to the exploitation of the economically vulnerable or to the destruction of the natural environment, or that a failure to adequately regulate individual conduct is promoting self-destructive behavior, or that the exercise of certain associational and expressive freedoms ("discrimination"; "hate speech") is entrenching existing inequalities. Third, we can work to intensify the enjoyment of republican freedom by making public actors and institutions more accountable and responsive within their existing sphere of authority: we might set out to change current patterns of participation and representation, to place administrative agencies under more effective public control, or to limit the political influence of certain kinds of private power. And finally, we can use our market freedom, singly or in solidarity with others, to try to convince our fellow citizens to change their ways – either directly through persuasion and protest, or simply by modeling what we take to be exemplary behavior.

Political polarization makes this kind of politics harder, and ultimately impossible, to sustain. The enjoyment of republican freedom requires that we allow people to hold and exercise political power even when we disagree with them, and even when their interests conflict with ours. There are many reasons that we might have for being willing to share power in this way, including a commitment to reciprocity and fair play, an ability to sympathize with the aims and aspirations of those who disagree with us, a recognition of the partiality of our understanding and the fallibility of our judgment, a confidence that our political opponents can be trusted not to abuse power when they hold it, an expectation that political losses and setbacks are temporary, an appreciation of the value and fragility of existing norms and institutions, or just a bare desire to preserve the peace and maintain social stability. These reasons are not mutually exclusive; indeed, they often reinforce each other in practice. Nevertheless, as polarization increases, our inclination to endorse them comes under increasing pressure: the commitment to reciprocity and mutual sympathy begins to fade, a sense of one's own fallibility and a confidence in the trustworthiness of other people becomes harder to sustain, and norms, institutions, and even social stability itself are increasingly experienced as so many barriers to the realization of one's own will.

Eventually the willingness to share political power comes to seem less like a display of civic virtue and more like a failure of nerve, at which point self-government is no longer a sustainable project and republican freedom is sacrificed to authoritarian or factional rule.

Likewise, the enjoyment of market freedom requires that we allow people to do as they please even when we find their behavior to be incomprehensible, offensive, or socially harmful. Here again, as we saw in Chapter 3, there are many reasons that we might have for being tolerant in this way, including a determination to keep regulatory power out of the hands of the state, a desire to maintain the conditions of pluralism and experimentation that are necessary for social progress, and a concern to show respect for individual choices and promote personal development. Moreover, in a liberal polity the question of how much market freedom people should enjoy has to be settled by republican means, which means that our commitment to toleration depends in part on our commitment to republican government itself. And here again as polarization increases we can expect our inclination to endorse these reasons to come under increasing pressure: some people's choices begin to seem less worthy of respect and their development less worthy of promoting, it becomes harder to remain open to certain points of view or receptive to certain kinds of pluralism, and it seems more important to give the state the means to pursue the "right" ends than to place principled limits on its power. Eventually the willingness to tolerate people with whom we disagree and behavior to which we object comes to seem less like a display of liberality and more like an accommodation to decadence, injustice, or bigotry, at which point toleration is no longer a sustainable practice and the domain of market freedom – and, in all likelihood, of republican freedom too – sharply contracts.

Of course, the outcomes that I have just described will only seem troubling to people who value republican and (or) market freedom in the first place, and needless to say this does not describe everyone. Some people and many states are not committed to the project of republican self-government, and while all states provide their citizens with at least a *de facto* domain of market freedom, in keeping with the first set of reasons that we considered in Chapter 3 (indifference, infeasibility, and so on), liberals hold that there are *principled* reasons to do so; reasons that depend on something more than the arbitrary will or administrative capacity of the state itself. An appreciation of the threat that political polarization poses to a liberal politics therefore helps to clarify what it means to be anti-liberal, and to distinguish different kinds of anti-liberalism from each other. Some people – *authoritarians* of various stripes – deny (often implicitly) that republican and market freedom are important political values, and some – *utopians* of various stripes – hold (often implicitly) that one or the other of them is a sufficient political value taken in itself. Within the latter group we can distinguish *socialist* utopians, who embrace republican freedom to the exclusion of market freedom, from *market* utopians, who embrace market freedom to the exclusion of republican freedom. This way of carving up the terrain will probably seem tendentious to anti-liberals themselves: authoritarians do not typically defend authority for its own sake, but rather for the sake of the things that it can be used to achieve or protect, and utopians (who are often authoritarians in practice) do not typically see their aims as "utopian" in the sense of being fanciful or quixotic. Nevertheless, focusing on the threat that political polarization poses to a liberal polity helps us to see more clearly what is at stake in the conflict between liberals and anti-liberals, and where the key political bets are being placed.

The task of distinguishing liberals from anti-liberals is complicated by the fact that contemporary critiques of liberalism tend to be immanent critiques; that is, they take liberals to task for failing to live up to, or for actively subverting, their own ideals. We find versions of this kind of critique on both sides of the ideological divide. Critics on the right argue that liberalism lacks a moral center of gravity; that it draws the boundaries of toleration so broadly that it corrodes the ethical foundations of social life and promotes an empty, anomic individualism. Critics on the left argue that liberalism's claim to the mantle of freedom masks a deeper complicity in the power structures of capitalism and imperialism, and call attention to the fact that many prominent liberal thinkers and societies have been deeply implicated in practices of economic exploitation and racial domination. "Liberalism, on both views," Adam Gopnik points out,

is the Cuisinart of culture, whipping around and pureeing what had once been coherent communities. The left says it does this mostly in pursuit of profit and on behalf of the capitalism that liberalism shelters (even as it smiles and pretends it does not); the right, that it does this in pursuit of perverse principles and on behalf of the monster state that liberalism idealizes (even as it frowns and pretends to love only freedom).[2]

---

[2] Adam Gopnik, *A Thousand Small Sanities: The Moral Adventure of Liberalism* (New York: Basic Books, 2019), p. 84.

In either case the central charge is one of hypocrisy; that liberalism's practical effects are at odds with its professed values. As Patrick Deneen puts it, "[a] political philosophy that was launched to foster greater equity, defend a pluralist tapestry of different cultures and beliefs, protect human dignity, and, of course, expand liberty, in practice generates titanic inequality, enforces uniformity and homogeneity, fosters material and spiritual degradation, and undermines freedom."[3]

In order to understand why critics who describe themselves as anti-liberal nevertheless take liberals to task for being unfaithful to their own ideals, we have to return to a question that we raised and set aside in Chapter 4: the question of how contractarianism, with its focus on inalienable rights and universal consent, came to be seen as the paradigmatic form of liberalism, and thus as the main target of anti-liberal criticism. I therefore begin (Section 5.2) by extending my capsule history of the liberal tradition through the middle decades of the twentieth century, with the aim of demonstrating on the one hand that the contractarian turn marked a departure from the mainstream of liberal thought up to that point, and on the other hand that it is poorly suited to the challenge of responding to the problem of polarization. I then turn to the two immanent critiques that I have just described: on the one hand, that liberalism leads in practice to a deracinated brand of decadent hedonism (Section 5.3), and on the other hand that it amounts in practice to a rapacious brand of capitalist imperialism (Section 5.4). In each case we find that contractarian liberalism opens up the ideological space for the critique in question, and that a more traditional freedom-centered approach puts critics on the horns of a dilemma: they either have to concede (as some have) that they occupy a position within the liberal fold – that they are also committed to striking an appropriate balance between republican and market freedom, albeit one that is substantially different from the status quo – or embrace (as some have) one of the authoritarian or utopian positions that I have just described. Although this may sound like a polemical conclusion, my intentions are irenic: I hope to show that liberalism is friendlier to, and better able to accommodate, many of the criticisms that are made of it than the critics themselves suppose. I conclude (Section 5.5) by considering whether and on what terms liberalism so understood can also accommodate its contractarian counterpart.

---

[3] Patrick J. Deneen, *Why Liberalism Failed* (New Haven, CT: Yale University Press, 2018), p. 3.

5.2 THE CONTRACTARIAN TURN

I pointed out in the Introduction to this book that social contract theory was moribund during the formative period for the liberal tradition, and that the publication of John Rawls's *A Theory of Justice* in 1971 brought about a sea change in liberal political thought. Up to that point twentieth-century liberals had largely followed their nineteenth-century predecessors in focusing on the problem of striking an appropriate balance between republican and market freedom, and in emphasizing that there is not a once-and-for-all answer to the question of how this might best be done. Indeed, a commitment to meliorism, fallibilism, and pluralism – to what the philosopher Karl Popper called "piecemeal social engineering"[4] – was often said to be the key thing that distinguished liberal polities from their illiberal rivals. Frank Knight, the right-leaning economist and founding member of the Mont Pelerin Society, held that

> there is no question of the exclusive use [or] entire abolition of any of the fundamental methods of social organization, individualistic or socialistic. Economic and other activities will always be organized in all the possible ways, and the problem is to find the right proportions between individualism and socialism and the various varieties of each, and to use each in its proper place.[5]

Reinhold Niebuhr, the left-leaning theologian and fervent Cold Warrior, agreed that "the degree of emphasis which must be put on planning or spontaneity, on control or freedom, cannot be solved in terms of fixed principles," and insisted that

> [r]esponsible parties, when not corrupted by demagogy and dishonesty, know that the economic and political life in a community cannot go too far in a collectivist direction without becoming prey to bureaucratic stagnation. Nor can it go too far in the direction of an uncontrolled economy without aggravating the perils of insecurity and the evils of inequality arising from centralization of power.[6]

The most eloquent spokesman for liberal pluralism during this period was the philosopher and intellectual historian Isaiah Berlin. Although he is best known for asserting the value of "negative" liberty against its

---

[4] Karl Popper, *The Open Society and Its Enemies* (Princeton, NJ: Princeton University Press, 1945), chapter 9.
[5] Frank Hyneman Knight, "The Ethics of Competition" (1923), in *The Ethics of Competition and Other Essays* (New York: Harper and Brothers, 1935), p. 58.
[6] Reinhold Niebuhr, "Liberalism: Illusions and Realities," *The New Republic*, July 4, 1955, p. 12.

"positive" counterpart, Berlin's theory of liberal freedom is in fact double-barreled in exactly the way that I have described here: "to be free to choose, and not to be chosen for," he argues, "is an inalienable ingredient in what makes human beings human," and

> underlies both the positive demand to have a voice in the laws and practices of the society in which one lives, and to be accorded an area, artificially carved out, if need be, in which one is one's own master, a 'negative' area in which a man is not obliged to account for his activities to any man so far as this is compatible with the existence of organised society.[7]

Berlin's worries about the first, "positive" dimension of liberal freedom do not arise from its association with self-government, but rather from the fact that it can also refer to the rule of a "higher" over a "lower" self, and thus provide "a cloak for despotism in the name of a wider freedom." However, as we saw in Chapter 1, a commitment to republican freedom does not entail a commitment to a metaphysics of free agency, and Berlin himself admits that this development of the idea was "not always [made] by logically reputable steps." Indeed, he emphasizes that the desire for positive liberty has "animate[d] the most powerful and morally just public movements of our time" (namely, "demands for national or social self-direction"), and that the pursuit of negative liberty "has played its part in generating great and lasting social evils" (via "unrestrained capitalist competition"). He concludes that the question of how much negative liberty people should enjoy "has been, and perhaps always will be, a matter of infinite debate," and that in the end liberals can only insist on the recognition of a "shifting, but always recognisable, frontier" between "public" and "private" life.[8]

While liberals like Popper, Knight, Niebuhr, and Berlin focused most of their attention on the "totalitarian" menaces of communism and fascism, they directed some of their critical fire at fellow-travelers who did not share their view of liberalism's open-ended and pluralistic nature. Niebuhr, for example, drew an unfavorable comparison between "academic liberalism with its abstract notions of liberty and equality" and

---

[7] Isaiah Berlin, "Introduction" (1969) to *Four Essays on Liberty*, in *Liberty*, ed. Henry Hardy (New York: Oxford University Press, 2002), p. 52. Berlin associates the "positive demand" with the desire to be recognized as a responsible agent: to enjoy positive liberty, he writes, is "above all to be conscious of myself as a thinking, willing, active being, bearing responsibility for my choices and able to explain them by reference to my own ideas and purposes": Berlin, "Two Concepts of Liberty" (1958/1969), ibid., p. 178.

[8] Berlin, "Introduction," p. 39; Berlin, "Two Concepts of Liberty," pp. 179, 214; "Introduction," p. 37; "Two Concepts of Liberty," pp. 173–4.

"realistic liberalism ... stripped of its utopian errors," and Berlin suggested that a failure to "allow for the variety of basic human needs" had "blinded some contemporary liberals to the world in which they live."[9] Popper insisted that any effort to provide a "clear and detailed description or blueprint of our ideal state" is "self-defeating, and ... leads to violence."[10] Knight held that "[i]t would go a long way toward clarifying discussion if it were generally recognized on both sides that there are no one-hundred-per-cent individualists and no one-hundred-per-cent socialists; that the issue is one of degree and proportion."[11] John Maynard Keynes wrote a tart letter to Friedrich Hayek after the publication of his seminal jeremiad *The Road to Serfdom* (1944), taking him to task for not wrestling seriously with the problem of striking a balance between individual liberty and public regulation. "You admit here and there," he points out,

> that it is a question of where to draw the line. You agree that the line has to be drawn somewhere, and that the logical extreme is not possible. But you give no guidance whatever as to where to draw it. In a sense this is shirking the practical issue. It is true that you and I would probably draw it in different places. I should guess that according to my ideas you greatly underestimate the practicability of the middle course. But as soon as you admit that the extreme is not possible, and that a line has to be drawn, you are, on your own argument, done for, since you are trying to persuade us that so soon as one moves in the planned direction you are necessarily launched on the slippery path which will lead you in due course over the precipice.[12]

Hayek's response to this line of criticism is revealing. "The main lesson which the true liberal must learn from the success of the socialists," he argues, "is that it was their courage to be Utopian which gained them the support of the intellectuals and therefore an influence on public opinion

---

[9] Niebuhr, "Liberalism: Illusions and Realities," p. 13; Berlin, "Two Concepts of Liberty," p. 208.
[10] Karl Popper, "Utopia and Violence" (1948), in *Conjectures and Refutations: The Growth of Scientific Knowledge* (New York: Routledge, 1963), p. 482.
[11] Knight, "Ethics of Competition," p. 47n.
[12] John Maynard Keynes to Friedrich Hayek, June 28, 1944, quoted in Daniel Stedman Jones, *Masters of the Universe: Hayek, Friedman, and the Birth of Neoliberal Politics* (Princeton, NJ: Princeton University Press, 2012), p. 67. Knight remarked along similar lines that "I do wish my friend Hayek had seen fit to give his readers some indication of what he means ... by 'socialism'," since "[f]rom other statements of his we know that he is by no means opposed to all positive political action in the economic field": Frank H. Knight, "World Justice, Socialism, and the Intellectuals," *University of Chicago Law Review* 16 (1949), p. 439.

which is daily making possible what only recently seemed utterly remote." He concludes that liberals

> must make the building of a free society once more an intellectual adventure, a deed of courage. What we lack is a liberal Utopia, a program which seems neither a mere defense of things as they are nor a diluted kind of socialism, but a truly liberal radicalism which does not spare the susceptibilities of the mighty (including the trade unions), which is not too severely practical, and which does not confine itself to what appears today as politically possible.[13]

Hayek's liberal utopianism departs from the liberalism of his more traditional contemporaries in two important ways. First, he draws a strict distinction between "true" or "radical" liberalism and the "diluted kind of socialism" that he associates with Keynes's "middle course." His writings provide an especially forceful statement of the view that liberalism has fallen into decline and should return to the purer ideals of its "classical" period. Second, he argues that it is more important to articulate liberal ideals in a way that transcends the circumstances of a given time and place than to focus on "practical issues" of the kind that Keynes appeals to. As we have seen, and as Hayek was of course well aware, this way of thinking flies in the face of the then-prevailing view that utopianism is a distinguishing feature of an *illiberal* politics.

Each of these features of Hayek's position is also found, *mutatis mutandis*, in Rawls's *Theory of Justice*, the most widely discussed work of liberal political philosophy in the latter part of the twentieth century. Like Hayek, Rawls criticizes his liberal contemporaries for giving insufficient weight to the claims of individual liberty, and like Hayek he proposes to recover an older tradition of thought which "denies that the loss of freedom for some is made right by a greater good shared by others." For Rawls, the position to be rejected is utilitarianism rather than socialism, and the tradition to be recovered is not the *laissez-faire* doctrine of the Manchester School but rather "the familiar theory of the social contract as found ... in Locke, Rousseau, and Kant." Nevertheless, Rawls's approach is "radical" in the sense that, like all social contract theories, it asks us to step back from existing practices and institutions, and thus from contemporary problems and debates, to focus on the abstract question of what justice – the "first virtue of social institutions" – requires. It therefore

---

[13] Friedrich Hayek, "The Intellectuals and Socialism," *University of Chicago Law Review* 16 (1949), pp. 432–3. I have reversed the order in which these two passages appear in the text.

abandons the traditional liberal project of provisionally balancing fundamental values against one another – justice, Rawls insists, is an "uncompromising" virtue – and the equally traditional liberal emphasis on the importance of historical context. A "well-ordered society" on this view is one in which "everyone accepts and knows that the others accept the same principles of justice," and "to see our place in society from [this] perspective ... is to see it *sub specie aeternitatis*: it is to regard the human situation not only from all social but also from all temporal points of view."[14] Rawls later described this approach to political philosophy as "realistically utopian" – "realistic" not in the sense that its ideals are likely to be achieved, but rather in the sense that it would not be unreasonable to hope that they might.[15]

Rawls's account of how a just society would function superficially resembles the liberal politics that I have described here: where a liberal polity grants its citizens a domain of market freedom within a framework of laws and regulations that results from the exercise of, and that is intended to promote, republican freedom, Rawls's "well-ordered society" leaves "individuals and associations ... free to advance their ends ... within the framework of the basic structure, secure in the knowledge that elsewhere in the social system the necessary corrections to preserve background justice are being made."[16] However, this superficial resemblance masks a more fundamental difference in approach. Traditional liberalism starts with practical politics: the enjoyment of republican freedom requires that we each play a role, directly or indirectly, in determining how social and political power is exercised, and the enjoyment of market freedom requires that we accept a certain degree of uncertainty about how social practices and norms of conduct will develop over time. Contractarian liberalism begins, by contrast, with an effort to identify pre-political principles that all people (suitably idealized) could accept, and that would generate a stable pattern of social and political conduct if implemented. I take no position here on the question of whether ideal theorizing of this kind might be – or need

---

[14] John Rawls, *A Theory of Justice* (2nd ed., Cambridge, MA: Harvard University Press, 1999 [1971]), pp. 3–4 (§1), 10 (§3), 514 (§87).
[15] John Rawls, *The Law of Peoples* (Cambridge, MA: Harvard University Press, 1999), pp. 6, 11–12. For an excellent analysis of Rawls's use of the phrase "realistic utopia" see Dana S. Howard, "The Scoundrel and the Visionary: On Reasonable Hope and the Possibility of a Just Future," *Journal of Political Philosophy* 27 (2019), pp. 294–317.
[16] John Rawls, *Political Liberalism* (2nd ed., New York: Columbia University Press, 1999 [1993]), p. 269.

be[17] – of practical use to individual citizens, either as a means of clarifying their own ideals or of motivating them to engage in the difficult work of trying to realize them in practice.[18] I do want to insist, however, that it is poorly suited to play the role that Rawls himself assigns to it: that of providing a "shared conception of justice" that can serve as the "fundamental charter" for a liberal polity[19] – especially one that is confronted, as ours is, by the problem of polarization.

Three basic features of the contractarian approach make it poorly suited to play this role. First and most obviously, by framing political debate as a matter of trying to reach consensus on fundamental principles, contractarians make it harder to respond constructively to, or even to properly recognize, the conflicting values and interests that are present in any actually existing liberal society.[20] This line of criticism is often exaggerated: no contractarian that I am aware of claims to have actually identified universally valid principles of justice that are beyond debate and that should therefore be imposed by fiat. Nevertheless, by making consensus on fundamental principles both the aim of and (somehow) the precondition for a liberal politics, the contractarian approach turns its back on the traditional liberal commitment to meliorism, fallibilism, and pluralism, and thus on the traditional liberal conception of politics as an arena in which conflicting values and interests are balanced against each other in a way that is unlikely to be fully satisfying to any of the parties concerned. Instead of seeing political decisions as opportunities to do the most foreseeable good (meliorism), it encourages us to see them as steps toward or away from the realization of a distant and ultimately uncertain ideal. Instead of seeing political setbacks as opportunities to question not

---

[17] For a defense of the view that political philosophy does not need to be of any practical use see David Estlund, *Utopophobia: On the Limits (If Any) of Political Philosophy* (Princeton, NJ: Princeton University Press, 2019).

[18] There has been a lively debate in recent years about the pros and cons of "ideal theorizing"; for a nuanced defense of the practice see A. John Simmons, "Ideal and Nonideal Theory," *Philosophy and Public Affairs* 38 (2010), pp. 5–36; for a notable critique see Charles Mills, "'Ideal Theory' as Ideology," *Hypatia* 20 (2005), pp. 165–84; for a useful survey of the terrain see Laura Valentini, "Ideal vs. Non-ideal Theory: A Conceptual Map," *Philosophy Compass* 7 (2012), pp. 654–64. For my own take on the issue see Eric MacGilvray, "Liberalism Before Justice," *Social Philosophy and Policy* 32 (2016), pp. 354–71.

[19] Rawls, *Theory of Justice*, p. 5 (§1).

[20] I do not think that this conclusion is undercut by Rawls's shift, in *Political Liberalism* and later writings, toward seeking what he calls an "overlapping consensus" among a "family of reasonable liberal conceptions of justice," because on inspection it turns out that the family is, as it were, very close-knit.

only the soundness of our tactics but also the validity of our beliefs (fallibilism), it encourages us to see them as deviations from that ideal. And instead of seeing political disagreement, even about matters of justice, as an inevitable and often valuable feature of life in a free society (pluralism), it encourages us to see it as a sign of unreasonableness in our fellow citizens – or (less likely) in ourselves.[21]

Second, by setting out to construct an overarching social system to whose authority every reasonable person would consent, contractarians make it harder to come to terms with the role that substate groups and institutions play, for better or worse, in shaping individual identity and structuring political conflict. Here again this line of criticism has often been exaggerated: contractarians are not committed, as their "communitarian" critics have sometimes claimed, to a purely voluntarist conception of selfhood or to a strictly individualist social ontology.[22] Nevertheless, the contractarian appeal to pre-political consensus limits the horizons of a liberal politics in two important ways. On the one hand, it rules out the possibility that there might be irreducible conflicts of interest between social classes or groups. As we have seen, liberals have traditionally held that any effort to harmonize capitalism and socialism will necessarily be imperfect and temporary. Contemporary contractarians hold, by contrast, that the interests of all citizens in a just society are, at a sufficient level of abstraction, aligned, and that with the provision of adequate *ex ante* opportunity and *ex post* redistribution economic hierarchy would yield no cause for legitimate complaint.[23] On the other hand, the contractarian appeal to the "basic structure" as the ultimate site and arbiter of justice rules out the possibility that we might have reason to tolerate and even to promote the existence of substate groups and institutions – local governments, churches, civic associations, cultural communities, and so on – whose

---

[21] For two recent works of liberal political philosophy, written from otherwise very different standpoints, that criticize justice-centered liberalism along these lines see Amartya Sen, *The Idea of Justice* (Cambridge, MA: Harvard University Press, 2009); and Gerald Gaus, *The Tyranny of the Ideal: Justice in a Diverse Society* (Princeton, NJ: Princeton University Press, 2016).

[22] See, for example, Michael J. Sandel, *Liberalism and the Limits of Justice* (2nd ed., New York: Cambridge University Press, 1998 [1982]), and the response by Amy Gutmann, "Communitarian Critics of Liberalism," *Philosophy and Public Affairs* 14 (1985), pp. 308–22.

[23] For an influential critique of this "distributive paradigm" see Iris Marion Young, *Justice and the Politics of Difference* (Princeton, NJ: Princeton University Press, 1990), especially chapters 1–3.

norms and practices challenge, or at least dissent from, those of the liberal state, and which therefore limit and check its authority. As we saw in Chapter 4, Tocqueville held that "intermediate powers" like this played a crucial role in preventing "democratic despotism" in the United States, and Victorian pluralists like Lord Acton, Neville Figgis, and Frederic Maitland likewise credited them with preserving English liberty. Contractarians hold, by contrast, that no group or institution can legitimately interfere with the relationship between reasonable individuals and the just social structure that they have willed into existence.[24]

Third and finally, by insisting that we have to step back from the contingencies of our own time and place to determine what justice requires of us, contractarians make it harder to think about how best to pursue positive political change in the present. The first premise of the contractarian position is that we need a fixed point of orientation – a regulating ideal – to guide our political conduct: as Rawls puts it, "until the ideal is identified ... nonideal theory lacks an objective, an aim, by reference to which its queries can be answered."[25] This line of argument, straightforward as it may seem, oversimplifies the challenge of bringing about positive political change in two important ways. First, in a society in which we disagree about what justice requires – and in which many people refuse or otherwise fail to comply with its demands even when we do agree – responsible political decision-making is not just a matter of comparing the available alternatives and choosing the one that (by my own lights) more closely approximates ideal justice. It also requires that I take into account the foreseeable consequences of my actions. Will voting for my preferred candidate make it more likely that my least-preferred candidate wins? Will implementing my preferred policy now create a backlash that moves the polity further from my ideal in the long run? Will accepting a political compromise hasten or delay progress toward the ideal? Second, even if we think that tactical considerations like this can be

---

[24] For a useful analysis of how contractarian "rationalism" obscures the existence and underestimates the importance of this "pluralist" strand of the liberal tradition see Jacob T. Levy, *Rationalism, Pluralism, and Freedom* (New York: Oxford University Press, 2015). For a defense of liberalism that treats freedom of association as a primary value see Chandran Kukathas, *The Liberal Archipelago: A Theory of Diversity and Freedom* (New York: Oxford University Press, 2003).

[25] Rawls, *Law of Peoples*, p. 90. Simmons puts the point more forcefully; "[t]o dive into nonideal theory without an ideal theory in hand," he argues, "is simply to dive blind, to allow irrational free rein to the mere conviction of injustice and to eagerness for change of any sort": Simmons, "Ideal and Nonideal Theory," p. 34.

accommodated within the parameters of ideal theory,[26] the contractarian approach fails to take into account the effect that political change itself will have on our existing beliefs. Our ideas about justice developed in response to a particular set of social and political circumstances and are likely to change as the circumstances themselves change in the pursuit of justice as we currently conceive of it. If they do not, this is as likely to be the result of stubbornness or lack of imagination as of moral clarity on our part.[27]

Taken together, these considerations raise serious doubts about the possibility that a contractarian theory of justice might serve as the "fundamental charter" for a pluralistic and increasingly polarized liberal polity. Any constructive response to the problem of polarization will require that we engage our fellow citizens in a spirit of meliorism, fallibilism, and pluralism, that we remain open to the possibility that conflicts of interest between certain classes and groups might be irreducible, that we be prepared to tolerate (at a minimum) the political influence of groups and institutions with which we profoundly disagree, and that we admit that the question of how best to chart a course toward a just society is complicated and uncertain enough to make the line between ideal and nonideal theory extremely difficult to draw. As we have seen, in rejecting these propositions contemporary contractarians depart sharply from the mainstream of the liberal tradition that stretches (roughly speaking) from Constant to Berlin. To be sure, none of these considerations provides conclusive grounds for abandoning the contractarian approach. A determined contractarian might bite the bullet and insist that reasoned consensus on basic principles of justice is both possible and desirable – or at least that we have a duty to seek it – and that the intuitions that I have tried to prime here should therefore be set aside. To move beyond this impasse, it will be helpful to consider some cases. I therefore turn back now to the two immanent critiques of liberalism that I sketched earlier: the claim, most closely associated with the political right, that it corrodes the

---

[26] Simmons offers some suggestions about how this might be done at "Ideal and Nonideal Theory," pp. 18–25.

[27] This emphasis on the historical contingency of our political ideals is a central theme in the political writings of Bernard Williams; see, for example, his essays "Realism and Moralism in Political Theory" and "In the Beginning Was the Deed," in *In the Beginning Was the Deed: Realism and Moralism in Political Argument*, ed. Geoffrey Hawthorn (Princeton, NJ: Princeton University Press, 2005), pp. 1–28. Richard Rorty develops a more rhetorical version of this line of argument in his *Contingency, Irony, and Solidarity* (New York: Cambridge University Press, 1989).

ethical foundations of social life, and the claim, most closely associated with the political left, that it is complicit in the power structures of capitalism and imperialism. Each of these critiques calls attention to an important source of political polarization, and in each case, as we will see, a freedom-centered liberalism offers a more constructive response than its justice-centered counterpart.

5.3 CORRUPTION AND COMMUNITY

Ever since liberalism first emerged as a distinct political ideology, critics have argued that the freedom that it offers, and the ethos of pluralism and toleration that it embodies and enforces, is incompatible with human flourishing. The oldest and most influential versions of this critique are religiously motivated. The papal encyclical *Libertas Humana* (1888), for example – one of a long line of papal polemics against liberalism that stretches from the time of the French Revolution to the Second Vatican Council – takes liberals to task for "ascrib[ing] to human reason the only authority to decide what is true and what is good," thereby opening the way to "universal corruption": "If unbridled license of speech and of writing be granted to all," it warns, then "nothing will remain sacred and inviolate," and "pernicious and manifold error, as too often happens, will easily prevail."[28] This line of argument has also been stated in secular terms; Leo Strauss warns, for example, of a "[l]iberal relativism" which "has its roots in the notion that everyone has a natural right to the pursuit of happiness as he understands happiness": "The more we cultivate reason," he concludes, "the more we cultivate nihilism" and "the less we are able to be loyal members of society."[29] Alasdair MacIntyre argues along similar lines that the liberal conception of political community as "an arena in which individuals each pursue their own self-chosen conception of the good life" is "inimical to the construction and sustaining of the types of communal relationships required for the best kind of human life": although "the tradition of the virtues was able to survive the horrors of the last dark ages," he warns, "[t]his time ... the barbarians are not waiting

---

[28] Pope Leo XIII, *Libertas Humana* (1888) §§16, 23. For a broader examination of the Church's evolving attitude toward liberal ideas in the nineteenth and twentieth centuries see Emile Perreau-Saussine, *Catholicism and Democracy: An Essay in the History of Political Thought*, trans. Richard Rex (Princeton, NJ: Princeton University Press, 2012 [2011]).

[29] Leo Strauss, *Natural Right and History* (Chicago: University of Chicago Press, 1953), p. 6.

beyond the frontiers; they have already been governing us for quite some time."[30]

A distinct but overlapping critique takes liberalism to task not for promoting individual autonomy but rather for undermining the conditions for its enjoyment. These critics accuse liberals of failing to understand that our individuality, and thus our capacity for free choice, is constituted by our social environment, and that to conceive of this environment as itself a matter of personal choice – and thus of public indifference – is both conceptually incoherent and practically disastrous. The conservative philosopher Roger Scruton argues, for example, that liberalism "isolates man from history, from culture, from all those unchosen aspects of himself which are in fact the preconditions of his subsequent autonomy"; "[i]t tries to stretch the notion of choice to include every institution on which people have conferred legitimacy, without conceding that their sense of legitimacy stems precisely from their respect for themselves as beings formed, nurtured and amplified by these things."[31] The social democratic philosopher Charles Taylor agrees that "the free individual can only maintain his identity within a society/culture of a certain kind," and so cannot "be concerned purely with his individual choices and the associations formed from such choices to the neglect of the matrix in which such choices can be open or closed, rich or meagre."[32] The communitarian philosopher Michael Sandel puts the point the other way around: "The triumph of the voluntarist conception of freedom," he argues "has coincided, paradoxically, with a growing sense of disempowerment," because "[e]ven as we think and act as freely choosing, independent selves, we find ourselves implicated in a network of dependencies we did not choose and increasingly reject."[33]

Contractarians have offered a consistent response to each of these critiques, from Locke's *Letter on Toleration* through to Rawls's *Political Liberalism*: disagreements about what (if anything) is the true religion, about what virtue consists in and how it should be cultivated, and about what kind of community is most conducive to human flourishing, are so deep, their implications for our lives so profound, and our disposition to

---

[30] Alasdair MacIntyre, *After Virtue: A Study in Moral Theory* (2nd ed., Notre Dame, IN: University of Notre Dame Press, 1984 [1981]), pp. 195, xv, 263.
[31] Roger Scruton, *The Meaning of Conservatism* (New York: Macmillan, 1980), p. 112.
[32] Charles Taylor, "Atomism" (1979), in *Philosophical Papers*, vol. 2: *Philosophy and the Human Sciences* (New York: Cambridge University Press, 1985), p. 207.
[33] Michael J. Sandel, *Democracy's Discontent: America in Search of a Public Philosophy* (Cambridge, MA: Harvard University Press, 1996), p. 202.

fight about them so strong, that the only defensible policy is one of individual liberty and mutual toleration. On this view, a liberal polity should focus on the protection of certain basic rights – to privacy, property, and bodily integrity; to belief, thought, and expression; to assembly, association, and movement; and so on – that define a domain of conduct within which individuals are free to pursue the good as they understand it. As contractarians have repeatedly emphasized, this does not amount to an endorsement of moral neutrality or relativism, because the reasons that liberals have for granting people this kind of freedom – to show them the respect that they are owed as reasoning creatures – are themselves moral in nature.[34] Contractarian liberals do not deny that religion, virtue, authenticity, and community are important human values; on the contrary, it is precisely because they *are* such important values that efforts to impose them politically are so objectionable in principle, and meet with such vigorous resistance in practice. In short, they emphasize that modern societies are pluralistic societies, and that liberalism as they conceive of it provides the only just and feasible response to this kind of pluralism.[35]

Despite its obvious attractions, this brand of liberalism is poorly suited for defending liberal principles in a time of political polarization. As we saw in the Introduction, contractarians hold that a political order is only legitimate if its authority rests on the consent of those who are subject to it, but emphasize that consent can be improperly given and improperly withdrawn. The key question from this point of view is not what the citizens of a given polity actually *have* consented to, but rather what a reasonable person *would* or *should* have consented to. The boundaries of reasonable consent – that is, the question of what rights citizens actually have – are therefore defined pre-politically (presumably by the liberal philosopher), and any citizen or polity that fails to respect those boundaries is *ipso facto* acting unjustly. This line of argument has two troubling implications. First and most obviously, it treats ordinary politics as a standing threat to individual liberty and sets up an irreducible tension between liberal principles and democratic government. Second and more

---

[34] See, for example, Charles Larmore, "The Moral Basis of Political Liberalism," *Journal of Philosophy* 96 (1999), pp. 599–625.
[35] Rawls argues, for example, that "the problem of political liberalism" is to show "that there may exist over time a stable and just society of free and equal citizens profoundly divided by reasonable religious, philosophical, and moral doctrines," and that "[e]xcept on the basis of ... equal liberty of conscience and freedom of thought ... firmly founded and publicly justified, no reasonable political conception of justice is possible": Rawls, *Political Liberalism*, pp. xxv–xxvi.

fundamentally, it frames political debate, insofar as it touches on questions of justice or right, as a matter of identifying not just the best policy, but the policy that any right-thinking person would endorse on reflection. Such an approach makes it tempting to see political disagreement, insofar as it touches on questions of justice or right, not as an expected feature of life in a pluralistic society, but rather as a sign of ignorance or bad faith in one's fellow citizens.[36] This is of course exactly the attitude that citizens of opposing views tend to adopt toward one another under conditions of political polarization.

Contractarian liberals therefore invert the liberal position that I have described here, and that was defended by the mainstream of the liberal tradition from its origins in the early decades of the nineteenth century through the middle decades of the twentieth. As we saw in Chapter 4, the liberal tradition began with the problem of reconciling the practice of republican self-government with the rise of social and political equality, and the first thinkers to call themselves "liberal" promoted market freedom in the broad sense of the term — freedoms of association, expression, exchange, and so on — as a means of limiting the power of the democratic state and of stimulating the energies of the democratic citizen. In this sense they were no less committed to the defense of individual rights than their contractarian forebears. However, as the harmful effects of the unregulated exercise of market freedom (especially, but not only, in the economic realm) came into clearer focus — and as the newly enfranchised working class gained the political power to do something about them — the pendulum began to swing in the other direction, and liberal polities set out to create the material and social conditions that are necessary to make the equal enjoyment of republican freedom possible, and its exercise meaningful. In each case liberal thinkers did not present their position as something that would or should be embraced by all reasonable people; rather, they engaged directly in the hard work of political mobilization, negotiation, and compromise, even as they admitted that there is not a definitive answer to the question of how the two kinds of freedom that they valued should be balanced against one another.

---

[36] Ironically, Rawls himself emphasizes that uncertainty about how to weigh conflicting evidence, define key terms, and balance competing value claims – what he calls the "burdens of judgment" – limits our ability to reach agreement on fundamental moral questions: ibid., pp. 54–8. It is not clear how this appreciation of the irreducibility of disagreement even among people of good will can be reconciled with a commitment to identifying principles of justice to whose legitimacy all reasonable people could consent.

In addition to more accurately reflecting the history of the liberal tradition, this account provides a more straightforward response to the claim that liberals value freedom over virtue and community. On the one hand, it reminds us that the nonresponsible choices – the market freedoms – that liberal citizens enjoy are secured through the exercise of their republican freedom. As we saw in Chapter 3, there is a wide range of reasons that liberal polities might have for allowing nonresponsible choice in a given domain: to maintain social stability, to limit the power of the state, to promote social progress, to foster personal development, and so on. The crucial point for our purposes is that in a liberal polity these freedoms are not imposed on "virtuous" or "organic" communities by ideological fiat; they are an expression of the political will of those very communities. Those of us who are unhappy with the amount or kind of market freedom that individuals enjoy – as, again, we all no doubt are in different ways and to different extents – can use our own republican freedom to work for change in the public sphere, or our own market freedom to try to change the "private" behavior of our fellow citizens – as indeed the critics cited above have each done. On the other hand, this account reminds us that all liberal polities place substantial limits on market freedom, and do so for reasons that are themselves liberal: to ensure that citizens have the resources and opportunities that are necessary for effective political participation, to protect them against the arbitrary exercise of power in "private" domains like the family and the workplace, and so on. To suggest that classical liberals like Constant, Tocqueville, and Mill – let alone "new" liberals like Green, Hobhouse, Hobson, and Dewey – did not understand that our capacity for free choice is constituted and shaped by the social environment in which our choices are made is to fail to grasp the most basic premises of their thought.

A further advantage of a freedom-centered liberalism is that by tracing the origins of the liberal tradition (correctly) to the rise of social and political equality over the course of the nineteenth and twentieth centuries, it allows us to distinguish liberal ideas and practices from early modern developments like the Protestant Reformation, the rise of experimental science, the "discovery" and exploitation of the New World, and the emergence of commercial societies. Critics of liberalism who are concerned about the social consequences of those developments – who complain, for example, about the rise of secularism, technocracy, colonialism, and capitalism – are not really objecting to *liberalism*; they are objecting to modernity itself: after all, nonliberal societies have been just as profoundly implicated in and affected by these developments as liberal ones. (It is telling that critics who argue along these lines often describe manifestly illiberal early modern thinkers like Machiavelli, Bacon, Descartes, and Hobbes as the true founders of liberalism.[37]) It is doubtful, to say the least, whether any political ideology can be credited with this kind of influence: surely modernity in all of its complexity is at least as much a product of technological innovation, rising levels of wealth and education, and increased contact between people from radically different backgrounds and cultures as of any organized set of political ideas, liberal or otherwise. The essential point for our purposes is that liberalism is not coextensive with modernity, it is a particular way of responding to the social and political forces that modernity has unleashed.

The critic might of course respond that the liberal response to modernity has been inadequate or misguided. As we have seen, a freedom-centered liberalism can accommodate this kind of criticism up to a point: protest and reform are central features of life in a liberal polity, and there are many different ways of balancing republican and market freedom – and of designing republican institutions themselves – within the horizon of a liberal politics. However, there are two more radical alternatives. One, which we might properly describe as *utopian*, holds that the only viable way to respond to the corruption of modern social and political life is to withdraw from politics altogether. This is presumably what MacIntyre has in mind when he suggests that "[w]e are waiting not for a Godot, but for another – doubtless very different – St. Benedict."[38] Liberals have no quarrel, as far as I can see, with this kind of quietism. A second response, which is *authoritarian* in practice but sometimes has utopian aims, holds that the only viable response to modern corruption is to submit the will of the people as expressed through republican institutions to that of a "higher" authority: a clerical hierarchy, as in ultramontane Catholicism or political Islamism; a privileged class, as in hereditary aristocracy or vanguardist socialism; or an idealized version of "the people" themselves, as in fascism or populism. A freedom-centered liberalism is of course fundamentally incompatible with, and irreconcilably opposed to, political ideologies like these, but it does not have a non-question-begging response to them; as I have said, all it can do is help us

---

[37] See, for example, chapter 1 of Deneen's *Why Liberalism Failed*, which presents in rather blunt terms a line of argument that is laid out more subtly by Strauss and his followers.
[38] MacIntyre, *After Virtue*, p. 263. This allusion to the founder of Christian monasticism helped to inspire a Christian countercultural movement known as the "Benedict Option": see in particular Rod Dreher, *The Benedict Option: A Strategy for Christians in a Post-Christian Nation* (New York: Sentinel, 2017).

see where the key political bets are being placed. At issue, ultimately, is the question of human equality: not the abstract and inflexible kind of equality that contractarians appeal to, but the concrete and contestable kind of equality that is imperfectly embodied in the practices of self-government and individual liberty – of republican and market freedom – that liberal societies have painstakingly developed and refined over the last two centuries; a kind of equality that is fundamentally threatened by the rise of political polarization.

5.4 CAPITALISM AND EMPIRE

The critique of liberalism that we have just examined boils down to the claim that liberal efforts to promote freedom and equality are excessive or ill-considered. A very different line of criticism holds that liberalism's claim to the mantle of freedom and equality is largely or entirely specious. Here again the critique takes two different but related forms. The first argues that liberalism promotes class domination; that by defining equality as formal equality before the law and freedom as the absence of constraint it clears the way for the exploitation of the poor and vulnerable in the endless pursuit of profit, and for the destruction of the natural environment in the endless pursuit of growth. Liberalism, according to this line of argument, provides an ideological mask for capitalism.[39] The second critique argues that liberalism promotes cultural and racial domination; that by making claims to equal freedom conditional on individual or civilizational maturity – or simply by providing a rhetorical fig leaf for national chauvinism and prejudice – it clears the way for the exploitation of non-European peoples; whether directly, through conquest and occupation, or indirectly, by legitimizing an international system that traps the formerly colonized "global south" in a subordinate position. Liberalism, according to this line of argument, provides an ideological mask for

---

[39] This line of argument can be traced back at least as far as Marx and Engels' sarcastic references to "bourgeois freedom" in the *Communist Manifesto* and elsewhere. The subsequent literature is of course vast and diverse; some notable twentieth-century contributions include Harold J. Laski, *The Rise of European Liberalism: An Essay in Interpretation* (London: George Allen and Unwin, 1936); C. B. Macpherson, *The Political Theory of Possessive Individualism: Hobbes to Locke* (New York: Oxford University Press, 1962); and Eric Hobsbawm's trilogy *The Age of Revolution: 1789–1848*, *The Age of Capital: 1848–1875*, and *The Age of Empire: 1875–1914* (New York: Vintage Books, 1962, 1975, and 1987).

imperialism.[40] Although they appeal to different features of the liberal position, these two lines of argument can be made to work together in a familiar way: insofar as imperialism can be said to advance the ends of capitalism and vice versa, liberalism serves as an all-purpose foil for movements seeking economic, racial, and global justice, and indeed as the leading ideological obstacle to radical social and political change.

Each of these critiques contains more than a kernel of truth: liberals have often been enthusiastic capitalists – and have almost always been at least half-hearted ones – and many liberal thinkers and polities have also been enthusiastic – or at least half-hearted – imperialists. However, there is an obvious asymmetry between them: almost all liberals are willing to avow their allegiance, however qualified, to some form of capitalism, but in the postwar period liberals have generally ignored or disavowed the liberal entanglements with empire.[41] Despite the close connections between these two lines of criticism, it therefore makes sense to consider them separately. Taken in itself the capitalism critique, as we might call it, can be dealt with fairly straightforwardly (though not of course conclusively). As we saw in Chapter 4, liberal thought and practice underwent a profound transformation over the course of the nineteenth century, as the early enthusiasm for market freedom as a tool for expanding opportunity, promoting prosperity, and limiting the power of the state was increasingly qualified by concerns about the horrific effects of industrialization on the economically vulnerable. Since the later decades of the nineteenth century the question for liberals has not been *whether* capitalism should be regulated but rather how and to what extent, and as we have seen liberalism is compatible with a wide range of responses to this question, ranging from the *laissez-faire* approach of the Manchester School to the "practicable socialism" of the "new" liberals – with actual

---

[40] Here again the literature, though of more recent origin, is vast and diverse. Three notable contributions that focus specifically on liberal political thought are Bhikhu Parekh, "Superior People: The Narrowness of Liberalism from Mill to Rawls," *Times Literary Supplement*, February 25, 1994, pp. 11–13; Bhikhu Parekh, "Liberalism and Colonialism: A Critique of Locke and Mill," in J. N. Pieterse and B. C. Parekh, eds., *The Decolonization of Imagination: Culture, Knowledge and Power* (London: Zed Books, 1995), pp. 81–98; and Uday Singh Mehta, *Liberalism and Empire: A Study in Nineteenth-Century British Social Thought* (Chicago: University of Chicago Press, 1999). See also more recently Onur Ulas Ince, *Colonial Capitalism and the Dilemmas of Liberalism* (New York: Oxford University Press, 2018) and Jeanne Morefield, *Empires Without Imperialism: Anglo-American Decline and the Politics of Deflection* (New York: Oxford University Press, 2014) which focus respectively on the origins and (putative) decline of liberal imperialism.
[41] A notable, if partial, exception is Niall Ferguson, *Empire: How Britain Made the Modern World and the Lessons for Global Power* (New York: Basic Books, 2002).

liberal practice tilting decidedly in the latter direction. The crucial point for liberals, again, is that the question of how to strike a proper balance between republican and market freedom – and thus, in the economic domain, between socialism and capitalism – must itself be decided by republican means and remain open to revision by republican means over time. A freedom-centered liberalism is therefore considerably more flexible – and considerably less receptive to claims about the inviolability of property rights or the immutability of schemes of distributive justice – than its contractarian counterpart.

The critic might respond that it is naive to think that capitalism can be subject to popular control, given its tendency to concentrate wealth in the hands of the capitalist class, and given the disproportionate political influence that that class is able to exert. This challenge has been magnified by the intensification of global trade, which threatens to create a "race to the bottom" dynamic in which states that muster the political will to regulate capitalism more closely become less economically competitive than states that give it freer rein. Again, these concerns are well-founded: republican polities have been wrestling with the problem of limiting the political power of the wealthy since classical antiquity, and liberals have been arguing about the domestic political implications of global trade since the eighteenth century. Nevertheless, we should not lose sight of the success that liberal polities have had in ensuring that the prosperity that capitalism generates is broadly shared, and in limiting the harms that it does to the working class, the poor, and the natural environment – even in the face of fierce and sometimes violent resistance. The basic model whose outlines we examined in Chapter 4 – combining free enterprise with consumer, workplace, and environmental safety regulations, social insurance programs, public provision or subsidy of essential goods like health care and education, and direct aid to the poor – has proven to be extraordinarily effective and resilient, and the wide variety of ways in which it has been adapted to fit the political, economic, and cultural circumstances of different times and places is a testament to the capaciousness of the liberal conception of freedom.

Many critics on the anti-liberal left will object that this model has fallen short in many cases and will point in particular to the rollback of regulations, the retrenchment of public services, the decline of labor unions, the rise of wealth and income inequality, and the reduction of social mobility in advanced democracies over the last several decades. Many liberals will heartily agree. The difference between the liberal and anti-liberal left – to the extent that there is a meaningful difference – boils down at this point to a question of tactics. The liberal will insist that economic reform, like all reform, should be pursued whenever possible through existing republican institutions – keeping in mind again that those institutions can themselves be reformed, and that institutional reform often depends on direct action via protests, acts of civil disobedience, strikes, boycotts, and so on. Liberals have three basic reasons for adopting this position, although different liberals weigh them in different ways. The first reason is moral: the liberal commitment to equality requires that all interests be represented in the making of public policy, including the interests of the powerful, and this is exactly what republican institutions are (or should be) designed to do – although again the question of *how* different interests should be represented is a matter of political debate, and subject to change. The second reason is epistemic: all reforms have unanticipated consequences, and requiring that they be enacted only after a process of public deliberation and negotiation in which a wide variety of interests are represented – and that they continue to pass the test of public accountability over time – makes it less likely that ill-considered policies will be enacted. The third reason is pragmatic: lasting political change depends, for better or worse, on the cooperation (or at least the acquiescence) of the powerful – keeping in mind that power comes in many forms – and this cooperation is most likely to be secured, for better or worse, when change is brought about through institutions in which their interests are represented, and through processes that they accept as legitimate.

Many critics on the anti-liberal left find this liberal commitment to pursuing reform, economic or otherwise, by working within existing political institutions to be exasperating and at times infuriating – as indeed politics generally is. There is an enormous amount of misery and injustice in the world, and to say that the victims should have the patience to wait for efforts at reform to play out – and the confidence to believe that those efforts will eventually succeed – is from this point of view to show extraordinary complacency in the face of human suffering. The liberal need not deny the premise to ask what alternative the critic has in mind. An authoritarian might argue that the only way to break the power of the economic elite – or of any elite – is to seize power from it by force and rule in the name of the downtrodden class (as we saw in Chapter 3, "neoliberals" have sometimes been inclined to seize power for the opposite purpose). A utopian – who, as I have pointed out, is often an authoritarian in practice – might argue that a decisive transformation of social relations or a cathartic act of political violence will purge human nature of the selfish, status-seeking, and dominating impulses that make meaningful change so hard to achieve. Again, a freedom-centered liberalism firmly rejects each of these positions but does not have a non-question-begging response to any of them; it can only help us to see where the key political bets are being placed. The liberal will insist that no party, group, or class can be trusted with unchecked power; that lasting political change requires widespread "buy-in," especially from the powerful, or else a level of repression whose costs would far outweigh any promised benefits; and that the perverse aspects of human nature can be channeled in more or less constructive ways but never entirely overcome. As we have seen, within those bounds a freedom-centered liberalism is compatible with a wide range of economic, social, and political arrangements.

The claim that liberal thinkers and polities are responsible for some of the many wrongs that have been done in the name of empire is harder to respond to, not because it is untrue, but because it is not clear how it should affect the way we think about liberalism today, or how it might help us to choose between liberalism and its ideological rivals – each of which has also had significant atrocities, imperial and otherwise, committed in its name. The basic force of the critique is easy to grasp: a political ideology that claims to stand for the equal enjoyment of freedom, in the dual sense of individual liberty and self-government, has not only been complicit in the conquest and subjugation of non-European peoples, but has ventured (at times) to defend those practices as a matter of liberal principle. As I have already pointed out, contemporary liberals are almost unanimous in disavowing colonialism and imperialism as they were practiced prior to the Second World War; indeed, one of the great achievements of the recent scholarly literature on the subject has been to break the silence that surrounded that ugly history and to call liberals (and others) to account for its legacy. The question for our purposes is whether the liberal entanglements with empire should be seen simply as signs of hypocrisy or moral blindness on the part of the thinkers and actors concerned – deplorable in themselves but otherwise detachable from liberalism properly speaking – or whether on the contrary there is a deeper connection between liberal ideals and what the political theorist Uday Mehta has described as "the urge to dominate the world."[42]

This question is hard to parse, in large part because the domination of weaker by stronger groups is such a depressingly ubiquitous practice in human history; one that almost all sufficiently powerful states and peoples have engaged in regardless of cultural background or political ideology.

---

[42] Mehta, *Liberalism and Empire*, p. 20.

Capitalism and Empire

"Modern" imperialism as practiced by European powers originated in the latter part of the fifteenth century – long before the earliest expressions of what were later called liberal ideas – and was a long-standing practice by the early decades of the nineteenth century, when the first thinkers to call themselves liberals began to respond to it. Liberal thinkers who wrestled with the question of empire, as nearly all of them did, were therefore not just discussing abstract matters of principle but also responding to an established pattern of facts: the question of whether a liberal polity should acquire an empire is very different from the question of what it should do about an empire that already exists. The issue is further complicated by the fact that the question of empire is often – even usually – framed as a question of national interest and is therefore strongly colored by considerations of *realpolitik*: the question of whether a liberal polity should acquire an empire takes a very different form when its geopolitical rivals (whether liberal or not) have already done so or are in the process of doing so. A further and related layer of complexity arises from the fact that empires are powerful symbols of national prestige which, like all powerful symbols, are often exploited for domestic political purposes. Many of the liberal responses to the question of empire were strategic interventions in political debates in which their opponents – especially on the political right[43] – were using jingoistic rhetoric to advance their own agendas.

These considerations do not mitigate or excuse the wrongs that have been done in the name of liberal (or European) imperialism, they just help us to see why it is hard to sort out the relationship between liberalism's guiding values and its imperial legacy. We can nevertheless distinguish four basic stances that liberals, *qua* liberals, have taken toward the question of empire. The first, which we might call *commercial liberalism*, puts commerce at the center of liberal foreign policy, and holds that liberal polities should shun the temptations of conquest and imperial rule and focus instead on promoting free trade and open markets. Adam Smith, with his support for American independence, his withering criticism of the East India Company, and his opposition to colonial mercantilism more generally, was an early and highly influential advocate of this way of thinking,[44] which was also endorsed by prominent liberal defenders of

---

[43] Especially, but not exclusively; see, for example, the election-year pamphlet *Fabianism and the Empire: A Manifesto by the Fabian Society*, ed. George Bernard Shaw (London: Grant Richards, 1900).

[44] Adam Smith, *An Inquiry into the Nature and Causes of the Wealth of Nations* (Oxford: Clarendon Press, 1979 [1776]), IV.vii.c; on the East India Company see also ibid. V. i.e.26–8.

laissez-faire such as Jeremy Bentham, Richard Cobden, Herbert Spencer, and Joseph Schumpeter.[45] A similar conviction animates Benjamin Constant's impassioned defense of the "spirit of commerce" against the "spirit of conquest."[46] In its more optimistic and expansive form commercial liberalism holds that commerce is the only humane and effective means of promoting liberal ideals abroad.[47] In its more cautious and insular form it calls attention to the fact that imperial rule always corrupts the imperial power itself.[48] In either case, commercial liberals hold that the costs of maintaining an empire far exceed any benefits that it might yield, and that liberal imperialism is, if not a contradiction in terms, then at least a profoundly misguided policy.

A second school of thought, which we might call *paternalistic liberalism*, holds that empire can be justified on liberal grounds if (and only if) it is administered for the benefit of the colonized peoples, and in particular if

---

[45] Jeremy Bentham, "Emancipate Your Colonies!" (1830 [1793]), in *Rights, Representation, and Reform: Nonsense Upon Stilts and Other Writings on the French Revolution*, ed. Philip Schofield, Catherine Pease-Watkin, and Cyprian Blamires (New York: Oxford University Press, 2002), pp. 289–313; Jeremy Bentham, "Rid Yourselves of Ultramaria" (1822), in *Colonies, Commerce, and Constitutional Law: Rid Yourselves of Ultramaria and Other Writings on Spain and Spanish America*, ed. Philip Schofield (New York: Oxford University Press, 1995), pp. 3–194; Herbert Spencer, *Social Statics* (London: John Chapman, 1851), chapter 27; Herbert Spencer, "Imperialism and Slavery," in *Facts and Comments* (New York: D. Appleton, 1902), pp. 157–71; Joseph Schumpeter, "The Sociology of Imperialisms" (1919), in *Imperialism and Social Classes: Two Essays*, trans. Heinz Norden (New York: Meridian Press, 1955), esp. pp. 64–98. On Cobden see Peter Cain, "Capitalism, War, and Internationalism in the Thought of Richard Cobden," *British Journal of International Studies* 5 (1979), pp. 229–47.

[46] Benjamin Constant, *The Spirit of Conquest* (1814), in *Political Writings*, ed. and trans. Biancamaria Fontana (New York: Cambridge University Press, 1988), pp. 51–83.

[47] Smith suggests, for example, that "[h]ereafter, perhaps, the natives of [non-European] countries may grow stronger, or those of Europe may grow weaker, and the inhabitants of all the different quarters of the world may arrive at that equality of courage and force which, by inspiring mutual fear, can alone overawe the injustice of independent nations into some sort of respect for the rights of one another. But nothing seems more likely to establish this equality of force than that mutual communication of knowledge and of all sorts of improvements which an extensive commerce from all countries to all countries naturally, or rather necessarily, carries along with it": Smith, *Wealth of Nations*, IV.vii. c.80.

[48] As Constant puts it, "[a] government given up to the spirit of invasion and conquest must corrupt a part of the population to secure its active service in its own enterprises ... it must also act upon the rest of the nation, demanding its passive obedience and sacrifices, in such a way as to disturb its reason, pervert its judgment and overturn all its ideas ... All these troubles will occur not for the sake of legitimate self-defence, but in order to acquire remote countries, the possession of which will add nothing to national prosperity, unless we choose to call national prosperity the vain, nefarious renown of a handful of men!": Constant, *Spirit of Conquest*, pp. 63–4, 67 (chapter 8).

Capitalism and Empire 193

(and only if) it seeks to prepare them for self-government, and thus for the enjoyment of liberal freedom. This brand of liberal imperialism adds a political dimension to the "civilizing mission" that European powers took themselves to be (or claimed to be) engaged in from the fifteenth century onward; one that also had important and overlapping religious (Christianizing) and economic (modernizing) dimensions. It was most notably applied in Victorian efforts to justify British colonial rule in India, and is most closely associated among canonical liberal thinkers with John Stuart Mill and his father James, each of whom held important positions in the East India Company.[49] Liberal paternalists often concede, as did both of the Mills, that colonies are a net economic loss to the imperial power, but hold that liberal polities nevertheless have a duty to improve the "backward" or "barbarous" societies with which they come into contact – a position that Rudyard Kipling famously apostrophized as the "White Man's burden." As Kipling's language suggests, the moral credentials of liberal paternalism are ambivalent at best, even if we set aside the fact that many of those who endorsed it did so cynically or hypocritically. On the one hand – this is its liberal side – it delegitimizes the ordinary imperial motivations of plunder and exploitation, and commits imperial powers to the more constructive project of creating the material, social, and institutional conditions for self-government among the colonized people.[50] On the other hand – this is its paternalistic side – its

---

[49] Mill infamously states near the beginning of *On Liberty* that "[d]espotism is a legitimate mode of government in dealing with barbarians, provided the end be their improvement and the means justified by actually effecting that end": John Stuart Mill, *On Liberty* (1859), in *Collected Works*, ed. J. M. Robson (Toronto: University of Toronto Press, 1963–91), vol. 18, p. 224 (chapter 1). He puts the point more bluntly in the contemporaneous essay "A Few Thoughts on Non-Intervention" (1859), where he argues that "nations which are still barbarous have not got beyond the period during which it is likely to be for their benefit that they should be conquered and held in subjection by foreigners," and concludes that "barbarians have no rights as a *nation*, except a right to such treatment as may, at the earliest possible period, fit them for becoming one": Mill, *Collected Works*, vol. 21, pp. 118–19 (original emphasis). Mill's views on colonialism and empire have attracted intense scholarly attention; three influential discussions, ranging from least to most sympathetic, are Mehta, *Liberalism and Empire,* chapters 2–3; Jennifer Pitts, *A Turn to Empire: The Rise of Imperial Liberalism in Britain and France* (Princeton, NJ: Princeton University Press, 2005), chapter 5; and Georgios Varouxakis, *Liberty Abroad: J. S. Mill on International Relations* (New York: Cambridge University Press, 2013), chapter 5.

[50] Mill held, for example, that imperial powers that fail to "improve" their colonies "are guilty of a dereliction of the highest moral trust which can devolve upon a nation: and if they do not even aim at it, they are selfish usurpers, on a par in criminality with any of those whose ambition and rapacity have sported from age to age with the destiny of

appeal to civilizational hierarchy can (and often did) slide into a smug faith in the innate superiority of European peoples, and thus into a convenient rationale for the domination of non-Europeans.[51]

A third school of thought, which we might call *heroic liberalism*, sees empire as a proving ground for the civic virtue of the imperial power, and as an essential tool for promoting political solidarity in the metropole. Needless to say, the effort to promote republican freedom through conquest, although it has an ancient pedigree,[52] is hard to distinguish in practice from ordinary militarism or nationalism, and thus from extra-liberal motivations like national pride and chauvinism.[53] These motivations are what ultimately led François Guizot, for example, to support the French occupation of Algeria despite his initial skepticism.[54] We nevertheless find in Tocqueville – Guizot's parliamentary nemesis – a more distinctively liberal defense of empire. Tocqueville believed that the July Monarchy, with its one-sided emphasis on the pursuit of wealth, was deliberately cultivating an attitude of political passivity among the French people, and thereby promoting the kind of "individualism" that he thought fatal to republican freedom in a democratic society. He became convinced that the conquest and colonization of Algeria provided an opportunity for his fellow citizens to transcend the self-centered materialism that he saw as characteristic of the age.[55] James Fitzjames Stephen

---

masses of mankind": Mill, *Considerations on Representative Government* (1861), *Collected Works*, vol. 19, pp. 567–8 (chapter 18).

[51] On the hardening of British attitudes toward colonized peoples in the later nineteenth century, see Karuna Mantena, *Alibis of Empire: Henry Maine and the Ends of Imperial Liberalism* (Princeton, NJ: Princeton University Press, 2010).

[52] The usual model is Rome, and the *locus classicus* in the modern period is Machiavelli's *Discourses on Livy*. For a useful discussion see David Armitage, "Empire and Liberty: A Republican Dilemma," in Quentin Skinner and Martin van Gelderen, eds., *Republicanism: A Shared European Heritage* (New York: Cambridge University Press, 2003), vol. 2, pp. 29–47.

[53] In calling these motivations "extra-liberal" I do not mean to suggest that liberals are not susceptible to them, just that they are not any more or less so than anyone else.

[54] "With nations as with individuals, greatness has its consequences and conditions from which they cannot withdraw themselves without decline ... The retention of Algeria was, I feel convinced, after 1830, a necessity of this kind; it involved a case of personal greatness for France, and a duty toward the future of the Christian world": François Guizot, *Memoirs to Illustrate the History of My Time*, trans. J. W. Cole (London: Richard Bentley, 1860), vol. 3, p. 242.

[55] Tocqueville's writings about Algeria are collected in Alexis de Tocqueville, *Writings on Empire and Slavery*, ed. and trans. Jennifer Pitts (Baltimore, MD: Johns Hopkins University Press, 2001). For discussion of his evolving position on the issue see Melvin Richter, "Tocqueville on Algeria," *Review of Politics* 25 (1963), pp. 362–98, and Pitts, *A Turn to Empire*, chapter 7, which follows Richter's analysis closely.

Capitalism and Empire

offered a similarly romantic defense of British rule in India, arguing that "ambition is the great incentive to every manly virtue," and that "conquest is the process by which every great state in the world ... has been built up."[56] Although heroic liberalism is not strictly incompatible with its paternalistic counterpart – Stephen seems to have embraced both projects – taken on its own it does not give any weight to the interests of the colonized people and thus does not place any limits, as paternalistic liberalism does, on how they are treated.[57]

A fourth and final school of thought, which we might call *internationalist liberalism*, shares commercial liberalism's hostility toward conquest and imperial rule, but sees international alliances rather than trade as the essential means of promoting and defending liberal ideals abroad. This is the position that was adopted by the "new" liberals in the early part of the twentieth century. Hobhouse and Hobson were each sharply critical of traditional imperialism; indeed, Hobson is best known for arguing that the "taproot of Imperialism" is neither national glory nor belief in a civilizing mission but rather the capitalist quest for profits, and that instead of serving the interests of the financial class by seeking out foreign markets to exploit, the British state should redistribute wealth in order to increase effective demand and improve standards of living domestically.[58] Hobhouse summed up this line of argument in a single sentence: "Militarism, based on Imperialism, has eaten up the national resources which should have gone to improve the condition of the people."[59]

---

[56] Quoted in Duncan Bell, *Reordering the World: Essays on Liberalism and Empire* (Princeton, NJ: Princeton University Press, 2016), p. 56; Bell refers to this way of thinking as "republican imperialism."

[57] Tocqueville, for example, could be shockingly nonchalant about the atrocities that the French were committing in Algeria, and had no patience for what he saw as the self-congratulatory moralism of his British counterparts; "[w]hat I cannot get over," he complains, "is their perpetual attempts to prove that they act in the interest of a principle, or for the good of the natives, or even for the advantage of the sovereigns they subjugate; it is their frank indignation toward those who resist them; these are the procedures with which they almost always surround violence": quoted in Pitts, *A Turn to Empire*, p. 223.

[58] J. A. Hobson, *Imperialism: A Study* (London: J. Nisbet and Company, 1902), quoted at p. 86 (part 1, chapter 6). Vladimir Lenin adopts the critical side of Hobson's analysis wholesale in his influential essay *Imperialism: The Highest Stage of Capitalism* (1917), although his proposed remedy is of course very different.

[59] L. T. Hobhouse, "The Imperial Idea," in *Democracy and Reaction* (London: T. Fisher Unwin, 1904), p. 31. Despite his domestic focus, Hobhouse was neither blind nor indifferent to imperialism's impact on the colonized peoples: "that spirit of domination which rejoices in conquest," he argues, "is by nature hostile to the idea of racial equality, and indifferent to political liberty ... The literature of Imperialism is openly

However, both Hobson and Hobhouse were enthusiastic about the prospect of creating a federation of "civilized" democracies to advance liberal ideals internationally. Here they drew upon, although they did not specifically defend, the legacy of British settler colonialism; that is, they saw the existence of cultural, linguistic, and (as they sometimes put it) racial ties between Britain, Canada, Australia, New Zealand, and the United States as a promising starting point for forming, in Hobhouse's words, "a model, and that on no mean scale, of the International State": "The old doctrine of absolute sovereignty is dead," he argued, and "[t]here exist the political conditions of a democratic alliance which it is the business of the British Liberal to turn to account."[60] Hobson agreed that "a voluntary federation of free British States, working peacefully for the common safety and prosperity, is in itself eminently desirable, and might indeed form a step towards a wider federation of civilized States in the future" – adding that "it will appear only natural that the earlier steps in such a process should take the form of unions of States most closely related by ties of common blood, language, and institutions."[61] The "inter-imperialist" idea, as Hobson called it, of promoting liberal ideals by fostering cooperation among "civilized" democracies anticipates the postwar turn away from national empires and toward institutions of global governance.[62]

Each of these liberal stances toward imperialism has obvious attractions and equally obvious pitfalls. Taken together, they demonstrate that there has never been a unified liberal position on the question of empire, any more than there has on the question of capitalism: indeed, the four

---

contemptuous – sometimes aggressively, sometimes patronizingly – of the 'coloured' races, and scoffs at the old Liberal conception of opening to them the road to self-development, and alternates between a sentimental insistence on the duties owed to them by the white man, and invective against any one who inquires how those duties are being performed": ibid., pp. 36–7.

[60] L. T. Hobhouse, *Liberalism* (1911), in *Liberalism and Other Writings* (New York: Cambridge University Press, 1994), pp. 115–16 (chapter 9). I have reversed the order in which these passages appear in the text.

[61] Hobson, *Imperialism*, p. 351 (part 2, chapter 6). Mill seems to have anticipated this idea: an alliance of the British settler colonies, he suggests, would "add[] to the moral influence, and weight in the councils of the world, of the Power which, of all in existence, best understands liberty – and whatever may have been its errors in the past, has attained to more of conscience and moral principle in its dealings with foreigners, than any other great nation seems either to conceive as possible, or recognise as desirable": Mill, *Considerations on Representative Government*, p. 565 (chapter 18).

[62] On the origins and early development of this way of thinking see Duncan Bell, *The Idea of Greater Britain: Empire and the Future of World Order, 1860–1900* (Princeton, NJ: Princeton University Press, 2007), and more recently *Dreamworlds of Race: Empire and the Utopian Destiny of Anglo-America* (Princeton, NJ: Princeton University Press, 2020).

Capitalism and Empire 197

positions that we examined most closely in Chapter 4 – those of Constant, Tocqueville, Mill, and the "new" liberals – reach four different conclusions on the matter. Moreover, the questions about empire that divided the liberal tradition in its formative period are the same questions that animate foreign policy debates in liberal polities today: whether free trade will bring about political liberalization, whether military force should be used to spread democracy or to protect vulnerable people, whether war can be a useful means of promoting civic virtue and political solidarity, and whether state sovereignty should be sacrificed to multilateral alliances or institutions of global governance. Liberals hold, and have always held, a wide range of positions on each of these questions. What binds them together in the realm of foreign policy is a shared concern for republican freedom: this, if anything, is the source of the liberal "urge" toward imperialism. From that common starting point the hard questions – whether freedom should be promoted through peaceful or coercive means, what effect efforts to promote freedom abroad are likely to have on the enjoyment of freedom domestically, what should be done about societies that lack the material, social, and institutional conditions for effective self-government, what weight should be given to the claims of national self-determination, and (above all) whether interfering with the affairs of another people is likely to do more harm than good – are ultimately matters of judgment rather than of principle, and the answers will vary from person to person and from case to case.[63]

Here again a freedom-centered liberalism is more flexible and context-sensitive than its contractarian counterpart: it is compatible, as we have seen, with a wide range of economic, social, and political arrangements, and is therefore able to admit, and indeed to expect, that the question of how to strike an appropriate balance between republican and market freedom will be answered in different ways in different times and places. Liberalism so understood is "anti-imperialist" in the limited but important sense that it is skeptical toward the idea that specific economic policies, political institutions, cultural norms, or principles of global justice should be exported to or imposed upon other peoples – although it has often been receptive to the idea that there are basic human rights that

---

[63] As Pitts puts it, "[n]o explanation that rests on some set of basic theoretical assumptions in the liberal tradition can possibly explain [its] flexibility on the question of empire ... Rather, we must investigate the pressures and anxieties of certain historical moments to understand how thinkers whom we understand to exist within a broad but identifiable tradition could have disagreed so thoroughly": Pitts, *A Turn to Empire*, p. 4.

liberal polities have at least a *prima facie* duty to protect. This brand of liberalism poses two questions to those who are inclined to take a firmer stance against "empire" in any of its forms. On the one hand, it asks whether we should simply accept the existence and influence of authoritarian regimes; that is, whether we should adopt a policy of noninterference toward such regimes not simply (as we often must) out of prudence, but as a matter of principle. On the other hand – assuming a negative answer to the first question – it asks what nonutopian means the anti-liberal has in mind, beyond the familiar mechanisms of economic development and exchange, global governance and international law, or military intervention, for promoting republican freedom, and thus genuine national self-determination, in places where it has been subverted or has never been enjoyed. In the absence of a clear response to each of those questions, liberals will insist that some combination of those policies – what combination, again, is a matter of debate – offers the only principled course of action for a liberal polity to pursue.

5.5 LIBERAL BOUNDARIES

Needless to say, the preceding discussion does not resolve any of the highly contentious issues that it touches on. I simply hope to have shown that a freedom-centered liberalism provides a shared moral vocabulary for discussing issues like these; that it makes it possible for us to talk about them, despite our disagreements, in a constructive way. Of course, to say that something is *possible* is not to say that it is inevitable or even likely: identifying a shared vocabulary is a necessary but far from sufficient condition for responding to the problem of political polarization. Two deeper challenges remain. The first is to restore a sense of shared civic narrative, and thus of shared fate, that binds the liberal polity together. The declining allegiance to such a narrative – or more precisely, the growing allegiance to competing narratives – is both a cause and an effect, I think, of the fact that many of us deliberately choose sources of information that reinforce rather than challenge our existing beliefs and are sometimes willing to pay significant personal and political costs in order to avoid admitting that we might be (or were) wrong. The second and related challenge is to restore a sense of civic trust, and thus a willingness to compromise and share power with people who disagree with us. The decline of trust is responsible, I think, for the fact that we are increasingly unwilling to accept the legitimacy of rule by our political opponents, and often seem to take perverse pleasure in painting them in the worst possible light.

Still, a necessary condition is still a necessary condition, and the central argument of this book has been that a freedom-centered liberalism offers a promising response to these challenges, and to the problem of polarization that they reflect and reinforce. Liberalism so understood holds that at a sufficient level of abstraction we do share a set of values with our political opponents; that we are committed in common to the pursuit and enjoyment of republican and of market freedom, that we recognize that neither kind of freedom is absolute or inviolable, that our political disagreements ultimately boil down to matters of judgment about how the balance between them should be struck, that these are matters about which reasonable people can disagree, and that to refuse to submit one's own judgments to the tribunal of republican institutions – recognizing, again, that those institutions can themselves be reformed – is to deny one's fellow citizens the status of equal citizenship on which their own republican freedom depends. As I have emphasized throughout this chapter, liberals do not have a non-question-begging response to those who deny that republican and market freedom are genuine values, or who insist that one of them should be entirely sacrificed to the other, or who hold that they have identified a way of harmonizing them that all reasonable people should accept. We can only appeal, as a matter of principle, to the superiority of discussion over force as a means of achieving positive political change, and, as a matter of experience, to the success that liberal polities have had over the last two centuries in making an imperfect and evolving, but nevertheless attractive and durable, form of freedom available to countless human beings. The only alternatives to a liberal politics, as far as I can see, are an authoritarian assertion of factional will or a utopian withdrawal – whether peaceful or violent – from politics as we know it.

I would like to conclude by considering two sets of questions that a contractarian liberal might raise about the freedom-centered view that I have developed here. The first set of questions has to do with the nature of its commitment to republican freedom. I have argued that, from a republican point of view, we are free if and to the extent that we have collectively authorized the social conditions under which we act or are able to supervise and control those who did. But what could it mean, the contractarian might ask, to say that we have authorized the social conditions under which we act, if not that we have in some sense consented to them? Doesn't a commitment to republican freedom therefore commit us to the contractarian ideal of reaching consensus among reasonable people? And doesn't this kind of consensus provide exactly the kind of "shared narrative" on which a liberal politics depends? The second set of questions has to do with the nature of the liberal commitment to market freedom. I have argued that republican freedom has priority over market freedom in the procedural sense that the trade-offs between them have to be made in publicly visible and contestable ways and for publicly avowable reasons. What limits, the contractarian might ask, does a freedom-centered liberalism place on how this balance is struck? How much market freedom does a liberal polity have to offer its citizens in order to count as "liberal"? Are any rights or freedoms inalienable or inviolable? If so, then doesn't a freedom-centered liberalism give priority to justice in at least that limited sense? If not, then does it really count as a liberal view? In either case, doesn't civic trust depend in part on our being confident that there are some things that the state cannot do to us, no matter what faction or coalition of our fellow citizens happens to control it?

These penetrating questions highlight what is, depending how we look at it, either the closest point of contact or the most basic point of contrast between a freedom-centered liberalism and its contractarian counterpart. The first set of questions brings us up against the central paradox of republican self-government: we are only free if we have collectively authorized (or consented to) the social conditions under which we act, but no social and political system has actually won the authorization or consent of all – or even, if we consider it in all of its complexity, of any – of its citizens. The contractarian solution to this paradox is, as we have seen, to retreat to idealization; the question is not what we actually *have* consented to, but rather what we *would* or *should* have consented to if we were fully reasonable. This is a fundamentally backward-looking conception of consent: it assumes that we already know, or could discover on reflection, what justice requires of us. The problem with this way of thinking is that political decisions involve the exercise of judgment, and the exercise of judgment involves making claims about the future: moral claims as well as empirical ones. That is, in defending a given course of action we are not only predicting that a given set of consequences will follow, but also that we and our fellow citizens will evaluate those consequences in a certain way. Needless to say, both kinds of claims are inherently fallible: what we think is going to happen does not always happen, and even when it does, we do not always evaluate the results as we expected.

Because political judgment is prospective and fallible in this way, so too must be our understanding of consent. I propose that we think about it in the following way.[64] Whenever a politically decisive coalition acts in the face of objections from some of its fellow citizens – that is to say, whenever political action is taken – its members must hold, if their decision is to be legitimate, that the dissenters could be brought to accept their position if sufficient arguments and evidence were made available to them – and they must have made, and must continue to make, a good faith effort to provide the necessary arguments and evidence. At the same time they have to admit that this prospective claim of justifiability could in principle be rebutted if sufficient arguments and evidence fail to emerge, or if countervailing arguments and evidence come to light – and, crucially, they have to ensure that the necessary conditions for free and open criticism of their own arguments and evidence are in place.[65] The dissenters assume the opposite set of practical commitments: pointing out the flaws in the acting coalition's arguments, the gaps in their evidence, the ways in which things have not worked out as they predicted, and so on – and of course they have to be prepared to admit that they too may be mistaken. In more personal terms, if you and I disagree about a matter of public policy, and if we each intend to try to impose our beliefs on the polity as a whole (for example, by voting), then I have to believe that you believe that you could persuade me that your preferred course of action is superior to mine if only you had enough time and information, you have to believe the same thing about me, and we each have to have an effective opportunity to persuade the other. We do not necessarily have to avail ourselves of that opportunity: liberalism does not require that we make politics into a full-time occupation. Nevertheless, this is the practical stance that we have to adopt toward one another as fellow citizens of a liberal polity: our republican freedom depends on it, because otherwise we cannot properly be held responsible for the various ways in which our actions are constrained by the exercise of political power.

Unlike a justice-centered liberalism, which requires that we settle certain fundamental questions before we engage in ordinary politics, a freedom-centered liberalism is essentially forward-looking: it combines

---

[64] Here and in the following paragraphs I draw on the discussion in MacGilvray, "Liberalism Before Justice," pp. 368–71, and more generally on Eric MacGilvray, *Reconstructing Public Reason* (Cambridge, MA: Harvard University Press, 2004), chapters 6–8.

[65] These include, but are not necessarily limited to, the freedoms of speech, press, petition, and assembly.

an appreciation of the fact that our judgment is always fallible with a commitment to improving it over time. Political legitimacy is, on this view, not an established state of affairs but rather an ongoing and open-ended project; one whose realization lies in the hands and minds of ordinary citizens. I do not mean to deny or downplay the fact that this is a demanding project: it is often hard to believe that our fellow citizens are people of good will who are acting according to their best lights, and it is often hard to commit ourselves to the hard work of trying to justify ourselves to those who disagree with us, not least because this means that we have to step outside of our ideological comfort zones – and because we often have reason to doubt that our interlocutors are really listening. But this is the shared narrative that we are committed to if we are committed to the project of building and living in a free society, and this is the kind of trust that the citizens of a liberal polity have to have in each other. This prospective conception of legitimacy defines the boundary conditions of a liberal politics: it tells us what we have to believe and do in order for such a politics to be possible.

This, then, is how we can honor the liberal commitment to republican freedom without committing ourselves to the contractarian norm of universal consent among reasonable people – or, to put the point in positive terms, this is how contractarian intuitions about consent can be accommodated within a more traditional freedom-centered framework. Does liberalism so understood place any limits on where a liberal politics can lead us? Is there some minimal amount of market freedom that a polity has to provide in order to count as liberal? We have already seen that a liberal polity has to allow free and open criticism of political beliefs and actions in order to offer genuine republican freedom to its citizens. Beyond that point different liberals will answer the question in different ways; I for one am inclined to bite the bullet and say no. The liberal tradition as I understand it is not bound together by a commitment to a set of extra-political rights or freedoms, but rather by a shared concern with a basic political problem: the problem of striking an appropriate balance between republican and market freedom. As with any problem, we have to start from where we are and work out from there. As I pointed out in the Introduction to this book, there are matters of settled judgment in liberal thought and practice as it currently stands: it is hard to imagine a liberal politics that did not give special weight, for example, to the claims of religious liberty, or that did not treat property rights with special respect. We can probably agree, here and now, that a polity that did not honor these commitments would not qualify as liberal. But what it *means* to honor these commitments – and indeed what qualifies something as a "religion" or as "property" in the first place – has always been a matter of debate. When we consider how profoundly liberal thought and practice on these questions has changed (for better or worse) over the relatively brief span of time that liberalism has been a going concern, it is hard to be confident that even our firmest convictions will not be subject to change in the future.

Contractarians want some assurance that the course of future inquiry and experience will not lead us to abandon certain values that we currently hold dear. A freedom-centered liberalism does not provide this kind of assurance: the only way to ensure that the values that we cherish today are not corrupted or abandoned is through our own efforts and those of like-minded people. This is not to say that we should be expected, here and now, to accept whatever outcomes a liberal politics might yield. Sometimes the strain on our belief in our fellow citizens' commitment to liberal values is too great, and sometimes our fellow citizens do not even pretend to honor those values; for example, when they are openly motivated by cruelty or bigotry. We have all had the experience of obeying laws that we not only disagree with, but that we have reason to believe were imposed in bad faith. In such cases we are not self-governing even in the indirect and long-term way that I have just described: we are obeying force – or, if we happen to be members of the acting coalition, we are compelling others to obey force. And sometimes, if the stakes are high enough, force is the appropriate response to such a situation. There is a distinguished tradition in liberal thought, stretching from John Locke in the 1690s to Martin Luther King in the 1960s, of defending the use of extra-legal means, whether violent or nonviolent, to advance liberal ends in certain circumstances. The question of when this kind of resistance is justified is of course beyond the scope of this book, but as the preceding discussion makes clear its aim should not be to replace but rather to regenerate the guiding values of a liberal politics.

Can we describe the liberal effort to balance republican and market freedom as a justice-*oriented* project? Might we say, in other words, that if we were to reach unforced and enduring agreement on how the balance should be struck – assuming for the sake of argument that this is possible – then we would also have answered the question of what justice requires? I have no objection to this way of putting the point. However, James Madison offers a useful word of caution in the epigraph to this chapter: "Justice," he writes, "is the end of government. It is the end of civil society. It ever has been, and ever will be pursued, until it be obtained, *or until liberty be lost in the pursuit*" (my emphasis). Justice, on this account, is something whose meaning and implications we have to work out together over time: it is the *end* of government and of civil society, not their "first virtue." As the rest of *Federalist* 51 reminds us, to give any authority, whether political or philosophical, the unilateral power to determine and enforce what justice requires, and thus to ignore or override the disagreements about justice that exist among ordinary citizens, is to ensure that liberty will be lost in its pursuit. Because each of us has at best a partial and fallible grasp on what justice requires, liberty remains for Madison, as it must remain for any liberal, the first political value. This way of thinking puts politics rather than philosophy at the center of the liberal project and helps us to see that the deepest worries that we might have about that project are in the end worries about politics itself. It is time to steer the practice – and the defense – of liberalism in this more fruitful direction.

Conclusion

Thanks for joining this call on short notice. You all heard about the accident. I'm going to need to put out a statement. Thoughts?

Thank you, Governor, this should be a short call. We need to widen that stretch of road and put some lighting in. Public safety comes first, it's that simple.

Due respect Governor, it's not that simple. People are diverting to that area because of congestion up in the city. If we widen the road, it's just going to draw more traffic and we'll be back where we started.

What's wrong with giving people choices? Aren't we supposed to help them get where they're going? Safely?

We built a bunch of highways fifty years ago and people chose to move to the suburbs. Now we've got a traffic problem, we've got a pollution problem, and sorry, but the city's got a tax base problem. This stuff isn't random – I've been saying it for years, we're subsidizing sprawl. We've got to draw the line somewhere.

And you want to draw the line at letting people die on country roads? We can't come out against the suburbs – for God's sake, Governor, those are the people who elected you!

Speaking of choices, that driver wasn't wearing a seat belt, was probably speeding, and for all we know might have been asleep at the wheel. Some better choices get made and we aren't even having this conversation.

Yeah, and the family decides to sue and we're having a whole other conversation. We knew that stretch of road was a problem before this happened. You want that to be the headline for the next few months?

Don't get me started on the tort laws. We're subsidizing sprawl and we're subsidizing buck-passing.

Can we stick to the point? We're talking about traffic safety.

It's all connected, isn't it? At least the ambulance chasers voted for the other guy.

All right, I've heard enough. Thank you everyone. You'll have my statement in the morning.

***

Hey, did you hear about that girl with the photos? Pretty sick.

That creep should go to jail, plain and simple. What he did to her was disgusting, and she deserves some justice. I'm tired of this crap.

You think he should go to jail for posting some photos? The guy's an asshole, but doesn't he have a right to do what he wants with his pics? What she did is on her.

You're seriously blaming *her*? What the hell did he think was going to happen? What do you think he *wanted* to happen? You don't have a right to ruin someone's life.

I'm not defending him, I just want to know what you think we should do about it.

How about this: posting sexual content without the person's consent should be against the law. Period.

So you think we should start censoring what people can put on the web? Isn't that kind of a slippery slope? What if I post an embarrassing story about someone, or some juicy gossip? What if I out someone, should that be against the law?

Here's a slippery slope: women already have to deal with sexual harassment, sexual violence, partner abuse, stalking, catcalling, now this. This wasn't just some random guy being an asshole, it's part of a pattern. Enough is enough.

I hear you. I just worry that if we start making it illegal to do stuff that other people find hurtful it's gonna end badly. This'll get hashed out by politicians and juries, not right-thinking people like yourself.

Ha ha. Look, we already stop people from hurting each other in lots of other ways. I'm not saying this is easy, but it seems like something we can do. It's the least we can do for people like her.

Well, you've got more faith in the system than I do. Anyway thanks, I've gotta get back to work.

***

Our guests tonight need no introduction, they're two of our leading voices on immigration and border control. Thanks to both of you for joining us.

What should we be thinking about what we've seen over the last few months?

Thanks for having me. Look, it's very simple: if we can't control the border – or if this Administration doesn't *want* to control the border – then we don't have a country any more. The citizens of this great nation should be the ones who decide who gets to become a citizen. That's how democracy is supposed to work.

Thanks, it's good to be here. Let's not forget that the citizens of this great nation are also immigrants or descended from immigrants. This country was built by immigrants. To say that we should turn people away who are just looking for a better life, and send them back to God knows what, that just isn't who we are.

This country was built on the Constitution and the rule of law. That's who we are, and that's what holds us together. I'm not against immigration. The vast majority of people in this country aren't against immigration. But people have to follow the rules.

The Constitution says that if you're born here, you're a citizen. That's the rule. So, you're talking about breaking up families, or sending kids, fellow citizens, off to live in a place they've never known. I'll say it again, that's not who we are.

I'm talking about controlling the border. Right now, if you can make it across the chances that you get sent back – hell, the chances that you even appear before a judge – are pretty darn low. And people know that. That's why they're coming in the first place. I don't understand how you can defend a system that works like that.

And I don't understand how you can be part of a political movement that beats the crap out of people and sets their houses on fire. You think it's an accident those people had certain last names and that house was in a certain neighborhood?

I'm not condoning violence ...

You say you're not condoning it but those are your supporters. You tell people "we" don't have a country any more and what do you expect them to do? Let's be honest, these aren't random incidents, this country has a long and ugly history of using violence against certain groups to keep things a certain way. We need to be better than that, and the dog whistles don't help.

The rule of law is the rule of law. People who cross the border illegally should be punished, and so should people who take the law into their own hands.

I don't have anything against enforcing the law. But we need to see the law in a broader context. We shouldn't do things that are obviously cruel, like breaking up families. And we shouldn't do things that make the problems we have with hatred and discrimination in this country even worse. That's all I'm saying.

Well, there's a lot more to say but we've got to go to a break. Always good to hear from the two of you, thanks for being here.

It was my pleasure.

Thanks.

***

Are you ready to talk about what happened?

It's pretty simple: I fell for a guy, I ended up in a situation I couldn't control, and I got rescued. I guess I was lucky? Anyway, I feel like an idiot.

You shouldn't blame yourself. Getting taken advantage of isn't the same thing as being an idiot.

Who am I supposed to blame, him? I'm not a child. He didn't kidnap me. He told me where to go and I went. He told me what to do and I did it. It's what I wanted. Or thought I wanted at the time.

Let's talk about that. What did you want? What were you looking for?

I don't know, someone to talk to, something to belong to. School never clicked for me. I don't really have friends. You already know about my parents. I think I just wanted to be part of something bigger. It sounds stupid when I say it out loud.

Bigger than what?

Bigger than, I don't know. Bigger than where I came from. Come from. I mean what's the point of this town, even?

You were feeling trapped. We all feel that way sometimes. And you made a bad choice. But you can't blame yourself for your background or for the opportunities that you didn't have. All you can do is try to learn from your mistakes and move forward.

Yeah, but if I don't blame myself then it feels like, I don't know. Like I'm not really a person. Like I'm just randomly getting pushed around by everything around me.

That's a pretty deep thought. Maybe you're not such an idiot after all.

It still feels that way but thanks for saying so.

I'll see you next week.

***

All right people, it sounds like we've got a lot of bad options here, talk to me.

I'll keep it simple: the market was down twenty percent at closing and it could drop another twenty in the morning if we don't do something. The futures look pretty grim.

Do what exactly?

Well for starters we've got a liquidity problem. We need to keep the banks afloat, so this doesn't get out of hand and tank the real economy.

You're saying we should bail out the same banks that got us into this mess.

I'm not saying I like it.

I tell you who's not going to like it, the voters. There's an election coming up.

Well, they're really not going to like what happens if we *don't* bail out the banks. Like you said, we've got a lot of bad options.

OK, so how do we spin this? What's our story?

We've got to explain that a free market and a free government have to work together. Bottom line, we've got a bunch of random people making choices, and a bunch of rules that are supposed to keep those choices from getting out of hand. Sometimes people make bad choices. Sometimes we've got bad rules. Sometimes the choices are fine on their own but add up to something that nobody wanted. Sometimes the rules are fine on their own but don't get enforced properly. Sometimes, like now, all of the above. So first off, we've got to clean up this mess, and then we've got to figure out how to fix the rules and the enforcement so something like this doesn't happen again. Then the voters get their say, which will either send us back to the drawing board or else make it the next guy's problem. And someone down the line will have to do this all over again when the next crisis rolls around.

Sounds pretty complicated.

Freedom usually is.

Index

accountability
  defined, 41
  market freedom, lack of in, 47, 48, 88
  relationship with attributability, 41–2, 44–5
  republican freedom and, 44
action-centered freedom
  as absence of preventing conditions, 19
  political use during modern period, 19–20
  relationship with person-centered freedom, 13, 20, 24
  utilitarianism and, 25–6
Acton, Lord (John Dalberg-Acton), 178
Adams, John, 61
American Revolution, 129
Anarchy, State, and Utopia (Nozick), 37
ancient liberty, 4, 134–5, 136–7
Anderson, Elizabeth, 117
anti-paternalism, market freedom and, 115
Aquinas, Thomas, 20, 28
Arendt, Hannah, 52
aretaic appraisal, 48
Aristotle
  person-centered freedom and, 80
  on political exclusion, 71–2
  virtue and, 12, 60
attributability
  defined, 41
  market freedom, lack of in, 49, 88
  relationship with accountability, 41–2, 44–5
  republican freedom and, 44

Auden, W. H., 34
authoritarianism
  as anti-liberal belief, 16, 169, 185
  imperialism and, 189
autonomy, 50–1, 181

Bacon, Francis, 185
Bayle, Pierre, 126
Becker, Gary, 97, 101–2
Bell, Duncan, 160
Bentham, Jeremy
  on action-centered freedom, 25
  contractarianism and, 8–9
  Hobbes compared, 25
  imperialism and, 191–2
  justice paradigm and, 7–8
  Locke compared, 34
  negative liberty and, 22
  on person-centered freedom, 26
  on rightful choice, 27
  on social utility, 27–8
Berlin, Isaiah
  justice paradigm and, 7–8
  liberal tradition and, 179
  on negative versus positive liberty, 4, 29, 134, 171–2
  pluralism and, 171–2
  value of market freedom for, 117
Brandeis, Louis, 153–4
A Brief History of Neoliberalism (Harvey), 100
Brontë, Charlotte, 122–4
Brown, Wendy, 95, 100

210

Index

Burke, Edmund
  conservatism and, 109
  justice paradigm and, 7–8
  liberal tradition and, 126
  on liberty, 134

capitalism
  association with liberalism, 169, 179–80, 186–7
  economic inequality and, 131
  global trade and, 188
  laissez-faire principle and, 148, 187–8
  overview, 16
  republican freedom threatened by, 127, 133
  socialism and, 157–8, 177
Carter, Ian, 29–32, 40
Christianity, 125
Churchill, Winston, 157–8
Cicero, 58, 60–1
civic trust, 198–9, 202
civil rights, 105–6
"classical" liberals, 134–47
Cobden, Richard, 191–2
Cohen, G. A., 36–7, 75
colonialism. *See* imperialism
command economy, incompatibility with republican freedom, 79–80
commercial liberalism, 191–2
communication
  need for shared values in, 3–4
  as remedy for polarization, 3
Condorcet, Nicolas de, 7–8, 31–2
Consent, contractarianism and, 10–11, 182–3, 200
Consent argument
  libertarianism and, 92
  overview, 91–2
  problems with, 94
  responsibility and, 92, 93
conservatism, market freedom and, 109–10
Considerations on Representative Government (Mill), 142, 149, 193–4, 196
Constant, Benjamin
  on ancient versus modern liberty, 4, 134–5, 136–7, 159
  on commerce as checking power of state, 62, 137, 162
  on equality, 145–6
  on freedom, 159, 184

  on free press, 138
  imperialism and, 192, 196–7
  individualist liberalism and, 142–3
  justice paradigm and, 7–8
  liberal tradition and, 162–3, 179
  on limiting political power, 135–7, 146
  on Locke, 160
  Mill compared, 141–3, 144, 145–7, 150
  on political exclusion, 149
  political involvement of, 128
  on public opinion, 137–8
  on Smith, 161
  on suffrage, 149–50
  Tocqueville compared, 139–40, 145–7
  on unregulated conduct, 146–7
  value of market freedom for, 117
The Constitution of Liberty (Hayek), 98, 99
contractarianism
  conflicting values, inability to accommodate, 176–7
  consensus and, 176–7
  consent and, 10–11, 182–3, 200
  criticism of, 170, 179–80
  defenses of, 181–2
  eclipse of, 8–10
  justice and, 35
  justice paradigm and, 7
  legitimacy and, 10–11
  nineteenth-century liberalism and, 161
  political change, inability to accommodate, 178–9
  positive liberty and, 10–11
  relationship of market freedom and republican freedom in, 183
  revival of, 8
  substate groups and institutions, inability to accommodate, 177–8
contracts, 102, 103
control
  discursive control, 58–9, 65–6, 68–9, 83–4
  rational control, 66, 67
  responsibility and, xiii
  volitional control, 66–8, 83–4
corruption
  commerce as leading to, 60–1
  criticism of liberalism on grounds of, 169, 180–1
  overview, 16

Dagger, Richard, 54, 64–5
Dahl, Robert, 64

Democracy in America (Tocqueville), 130–1, 138, 140, 142, 160–1, 162
democratic despotism, 138–9, 140, 178
democratization of public life
  liberal response to, 132–3
  overview, 127
  in politics, 129–30
  in social relations, 130–1
Deneen, Patrick, 124, 170
Descartes, René, 185
Dewey, John
  on "classical" versus "new" liberals, 156
  contractarianism and, 9
  on freedom, 152–3, 156, 184
  justice paradigm and, 7–8
  on liberalism, 158
  liberal tradition and, 162–3
  political involvement of, 128
  value of market freedom for, 117
Digest (Justinian), 19
discourse model
  discursive control and, 58–9, 65–6, 68–9, 83–4
  interest model, superiority over, 71–2
  markets and, 70–1, 72
  overview, 58–9
  person-centered freedom and, 75–6, 80
  public versus private spheres and, 81–2
  rational control and, 66, 67
  virtue model, superiority over, 71–2
  volitional control and, 66–8, 83–4
discursive control, 58–9, 65–6, 68–9, 83–4
dispersion of power, market freedom and, 112
diversity, market freedom and, 112–13
division of labor, 132
Douglass, Frederick, 7–8
Dworkin, Ronald, 37, 38

East India Company, 191–2, 193
efficiency argument
  market freedom and, 114–15
  neoliberalism and, 92–3
  nonresponsibility and, 92–3
  overview, 92
  problems with, 94
  trade-offs and, 83
Engels, Friedrich
  as anti-liberal, 124
  imperialism and, 186
  socialism and, 147
epistemic modesty, market freedom and, 110–11
equality, relative importance of freedom versus, 1
equal liberty principle, 35–6
An Essay Concerning Human Understanding (Locke), 34, 160
experimentalism, market freedom and, 113
externalities, 103–4
eyeball test, 75, 77–8

Fawcett, Edmund, 124, 126
The Federalist (Madison, Hamilton, and Jay), 162, 165, 204
Ferguson, Adam
  on commerce as leading to corruption, 61
  contractarianism and, 9
  on markets, 47–8
Figgis, Neville, 178
Forrester, Katrina, 7
Foucault, Michel, 87, 95
Fragment on Government (Bentham), 25
Frankfurt, Harry, 67
Freeden, Michael, 153
freedom
  action-centered (*See* action-centered freedom)
  association of justice with, 33–4
  embedding of in social and legal framework, xii
  in liberal polity, xii
  market freedom (*See* market freedom)
  neoliberalism and, 100–1
  nonspecific value of, 31–2, 40
  person-centered (*See* person-centered freedom)
  as political value, 29
  relative importance of equality versus, 1
  relative importance of justice versus, 1, 12–13, 16, 120–1
  republican freedom (*See* republican freedom)
  subordination to justice, 32–40
Freeman, Samuel, 119–20
free press, 138
French Revolution, 129, 134, 180
Friedman, Milton
  on competition, 96
  consent argument and, 92
  libertarianism and, 86, 94–5

Index

marketplace of ideas and, 101–2
neoliberalism and, 95
on social values, 96–7

Gaus, Gerald, 57
German idealism, 152–3
Gilded Age, 132
Glorious Revolution, 161
Goodhart, Michael, 7
Gopnik, Adam, 158, 169
Gourevitch, Alex, 57–8
Green, T. H.
   on "classical" versus "new" liberals, 155
   contractarianism and, 9
   on freedom, 152–3, 159
   German idealism and, 152–3
   justice paradigm and, 7–8
   liberal tradition and, 162–3
   on Locke, 160–1
   political involvement of, 128
   on role of state, 154
   value of market freedom for, 117
Guizot, François
   imperialism and, 194
   justice paradigm and, 7–8
   on *laissez-faire* principle, 147
   Mill compared, 150
   on suffrage, 150
   Tocqueville versus, 194

Hamilton, Alexander, 7–8
Harcourt, William, 156
Hart, H. L. A., 36
Harvey, David, 100
Hayek, Friedrich
   on arbitrary power, 77
   on coercion, 98–9
   on commercial markets, 96
   on competition, 96, 97–8
   contractarianism and, 9
   criticism of, 173
   criticism of other liberals, 174
   on efficiency, 83
   on Ferguson, 9
   on freedom, 59
   on Hume, 9
   justice paradigm and, 7–8
   on law, 98
   liberal utopianism and, 173–4
   libertarianism and, 86, 94–5

marketplace of ideas and, 101–2
on markets, 57, 72–3, 78
neoliberalism and, 95
on nonresponsibility, 93
nonspecific value of freedom and, 31–2
Pettit compared, 59, 73–4
Rawls compared, 174
on responsibility, 76–7, 94
on Smith, 9
on social safety net, 73
on trade-offs, 82–3
heroic liberalism, 194–5
Hicks, John, 86
Hobbes, Thomas
   Bentham compared, 25
   conflation of person-centered freedom with action-centered freedom, 24
   on freedom as political value, 29
   on justice, 33, 36
   justice paradigm and, 7
   liberal tradition and, 162–3
   Locke compared, 34
   negative liberty and, 22, 31
   as nonliberal thinker, 160–1
   on person-centered freedom, 26
   on rightful choice, 27
   on social utility, 27–8
Hobhouse, L. T.
   on "classical" versus "new" liberals, 155
   on freedom, 152–3, 159, 184
   German idealism and, 153
   imperialism and, 195–6
   justice paradigm and, 7–8
   liberal tradition and, 162–3
   on Locke, 161
   nonspecific value of freedom and, 31–2
   political involvement of, 128
   on role of state, 154–5
   on socialism, 156–7
   value of market freedom for, 117
Hobson, J. A.
   on "classical" versus "new" liberals, 155–6
   on freedom, 152–3, 159, 184
   imperialism and, 195–6
   justice paradigm and, 7–8
   on liberalism, 158
   liberal tradition and, 162–3
   political involvement of, 128
   on socialism, 157

Hobson, J. A. (cont.)
  on wage labor, 154
homo economicus, 90, 95, 97
Humboldt, Wilhelm von
  justice paradigm and, 7–8
  nonspecific value of freedom and, 31–2
  value of market freedom for, 117
Hume, David
  contractarianism and, 8
  justice paradigm and, 7–8
  liberal tradition and, 126, 162–3

idealism. *See* German idealism
imperialism
  authoritarianism and, 189
  commercial liberalism and, 191–2
  criticism of liberalism on grounds of, 169, 179–80, 186–7
  disavowal by liberals, 190
  global trade and, 188
  heroic liberalism and, 194–5
  historical background, 190–1
  internationalist liberalism and, 195–6
  lack of unified liberal position on, 196–8
  laissez-faire principle and, 187–8, 191–2
  national interest and, 191
  overview, 16
  paternalistic liberalism and, 192–4
  realpolitik and, 191
indifference, market freedom and, 108–9
individualism, 139–40
industrialization
  inequality and, 131–2
  liberal response to, 133–4
  overview, 127
Industrial Revolution, 123–4, 131
infeasibility, market freedom and, 110
interest model
  commerce as fostering good government, 62–3
  commerce as mean of checking power of state, 62, 162
  defined, 61–2
  discourse model, superiority of, 71–2
  overview, 58, 59
  rejection of, 64–5
intermediate powers, 178
internationalist liberalism, 195–6
International Monetary Fund, 99–100
invisible hand, 93–4

Jane Eyre (Brontë), 122–4, 163–4
Jefferson, Thomas, 61
July Monarchy, 132, 150, 194
justice
  consent and, 10–11
  contemporary theories of, 37–8
  contractarianism and, 7, 35
  equal liberty principle and, 35–6
  feminist theory of, 37, 38
  justification and, 11–12
  legitimacy and, 10–11
  morality and, 34–5
  political exclusion and, 39
  as proper balance between republican freedom and market freedom, 203
  reasonableness and, 39–40
  relative importance of freedom versus, 1, 12–13, 16, 120–1
  rightful choice and, 39
  subordination of freedom to, 32–40
  utilitarianism and, 8, 32–3, 36
justice paradigm
  dominance of in academic liberalism, 6–7
  historical objections to, 7–10
  relationship with freedom-centered liberalism, 1–2, 201–2
  theoretical objections to, 10–12
justification, 11–12

Kant, Immanuel
  contractarianism and, 10, 35, 174
  on justice, 34–5
  justice paradigm and, 7
  liberal tradition and, 126, 159–60
  Locke compared, 34–5
  nonspecific value of freedom and, 31–2
  political exclusion and, 39
  positive liberty and, 22
  Rawls compared, 35–6
Keynes, John Maynard
  on Hayek, 173, 174
  on *laissez-faire* principle, 148
King, Jr., Martin Luther, 203
Kipling, Rudyard, 193
Knight, Frank
  criticism of other liberals, 173
  on Hayek, 173
  pluralism and, 171
Kramer, Matthew, 31

Index

Krause, Sharon, 117
Kymlicka, Will, 37

laissez-faire principle
  capitalism and, 148, 187–8
  imperialism and, 187–8, 191–2
  market freedom and, 145, 147, 148
Lassalle, Ferdinand, 147
Lectures on the Principles of Political Obligation (Green), 160–1
legitimacy, 10–11, 201–3
Letter on Toleration (Locke), 181–2
Leviathan (Hobbes), 24, 27, 28
Lewis, George Cornewall, 160
liberal freedom. *See specific topic*
The Liberal Imagination (Trilling), 1
liberalism
  class domination and, 186
  commercial, 191–2
  corruption, criticism on grounds of, 169, 180–1
  cultural/racial domination and, 186
  defined too loosely, 124
  defined too rigidly, 124
  heroic, 194–5
  internationalist, 195–6
  negative liberty and, 29
  polarization, threat from, 168–9
  republican freedom as compatible with, 54–5
  republican freedom as incompatible with, 52–3
  socialism and, 147, 156–8
Liberalism: The Life of an Idea (Fawcett), 126
Liberalism (Hobhouse), 156, 157, 161
Liberal Party (UK), 152
liberal polity
  basic rights in, 182
  civic trust and, 202
  defined, xii
  freedom in, xii
  imperialism and, 191
  nonresponsibility in, 82
  polarization, threat from, 169
  political debate in, 185, 202
  public versus private spheres in, 166
  relationship of market freedom and republican freedom in, 21–2, 49–50, 88–9, 90–1, 100–1, 184
  shared civic narrative and, 198
  trade-offs in, 119
liberal tradition
  Christianity and, 125
  "classical" liberals, 134–47
  contractarianism and, 161
  defined too loosely, 124
  defined too rigidly, 124
  historical context, sensitivity to, 159
  incorporation of early modern thinkers into, 160, 162–3
  industrialization and (*See* industrialization)
  liberty, centrality to, 159
  "new" liberals, 147–58
  overview, 15–16
  practical focus of, 159
  relationship between market freedom and republican freedom in, 125–8, 159
liberal utopianism, 173–4
libertarianism
  consent argument and, 92
  defense of markets, 89–90
  market freedom and, 89–90
  neoliberalism versus, 95
  origins of, 86
Libertas Humana (Papal encyclical), 180
liberty
  ancient, 4, 134–5, 136–7
  equal liberty principle, 35–6
  liberal tradition, centrality in, 159
  modern, 4, 134–5, 136–7
  negative (*See* negative liberty)
  positive (*See* positive liberty)
license. *See* corruption
Lind, John
  on action-centered freedom, 25
  on American independence, 26
  on person-centered freedom, 26
Locke, John
  Bentham compared, 34
  contractarianism and, 8, 10, 35, 174, 181–2
  on equality, 128–9
  on extra-legal resistance, 203
  Hobbes compared, 34
  on justice, 33–5
  justice paradigm and, 7
  Kant compared, 34–5
  liberal tradition and, 126, 128, 159–61, 162–3
  on natural rights, 161

Locke, John (cont.)
　political exclusion and, 39
　positive liberty and, 22
　Rawls compared, 35–6
　on separation of powers, 129
Long, Douglas, 28, 144
The Lost History of Liberalism
　(Rosenblatt), 125

Machiavelli, Niccolò, 185
MacIntyre, Alasdair, 180–1, 185
Madison, James
　on justice, 165, 203–4
　justice paradigm and, 7–8
　liberal tradition and, 126
　on liberty, 204
Maitland, Frederic, 178
Manchester School, 174, 187–8
Manent, Pierre, 158–60
Manifesto of the Communist Party (Marx
　and Engels), 124, 186
market freedom
　accountability and, 47, 48, 88
　anti-paternalism and, 115
　aretaic appraisal in, 48
　attributability, lack of, 49, 88
　commercial markets and, 88, 89, 96
　consent argument (*See* consent argument)
　conservatism and, 109–10
　contractarian liberalism and, 183
　contracts and, 102, 103
　critique of, 87
　defined, 47
　dependence on social and legal
　　framework, 87–9
　dichotomy with republican freedom, 4–5,
　　91, 118–19, 166
　as dimension of liberal freedom, 21–2,
　　46–51, 85, 91, 100–1, 125–8, 159, 184,
　　200
　dispersion of power and, 112
　diversity and, 112–13
　efficiency and, 114–15 (*See also* efficiency
　　argument)
　epistemic modesty and, 110–11
　evaluation of nonresponsible choices in,
　　48
　expanding, 166–7
　experimentalism and, 113
　free press and, 138
　ideal markets and, 102–3
　impersonal nature of markets, 72–6
　indifference and, 108–9
　infeasibility and, 110
　invisible hand and, 93–4
　laissez-faire principle, 145, 147, 148
　libertarianism and, 89–90 (*See also*
　　libertarianism)
　limits of, 90–1, 118–21
　as means of checking power of state, 117
　as means of promoting individual
　　development, 117
　as means of promoting social progress,
　　117
　neoliberalism and, 90 (*See also*
　　neoliberalism)
　nonresponsibility and, 4, 103–4, 107
　overview, 14–15
　perfectionism and, 115–16
　as person-centered conception of
　　freedom, 49–50, 88
　persuasion and, 167
　polarization, threat from, 168
　prices as externalities, 103–4
　privacy and, 116
　prudence and, 111
　regulation of markets and, 103
　scope of, 90, 101–2
　serendipity and, 113–14
　sovereignty and, 116
　stability and, 111–12
　state and, 119
　suffrage and, 130
　superiority of liberal conception, 1, 23–4
　trade-offs in, 5, 82–3, 119
　tradition and, 109
　value of, 90, 107–8
　voluntary associations and, 140–1
marketplace of ideas, 104–5
market utopianism, 16, 169
Marshall, T. H., 149
Marx, Karl
　as anti-liberal, 124
　imperialism and, 186
　socialism and, 147
Mehta, Uday, 190
Mill, James, 193
Mill, John Stuart
　on action-centered freedom, 25
　on boundaries of freedom, 6
　Constant compared, 141–3, 144, 145–7,
　　150

contractarianism and, 9
on democracy, 133
on education, 152
on equality, 145–6
on freedom, 21, 51, 99, 159, 184
Guizot compared, 150
imperialism and, 193–4, 196–7
justice paradigm and, 7–8
on Kant, 34
on *laissez-faire* principle, 145, 147
liberal tradition and, 162–3
on liberty, 18, 144
on limiting political power, 146
on Locke, 160
on nonconformity, 144
nonspecific value of freedom and, 31–2
on political exclusion, 149
political involvement of, 128
progressive liberalism and, 142–3
on public opinion, 142
on Smith, 161
on social expectations, 105
on social progress, 142–4, 145–6, 159
on suffrage, 150–2
Tocqueville compared, 142–3, 144, 145–7, 151–2
on truth, 104
on unregulated conduct, 146–7
utilitarianism and, 144–5
value of market freedom for, 117
on women's suffrage, 146, 150
Milton, John, 129
Mises, Ludwig von
libertarianism and, 86
on socialism, 147–8, 156
modernity, 184–5
modern liberty, 4, 134–5, 136–7
Montaigne, Michel de, 126
Montesquieu, Charles de
on commerce as checking power of state, 62
justice paradigm and, 7–8
liberal tradition and, 126, 162–3
Tocqueville compared, 162
Mont Pelerin Society, 86, 171
Mouffe, Chantal, 124

Nagel, Thomas, 43
Napoleon, 136
Napoleonic Charter of 1815, 136
negative liberty
liberalism and, 29

modern liberty compared, 134
person-centered freedom and, 22
positive liberty versus, 4, 29, 134, 171–2
utilitarianism and, 29–32
neoliberalism
coercion and, 97–9
competition and, 94–8
critique of, 87
defense of markets, 90
efficiency argument and, 92–3
freedom and, 100–1
imposition without consent, 99–100
liberal tradition, departure from, 95
libertarianism versus, 95
market freedom as moving beyond, 90
neoliberal polity, 119
spontaneity and, 97–9
"new" liberals, 147–58
Niebuhr, Reinhold, 171, 172–3
nondomination, 55, 69–70, 71–9
nonresponsibility
autonomy and, 50–1
as dimension of liberal freedom, 23–4
efficiency argument and, 92–3
in liberal polity, 82
market freedom and, 4, 103–4, 107
markets and, 81, 82
person-centered freedom and, 49–50
republican freedom as threat to, 71
superiority of liberal conception, 46–51
nonspecific value of freedom, 31–2, 40
Nozick, Robert
consent argument and, 92
on justice, 36–7, 38, 39

Okin, Susan, 37, 38, 39
The Old Regime and the Revolution (Tocqueville), 160–1
On Liberty (Mill), 18, 104, 142, 143, 145, 193
On Violence (Arendt), 52
orthonomy, 71–2

Paine, Thomas
justice paradigm and, 7–8
on liberty, 134
on natural rights, 161
Paley, William, 25, 27
Pareto efficiency, 103–4
paternalistic liberalism, 192–4
perfectionism, market freedom and, 115–16

person-centered freedom
  action-centered freedom distinguished, 13, 20
  challenges in applying to liberalism, 20–1
  discourse model and, 75–6, 80
  egalitarianism and, 20–1
  freedom as political value and, 21, 29
  market actors and, 21–2
  market freedom and, 49–50, 88
  negative liberty and, 22
  nonresponsibility and, 49–50
  as original conception of freedom, 19–20
  positive liberty and, 22
  preferred to action-centered freedom, 22, 50
  property rights and, 80
  relationship with action-centered freedom, 24
  republican freedom and, 21–2, 49–50, 56, 75–6
  responsibility and, 49–50
  rightful choice and, 39
  social status and, 19
  utilitarianism and, 26–7
Pettit, Philip
  on arbitrary power, 73–4
  on conditions for republican political rule, 56
  discourse model (*See* discourse model)
  on discursive control, 58–9, 65–6, 68–9
  on environmental harm, 74
  eyeball test, 75, 77–8
  on freedom and responsibility, 42–3
  Hayek compared, 59, 73–4
  interest model, rejection of, 64–5
  on liberalism and republicanism, 55
  on markets, 56–7, 75, 78
  nondomination and, 55, 69–70, 71–9
  on rational control, 66, 67
  republican freedom and, 13–4
  on social safety net, 73
  tough luck test, 70
  virtue model, rejection of, 63–4
  on volitional control, 66–8
Plato
  on freedom, 20
  person-centered freedom and, 80
  on virtue, 60–1
pluralism, 84, 171–2
Pocock, J. G. A., 81, 163
polarization
  causes of, 2
  communication as remedy for, 3
  liberal freedom as remedy for, 165–6, 199
  liberalism threatened by, 168–9
  market freedom threatened by, 168
  overview, 16
  problem of, 2–3
  republican freedom threatened by, 167–8
political exclusion, 39, 71–2, 148–50
Political Liberalism (Rawls), 176, 181–2
Politics (Aristotle), 71–2
Popper, Karl
  criticism of other liberals, 173
  justice paradigm and, 7–8
  pluralism and, 171
positive liberty
  ancient liberty compared, 134
  contractarianism and, 10–11
  negative liberty versus, 4, 29, 134, 171–2
  person-centered freedom and, 22
Price, Richard, 26
Principles of Moral and Political Philosophy (Paley), 25
Principles of Political Economy (Mill), 142, 145, 147, 161
Principles of Politics (Constant), 150, 161
privacy, market freedom and, 116
property rights
  person-centered freedom and, 80
  virtue model and, 81
Protestant Reformation, 185
prudence, market freedom and, 111
public versus private spheres
  capitalism and, 127
  changing boundaries of, xiii–xiv
  civil rights and, 105–6
  discourse model and, 81–2
  employment contracts and, 106
  in liberal polity, 166
  sexual misconduct and, 105–6
  social expectations and, 105, 106–7
  vices, regulation of and, 106

The Rake's Progress (Auden), 34
rational actor model, 97
rational control, 66, 67
Rawls, John
  contractarianism and, 10, 35, 171, 174–6, 181–2
  criticism of other liberals, 174
  on freedom, 10–11
  Hayek compared, 174

on justice, 7, 32, 36, 38, 39, 120
justice paradigm and, 7
Kant compared, 35–6
on liberalism and republicanism, 54
liberal tradition and, 126, 128
Locke compared, 35–6
on reasonableness, 11
on well-ordered society, 174–6
Raz, Joseph
on justice, 37, 39
on perfectionist state, 38
Reagan, Ronald, 86–7
realpolitik, 191
reasonableness, 39–40, 182–3
Reflections on the Revolution in France (Burke), 134
Reform Bills (UK), 130
republican freedom
accountability and, 44
arbitrary power and, 56, 73–4, 77
attributability and, 44
capitalism, threat from, 133
command economy, incompatibility with, 79–80
communitarianism and, 53–4
as compatible with liberalism, 54–5
contractarian liberalism and, 183
defined, 42
dichotomy with market freedom, 4–5, 91, 118–19, 166
as dimension of liberal freedom, 21–2, 40–6, 49–50, 85, 91, 100–1, 125–8, 159, 184, 199–200, 202
discourse model (*See* discourse model)
expanding, 167
German idealism and, 152–3
as incompatible with liberalism, 52–3
intensifying, 167
interest model (*See* interest model)
markets and, 56–8, 75–6, 84–5
nondomination and, 55, 69–70, 71–9
nonresponsibility, as threat to, 71
overview, 13–14
as person-centered conception of freedom, 45–6, 49–50, 56, 75–6
polarization, threat from, 167–8
political exclusion and, 148–52
political rule, conditions for, 56
responsibility and, 4
revival of, 53

role of state in promoting, 154–5
socialism and, 147, 156–8 (*See also* socialism)
superiority of liberal conception, 1, 22–3
trade-offs in, 5
virtue model (*See* virtue model)
wage labor and, 57–8, 153–4
women's suffrage and, 146, 150
republican government
liberal polity and, 90–1
necessary for security, 119–20
responsibility not coextensive with, 43–4
Republicanism (Pettit), 55, 64–5, 74, 76
Republic (Plato), 20
responsibility
capacity to act and, 42
consent argument and, 92, 93
control and, xiii
as dimension of liberal freedom, 40–6
person-centered freedom and, 49–50
republican freedom and, 4
republican government, not coextensive with, 43–4
social context of action and, 42
social practice of, 41
superiority of liberal conception, 22–3
Rigby, Elizabeth, 164
The Rights of Man (Paine), 134
The Road to Serfdom (Hayek), 73, 82–3, 173
Rosenblatt, Helena, 124, 125, 147
Rousseau, Jean-Jacques
on commerce as leading to corruption, 61
contractarianism and, 35, 174
on equality, 145–6
justice paradigm and, 7
liberal tradition and, 162–3
as nonliberal thinker, 160–1
on political power, 135
Ryan, Alan, 124

Sandel, Michael
on autonomy, 181
critique of liberalism, 124
on liberalism and republicanism, 54–5
on virtue model, 63–4
Scanlon, T. M., 10, 11
Schumpeter, Joseph, 191–2
Scruton, Roger, 181
Second Treatise of Government (Locke), 33–4, 128–9

Second Vatican Council, 180
separation of powers, 129
serendipity, market freedom and, 113–14
sexual misconduct, 105–6
shared civic narrative, 198, 202
Shklar, Judith, 117
Sidgwick, Henry
  on action-centered freedom, 25–6
  justice paradigm and, 7–8
  on rightful choice, 27
Simmons, A. John, 178
Smith, Adam
  on commerce as checking power of state, 162
  on commerce as promoting good government, 62–3
  contractarianism and, 8, 9
  on division of labor, 132
  on efficiency, 83
  on imperialism, 191–2
  on invisible hand, 93–4
  justice paradigm and, 7–8
  on *laissez-faire* principle, 145
  liberal tradition and, 95, 126, 161, 162–3
  on markets, 91, 92
social contract. *See* contractarianism
social expectations, 105, 106–7
socialism
  capitalism and, 157–8, 177
  criticism of, 147–8, 156
  liberal, 157
  liberalism and, 147, 156–8
  mechanical, 157
  official, 157
  practicable, 187–8
  republican freedom and, 147, 156–8
  socialist utopianism, 16, 169
sovereignty, market freedom and, 116
Spencer, Herbert, 191–2
The Spirit of Conquest and Usurpation (Constant), 192
The Spirit of the Laws (Montesquieu), 162
stability, market freedom and, 111–12
Staël, Germaine de, 7–8, 134
Stedman, Daniel, 95
Steiner, Hillel, 29–30
Stephen, James Fitzjames, 152, 194–5
Steuart, James, 62, 162
Stiglitz, Joseph, 100
Strauss, Leo, 180
Strawson, P. F., 41

suffrage, 130, 149–52
Summa Theologiae (Aquinas), 20, 28
Sunstein, Cass, 54, 64–5
Swift, Adam, 39–40
Sydney, Algernon, 129

Taylor, Charles, 181
Thatcher, Margaret, 86–7, 100
A Theory of Freedom (Pettit), 66, 83–4
A Theory of Justice (Rawls), 35, 36, 38, 120, 128, 171, 174
The Theory of Moral Sentiments (Smith), 161
Tocqueville, Alexis de
  Constant compared, 139–40, 145–7
  on democracy, 133
  on democratic despotism, 138–9, 140, 178
  on division of labor, 132
  on equality, 145–6, 159
  on freedom, 159, 184
  Guizot versus, 194
  imperialism and, 194, 195, 196–7
  on individualism, 139–40
  on industrialization, 131–2, 133
  on intermediate powers, 178
  justice paradigm and, 7–8
  liberal tradition and, 162–3
  on limiting political power, 146
  on Locke, 160–1
  Mill compared, 142–3, 144, 145–7, 151–2
  Montesquieu compared, 162
  political involvement of, 128
  on Smith, 161
  on social relations, 130–1
  on suffrage, 150, 151–2
  tragic liberalism and, 142–3
  on unregulated conduct, 146–7
  value of market freedom for, 117
  on voluntary associations, 140–1
Tomasi, John, 93, 99
totalitarianism, 172
tough luck test, 70
tradition, market freedom and, 109
Trilling, Lionel, 1
Two Treatises of Government (Locke), 160

utilitarianism
  action-centered freedom and, 25–6
  freedom as political value and, 29
  justice and, 32–3, 36

justice paradigm and, 8
liberal freedom and, 24–32
negative liberty and, 29–32
person-centered freedom and, 26–7
rightful choice and, 27
social utility and, 27–8
utopianism
as anti-liberal belief, 16, 169, 185
imperialism and, 189–90
liberal, 173–4
market, 16, 169
socialist, 16, 169

vices, regulation of, 106
virtue model
commerce as leading to corruption, 60–1
defined, 59–60
discourse model, superiority of, 71–2
domination in, 81
overview, 58, 59

property rights and, 81
rejection of, 63–4
separation of politics and economics in, 59–60
volitional control, 66–8, 83–4
Voltaire, 126
voluntary associations, 140–1

wage labor, 57–8, 153–4
Waldron, Jeremy, 8
Washington Consensus, 86–7, 99–100
Watson, Gary, 41, 48
The Wealth of Nations (Smith), 62–3, 161, 192
Webb, Beatrice, 148
Weber, Max, 7–8, 117
Williams, Bernard, 179
Wollstonecraft, Mary, 7–8
women's suffrage, 146, 150
World Bank, 99–100